THE SPIRIT AND THE FLESH
IN SHANDONG, 1650–1785

THE SPIRIT AND THE FLESH IN SHANDONG, 1650–1785

D. E. Mungello

ROWMAN & LITTLEFIELD PUBLISHERS, INC.
Lanham • New York • Boulder • Oxford

ROWMAN & LITTLEFIELD PUBLISHERS, INC.

Published in the United States of America
by Rowman & Littlefield Publishers, Inc.
4720 Boston Way, Lanham, Maryland 20706
www.rowmanlittlefield.com

12 Hid's Copse Road
Cumnor Hill, Oxford OX2 9JJ, England

British Library Cataloguing in Publication Information Available

Library of Congress Cataloging-in-Publication Data

Mungello, David E., 1943–
    The spirit and the flesh in Shandong, 1650–1785 / D. E. Mungello
      p. cm.
    Includes bibliographical references and index.
    ISBN 0-7425-1163-4 (alk. paper). — ISBN 0-7425-1164-2 (pbk. : alk. paper)
    1. Shandong Sheng (China)—Church history.   2. China—History—Ch'ing
dynasty, 1644–1912.   I. Title.

  BR1286.M86   2001
  275.1'1407—dc21   00-065323

Printed in the United States of America

 ♾ ™ The paper used in this publication meets the minimum requirements of
American National Standard for Information Sciences—Permanence of Paper for
Printed Library Materials, ANSI/NISO Z39.48–1992.

Contents

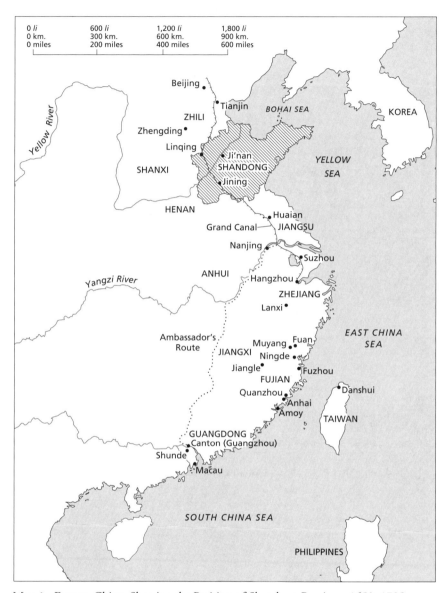

Map 1. Eastern China, Showing the Position of Shandong Province, 1650–1785

Map 2. Mission Sites in Western Shandong and Southern Zhili Provinces, 1650–1785

Illustrations

Preface

This book began in 1993 with my growing interest in the Chinese Christian literatus Shang Huqing (1619–after 1698). Over the following seven years, the project evolved into a study of Christianity in the region of Shandong. During that time, numerous friends, colleagues, and associates helped me by providing information, materials, translation assistance, and critiques of the emerging manuscript. Some of them went far beyond the bounds of scholarly courtesy and were extremely generous with their time. Without their help, this book would never have been completed. I would like to take this opportunity to recognize several individual contributions.

Dr. Adrianus C. Dudink, currently of Leuven, Belgium, assisted me by sharing the transcribed copy of Shang Huqing's *Bu Ru wengao (A Warning to Repair the Deficiencies of the Literati)* (1664) made from the Zikawei Library (Shanghai) copy. The copy belongs to the Sinologisch Instituut of Leiden University. In addition, he patiently helped me with numerous translation problems in deciphering this text. The *Bu Ru wengao* is a long, difficult text and I make no pretense to a comprehensive treatment of it. Father Albert Chan, S.J., of the University of San Francisco helped me with general information about Shang Huqing. Dr. Mi Chu Wiens promptly responded to my queries about rare materials in the Library of Congress (Washington, D.C.). Dr. R. G. Tiedemann of the University of London gave me extensive assistance in tracking down biographical citations of Shang Huqing.

I am indebted to several scholars for their assistance in helping me to translate difficult Chinese terms. These include Professor Derk Bodde of the University of Pennsylvania, Dr. Han Qi of the Chinese Academy of Social Sciences (Beijing), Professor Erik Zürcher of the University of Leiden, Professor Giuliano Bertuccioli of the University of Rome (Sapienza), and Dr. Vincent Yang of Baylor University. In addition, Dr. Elisabetta Corsi of the Colegio de México and Professor Manual J. Ortuño of Baylor University assisted with translation problems in European languages.

Several scholars and archivists offered indispensable assistance in helping me to obtain copies of manuscripts. These include Father Wiktor Gramatowski, S.J., of the Archivum Romanum Societatis Iesu and Father Luis M. Cuña Ramos of the Propaganda Archives (Rome). Professor Michele Fatica of the Instituto Universitario Orientale (Naples) was instrumental in helping me to obtain materials from the Biblioteca Nazionali Napoli. The late Father Bernward H. Willeke, O.F.M., was generous in sharing unpublished material that he had compiled on eighteenth-century Franciscan missionaries to Shandong. Father Arnulf Camps, O.F.M., kindly obtained a copy of Father Matteo Ripa's 1719 drawing of the Ji'-nan West Church floor plan from the General Archives of the Franciscans in Rome. Father Ponciano Macabalo, O.F.M., the vice secretary general for missionary evangelization of the Curia Generalis Ordinis Fratrum Minorum in Rome assisted me in obtaining permission to reproduce this drawing of the floor plan of Father Franchi's funeral. Professor Jonathan Chaves of George Washington University assisted me in obtaining a copy of an inaccessible article in Chinese. Professor Zhang Xiping of the Beijing Foreign Studies University assisted me in obtaining a copy of a map of Ji'nan from the National Library of China. The staff of the Shandong Provincial Library (Ji'nan) assisted me in searching for gazetteers in their collection. Dr. Claudia von Collani of the Universität Würzburg obtained copies of documents for me, and Professor T. Kaori Kitai of Swarthmore College assisted me in obtaining an illustration.

I am indebted to Dr. Dudink, Dr. Tiedemann, and Father Professor Nicolas Standaert, S.J., of the Katholieke Universiteit Leuven for reading an early version of the manuscript and for their suggestions for improving the manuscript. I would like to make a special note of thanks to Professor Bertuccioli, whose assistance was instrumental in the completion of this book. Finally, I would like to express my gratitude to all the Franciscan fathers who have contributed over the years to the wonderful multivolume *Sinica Franciscana*. Without access to all the rich and careful documentation in these volumes, this work would have been impossible to write.

Once again I would like to thank the Rowman & Littlefield staff for their assistance, particularly Mr. Stephen M. Wrinn, executive editor; Ms. Mary Carpenter, assistant editor; Ms. Lynn Weber, production editor; and Ms. Cheryl W. Hoffman of Hoffman-Paulson Associates, copyeditor.

Baylor University has been generous in providing financial support for this project. This has included a travel grant to visit Ji'nan in March 1997, a travel grant to visit Rome in October 1999, and sabbatical leave during the spring and summer of 1999.

Most distances in the seventeenth- and eighteenth-century documents that I used were expressed in *leguas* (leagues), an imprecise measurement that differed by time and place. While a league is approximately equal to 3 statute miles or 4.83 kilometers, many of the references to leagues in this work seem to refer to a somewhat lesser distance.

One of the problems in doing regional history involves locating remote place names, some of which are so obscure that they have disappeared over time. This explains why some of the sites mentioned are not found on the maps in this book. In addition, place names are sometimes duplicated at different geographical and administrative levels. For example, Ji'nan was not only the name of a city that was the capital of Shandong province but also the name of a prefecture (*fu*) that extended far beyond the city. At the time of the Qing dynasty (1644–1911), the administration of Chinese territory from the capital in Beijing was subdivided into eighteen provinces (*sheng*), such as Shandong, each of which was administered by a governor (*xunfu*). However, in most provinces (for example, in Zhili, but not in Shandong) the governor was subordinate to a governor-general (*zongdu*).

Within each province, local administration was divided into prefectures (*fu*) headed by prefects *(zhifu)*, subprefectures *(ting)* headed by subprefectural magistrates *(tongzhi)*, departments *(zhou)* headed by department magistrates *(zhizhou)*, and, at the lowest level, districts *(xian)* headed by district magistrates *(zhixian)*. There were slight variations in this system, but these complications go beyond our needs. For more detail, I refer the reader to *A Dictionary of Official Titles in Imperial China*, by Charles O. Hucker.

For the sake of simplicity, I have minimized references to the formal administrative categories, but the reader should be aware that most of the references to the towns in this work involve the lowest administrative level, namely, districts (xian). However, some place names refer to villages so obscure that they are merely part of a district. I am afraid that at times there may be some confusion, but this merely reflects the obscurity of many of the people and places treated in this work. From the perspective of the capital in Beijing, these people and places were of minor significance.

This book is dedicated *ab imo pectore* to my twin grandsons, Dylan George Pflum and Jordan David Pflum.

Introduction

In the seventeenth century, the encounter of Chinese and European cultures penetrated beyond the urban centers of China into the provincial cities and remote villages, where it touched many Chinese. These were, for the most part, humble and uneducated people. And although antiforeign hostility is often associated with the poor and unsophisticated, this did not prevent many of them from adopting a foreign religion. It was an encounter of cultures through the medium of religion. The missionaries brought a Europeanized form of Christianity to China, but they had to accommodate it to a very different culture and society there. This situation presented enormous challenges to both sides.

The frustrations and failures of Christianity in China have been widely noted by historians, but the dynamics of provincial conversions have not been well understood. The resurgence of Christianity in recent years in China has caused historians to reexamine this period and to recognize that in spite of the failures, the movement also produced some remarkable successes in the form of conversions of villages that have remained faithful to Christianity down through the years. However, since these successes were largely in rural areas, their importance has been minimized by high-culture historians.

In the cosmopolitan centers of China, the Jesuits, who were part of the intellectual elite of Europe, had long and serious (although ultimately unsuccessful) dialogues with their intellectual, social, and political counterparts in China, the literati. The story of this contact is a fascinating one and has been treated in numerous books. By contrast, the encounters of missionaries in the Chinese provinces have been barely touched upon, although abundant archival material is available for research. The missionaries active in the provinces were, on the whole, not Jesuits, but rather Franciscans, Dominicans, Augustinians, and secular priests who were associated with missionary bodies, such as Propaganda in Rome or the Missions Étrangères of Paris. They tended to be less learned than the Jesuits and more focused on missionary work. Their detailed lists of baptisms indicate that some of them measured success in terms of the quantity, rather than the quality, of their conversions, but others among them were more concerned with the nature and depth of their conversions.

If China were to become a Christian land, something many missionaries prayed would happen, it would have to involve large numbers of conversions. But there were different ways of arriving at that goal. The Jesuits tended to cultivate the most powerful and distinguished members of society in the hopes of first converting members of this elite and then using their power and influence to convert the rest of China. The non-Jesuit missionaries tended to approach the goal of a Christian China by converting large numbers of common people. This difference of approach was due in part to differing philosophies and in part to practical realities. The Jesuits had arrived in China first and had acquired a monopoly, reinforced by the Portuguese *padroado,* on missionizing the seats of power. (The early world explorations and colonizations of the Iberian powers gave them papally authorized monopolies on missionary activities in their respective spheres, the Portuguese padroado and the Spanish *patronato.*) The Jesuits' reluctance to share their monopoly—sometimes for good reasons involving superior knowledge of China rather than mere jealousy—forced the other orders to seek converts in the provinces.

For most missionaries in the provinces of China, with a few notable exceptions, conversions were made slowly and involved a great deal of hardship.[1] Moreover, new Christians often apostacized under the strain of a hostile imperial government and the pressure of local scholar–officials, who viewed Christianity as an alien and subversive force. Since the Manchu rulers who conquered China in 1644 were vastly outnumbered by the native Chinese population, they were hypersensitive about any threats to their authority. After an initial friendliness toward the missionaries under the first two Manchu emperors, the rulers turned against Christianity around 1700. In spite of this hostile climate, which eventually included (after 1724) a ban on missionaries in the provinces, missionaries continued to enter these areas surreptitiously and to conduct an underground church. Baptisms continued, sometimes involving whole villages. In terms of establishing the foundations of Christianity in China, these baptisms of obscure people in the provinces were as important as the conversions of eminent Chinese in Beijing and other urban centers.

This book looks at one of the provincial regions where these missionary activities occurred, specifically, the region of central and western Shandong province and neighboring southern Zhili (modern Hebei) province during the years 1650 to 1785. Although this is not intended as a study of Spanish Franciscan missionaries in China, the period parallels the missionary activities of the Spanish Franciscans in Shandong. In October 1650, the Franciscan Father Antonio Caballero arrived in the capital of Shandong province, filled with hopes as bright as the fields of sunflowers he had passed through on his way to Ji'nan. Some 135 years later, the Great Persecution of 1784–1785 demoralized Christians in Shandong and led eventually to the Spanish government's decision to discontinue its support of the China mission. The religious province of San Gregorio, based in Manila, abandoned Shandong with the death of the last Franciscan missionary there around 1801 and withdrew its mission from China in 1813.

The title *The Spirit and the Flesh in Shandong* was chosen to highlight the antithesis between the spirituality and moral ideals that inspired these Christians and the human weaknesses and temptations that brought about their downfall. On one hand, incredible acts of self-sacrifice were displayed not only by the European missionaries but also by humble Chinese Christians who undertook enormous risks (especially after 1724) in aiding and sheltering priests and who often suffered terrible consequences for doing so. In stark contrast to these instances of self-sacrifice were the endless personal squabbles among the missionaries and Chinese Christians, involving not only missionary politics but also simple human pettiness. There were also cases of more shocking behavior, including two priests who abused their priestly authority to seduce several of their youthful parishioners, scandalizing the Chinese Christians. This is a sexual scandal that, although known in its barest outline, has never been treated in any detail. The spirit and the flesh also converged in Shandong in the little-known practice of the penitential rite of self-flagellation among the Chinese members of the Confraternity of the Passion. Yet another contrast between the spirit and the flesh is found in accounts of, on one hand, divine power in miraculous events in Shandong and, on the other, human powerlessness experienced by Christians who suffered imprisonment and death. And yet, I am not sure that the spirit and the flesh are always in antithesis. In one sense, they seem to be symbiotic and in need of one another. Because of this, I have come to doubt that the great and inspirational acts of martyrdom could exist without both elements. In all, I have found these struggles between the spirit and the flesh to be a remarkable story. I hope that the reader will also.

Prelude: Wondrous Signs

In the early evening between eight and nine o'clock of August 9, 1658, on the eve of the feast of San Lorenzo, "a very large and brilliant cross" *(una mui grande y luçida cruz)* appeared in the sky over Ji'nan.[1] The sky was peaceful and clear, and the cross was very large and well formed in white with its pedestal on the ground. The cross was situated in the northeast, facing toward the southwest. It was seen by many people, both Christians and non-Christians of both sexes. The Christians worshipped, kneeling, while the non-Christians asked what it meant. Father Antonio Caballero wrote that the non-Christians "do not believe even though they see, nor do they perceive the truth even though they hear it."[2] Rather, they believed in the "ancient Pythagorean fantasy" *(chimera antigua pithagorica)* of the transmigration of the soul in Buddhism. The cross was visible throughout the city, where Caballero had been joined by the Jesuit Father Jean Valat. Although the cross's whiteness appeared to denote peace, Caballero interpreted the cross to denote a state of tribulation without bloodshed. This reading was confirmed a short time later when the Shunzhi Emperor (r. 1644–1661), who had previously been very friendly toward Father Schall, cooled in his affection for Christianity and began favoring the Buddhists.[3] There was even a rumor that the emperor had slapped Schall on the face and had begun destroying Christian churches.

Visions were part of the religious experience of Shandong Christians from the beginning. One such vision occurred four years after the missionaries Caballero and Valat had been expelled from Ji'nan. It was later reported by Father Paschale, who had heard about it. At midday on February 14, 1669, a twelve-year-old girl, the daughter of Christian parents, saw a procession in the sky over Ji'nan.[4] This procession was also seen, though less clearly, by many nonbelievers, Muslims, and Christians who had been baptized by Caballero before he was expelled in 1665. The procession consisted of pairs of men on donkeys, carrying banners. They were followed by many women dressed in white with their hair loosened and carrying crosses in their hands. The last of these women carried a child in her arms and appeared to be the Virgin Mary. Behind her were many men on foot, some carrying banners and others carrying crosses in their hands. Jesus appeared in the procession carried by two people supporting him at the arms, in the manner in which he was portrayed in the vivid European-style paintings of the Crucifixion and Resurrection that adorned the Christian churches in China. Other men followed, and the procession was concluded by a man carrying a staff across his shoulders with two baskets hanging at either end; in each basket was a live lamb whose head poked above the rim of the baskets, looking around.

Nearly fifty years later, on the night of September 8, 1718, during the Feast of the Birth of the Blessed Virgin Mary, a cross was again sighted in the sky above Ji'nan.[5] Father Fernández-Oliver sent news of this cross to Beijing, along with a detailed sketch of the apparition. There was immediate skepticism. Bishop Della Chiesa was unable to confirm the sighting, and Father M. Ripa, a Propaganda missionary, seized upon contradictions in the reporting of the event to claim that it was a fabrication by Fernández-Oliver.[6] In writing to Ripa about the event, Fernández-Oliver said that certain nonbelievers claimed to have seen the character *Tian* (Heaven) at the top of the cross, the character *zhu* (Lord) at the center of the cross, and a third, indistinguishable character at the base of the cross. Other observers claimed that they were able to clearly read in the apparition the phrase *Tianzhu Shangdi zhi hao* (The name of the Lord of Heaven Lord-on-High). However, Fernández-Oliver noted that by the time he, Father Nieto-Díaz, the servants, and other Christians saw the apparition, it was ending and none of these words were visible to them.

Miraculous rainfall sometimes followed prayers for rain by Christians in China. After the area of Ji'nan had suffered from droughtlike conditions for two years, the provincial governor and other important officials were at a Buddhist or Daoist temple to pray for rain.[7] The governor sent two men with a horse to the East Church and called Father Ibáñez to the temple. (Caballero was at this time absent, ministering to Christians in a village twenty leagues from Ji'nan.) The governor asked Ibáñez to pray for rain, which indeed fell four days later.[8]

The missionaries frequently were forced to deal with unorthodox forms of spirituality from poor people who claimed unique powers. In one such case, a woman in Ji'nan in 1680 claimed that the Mother of God appeared to her and commanded her also to take the name of the Mother of God.[9] Her claim to miraculous powers was based primarily on one famous incident. During a drought and before the wife of an official of Ji'nan, she recited some prayers that were followed by rain. On this basis she had built a following of two thousand people. Paschali also recounted a story of conversion that he regarded as near miraculous and a sign of God's blessing. A literatus who had been hostile to Christianity, to the point of twice striking a Christian slave of his with a club to force him to apostatize, was eventually converted by the slave's example and was baptized.[10]

1

The Trials and Endeavors of Father Antonio

False Start

No one played a greater role in introducing Christianity to Shandong than the Spanish friar Antonio de Santa Maria Caballero (Li Andang, honorary name Kedun). He was born in the village of Baltanás in the province of Palencia on April 20, 1602, and studied at the University of Salamanca.[1] There on March 24, 1618, one month before his sixteenth birthday, he entered the Order of the Friars Minor (Franciscans) at the Calvario convent of the religious province of San Pablo. He completed his studies at the university and volunteered for the Franciscan Japanese mission. After his ordination, he was assigned to Castroverde. From there he departed for the Philippines by way of Mexico in 1628 in the company of twenty-nine other Franciscans and arrived in Manila in 1629. He was appointed to teach rhetoric and theology at the San Francisco convent in Manila. In addition, he studied the Japanese language and ministered to the Japanese lepers at Balete. At that time the religious province of San Gregorio, based in Manila, had initiated a missionary effort in China that would continue until 1813 (although the last Spanish Franciscan in Shandong died in 1801).[2] Caballero was ultimately assigned to the China mission.

Caballero's work in China may be divided into two phases. The first phase, from 1633 to 1636, was contentious and ultimately abortive. Had Caballero not returned to China for a second time, he certainly would not be regarded as the pioneering and outstanding Franciscan missionary in China in the seventeenth century. It was during the second phase, from 1649 to 1669, and mainly in Shandong that Caballero's reputation was made. The situation of the Spanish Franciscans and Dominicans in regard to China was precarious. They were excluded by the Portuguese padroado from entering China through its main port for Europeans, Macau. Their awkward but persistent efforts to enter China through pirate-infested ports in Fujian province caused them to be viewed by the

Jesuits as a nuisance who threatened the fragile and hard-earned acceptance of Christian missionaries by the Chinese government.

Caballero's first entry into China was the result of an appeal for assistance sent from Fuan to the Philippines in December 1632 by the Dominican Father Angelo Cocchi (1597–1633).[3] In response, Caballero, along with Francesco Bermudez, O.F.M., and the Dominican Juan Bañeza de Morales (Li Yufan) (d. 1664), departed from the Philippines on March 9, 1633, and arrived in Danshui, Taiwan, on April 2.[4] There Caballero and Morales were picked up by a boat sent by Father Cocchi and brought to Fuan in Fujian province on July 2. Caballero then set out on his own in search of a base. At Jianchang in Jiangxi province and at Nanjing, he was treated by the Jesuits as more of a problem than a fellow missionary and, given the difficulties of official Chinese acceptance of foreign missionaries, he *was* a problem. Nevertheless, the Jesuits' treatment of him fell considerably short of what might be called Christian love. When Caballero's porter left him, the Jesuit vice-provincial Manuel Dias provided him with a substitute named Andrew Siao Leu, who on Dias's orders harassed rather than helped Caballero. Finally, on Dias's command, three Jesuit servants bound and kidnapped Caballero, putting him on a boat that, after six months of wandering, brought him back to where he began—Fuan.

In November 1634, the Dominicans and Franciscans came to an agreement by which the Dominicans would minister in Fuan while the Franciscans took Dingtou. Caballero then founded a new mission at nearby Ningde. At Dingtou he baptized his first and most famous convert, Luo Wenzao (Gregorio Lopez), O.P., who was born in the village of Luojia, near Dingtou.[5] Luo later entered the Dominican order in 1650 at Manila and was ordained a priest in 1654. Luo was named vicar apostolic of Nanjing on January 4, 1674, and consecrated bishop on August 28, 1685, by the Propaganda bishop Bernardino Della Chiesa. He died at Nanjing on February 27, 1691.[6]

In order to resolve troublesome issues of the Chinese rites to ancestors and Confucius, the Franciscans met in two long sessions at Dingtou in 1635 and 1636, and Caballero was selected to carry the minutes of these meetings back to their superiors in Manila.[7] However, his journey was plagued by shipwreck in the Taiwan Straits, capture by the Dutch from their base at Castle Zeelandia (in Taiwan), and imprisonment in Batavia and Ternate. After eight months, he was released at Malacca and found his way back to Manila by June 1637. So ended his adventurous but not very productive entry into China.

In 1640, he went to Macau, from which he and all other Spaniards were expelled in 1644. After the ship was carried off course, he and seven nuns arrived in Danang, Cochinchina, where they were sentenced to death. The sentence was commuted, and Caballero proceeded to baptize two thousand people, including the king's brother. Back in Manila by mid-1645, Caballero was noted for aiding earthquake victims and preaching against vices in public life. His preaching was rewarded by the governor with confinement and fasting in the mountains of the Philippines. Meanwhile, his Dominican associate, Morales, returned from Rome with decrees appointing both Morales and Caballero prefects apostolic in their respective missions.[8]

The Road to Ji'nan

In response to a plea from Dominicans in China, Caballero entered China for a second time in 1649. He was accompanied by three other Franciscans from the province of San Gregorio in the Philippines (island of Luzon)—Buenaventura Ibáñez, José Casanova, and Brother Diego—as well as several Dominicans, including Morales.[9] They traveled on board a junk owned by Zheng Zhiguan, an uncle of the famous pirate and Ming loyalist Zheng Chenggong (Koxinga) (1624–1662), and landed at the seaport of Anhai (also known as Jinjiang), located south of Quanzhou on the southern Fujian coast (see map 1). Because the Manchu conquest of China had recently extended into the Fujian coast, the situation there was chaotic and dangerous. Writing to the Franciscan provincial on November 20, 1649, Caballero complained that his lack of knowledge of the Chinese language was impeding evangelization.[10]

They remained at the port for one year, and in July 1650 Caballero departed by sea in the company of two Chinese menservants with the intention of establishing a mission in Korea. En route, Caballero was afflicted with an illness from which he was relieved only when kneeling or standing.[11] Finding the port at Tianjin closed to passage to Korea, Caballero heard that Korean merchants visited the capital, Beijing, twenty-five leagues (approximately seventy-five miles) away and decided to go there. With some difficulty he obtained entry through a gate at Beijing and located the house where the Korean merchants resided when they were in the capital, but they were no longer there. Caballero found some Korean tanners nearby, but they would not allow him to lodge with them, no matter how much money Caballero offered, because they feared that the presence of an illegal alien would get them into trouble with the law. Caballero found lodging in a Manchu's house, but his host became so fearful of being punished for lodging an unauthorized foreigner that he helped Caballero locate the residence of the Jesuit Father Schall, who served the throne in the Bureau of Astronomy and who received him kindly.[12] This was the beginning of a fruitful relationship in which Schall assisted Caballero in numerous ways.

Schall explained to him that it was impossible to go to Korea at that time because of hostilities between Koreans and the Manchus. Instead, he proposed that Caballero go to Ji'nan, the capital of Shandong province (see maps 1 and 2), where there lived a small number of Christians who had recently been abandoned by the departure of a Jesuit priest. Previously, Father Longobardo (1565–1655) had lived in Ji'nan for seventeen years.[13] More recently the Jesuit Father Giovanni Francesco De Ferrariis (Ferrari) (1609–1671) had lived there in solitude. Schall offered to write a letter of introduction to a literatus acquaintance in Ji'nan, and Caballero accepted the proposal, out of necessity rather than enthusiasm. His heart was still set on Korea when he climbed into an upper story of Schall's residence. On the wall was an image of the Savior, and at that moment he heard an inner voice saying, "Since I want you to go to Shandong and minister to all my sheep, will you not go willingly?" Caballero submitted to what he took to be the will of God, but there remained some reluctance. On the way to Ji'nan he passed through fields of wild sunflowers, something he had never before seen in China, and he was reminded of the sunflowers in Spain.[14] He took the beauty of the scene and the joy it inspired in him as a sign of Providence guiding him to Ji'nan.

Upon arriving in the city at the end of October 1650, Caballero sought out Schall's literatus acquaintance and presented him with Schall's letter as well as some small gifts (a case with two knives and a pair of scissors, four sheets of paper from Castile, and fifteen brooches from Castile).[15] In return, Caballero received two taels of silver with the promise of fifty more in order to buy a building for a church. One tael or *liang* was equivalent to 1.1 ounces or 31.25 grams of silver. The value of taels was often expressed by the Spanish missionaries in terms of a peso, a former silver coin of Spain and Spanish America equal to eight reals. Their relative value was approximately three taels to four pesos.

Caballero also visited two literatus friends of this first literatus, offering them similar small gifts (a tiny piece of soap from Mexico and two large handkerchiefs). The three literati gave Caballero a total of 130 taels for a church, and they also helped him obtain the deed for a Franciscan residence. During the interim, Caballero lived in the Jesuit house.[16] Finally, in 1651 he moved into the Franciscan residence, which he dedicated to Domina Angelorum (Lady of the Angels), that is, the Virgin Mary. When Caballero first arrived in Ji'nan, there were less than thirty Christians there and only ten to twelve of them attended mass.[17] During his first year in Ji'nan, he went on a journey to visit the Christian communities in outlying areas. Traveling two days from Ji'nan, he found a flock that had not seen a priest for seven years and whose religious beliefs had become unorthodox, blending with Chinese folk religion.[18] Caballero spent a month and ten days on this journey.

From Ji'nan he sent letters with his manservant to the two Franciscans he had left behind in the port of Anhai. In December 1651 Father Buenaventura Ibáñez (Wen Dula, Daoji) (1610–1691) arrived in Ji'nan, while the other Franciscan remained in Anhai to receive shipments from Manila. Ibáñez did not bring the vestments and chalices needed to serve mass because the provincial in Manila had ordered the Franciscans to go no farther than twenty leagues (approximately sixty miles) inland from Anhai. However, Caballero and Ibáñez decided that since the provincial had made this restriction before they had secured a residence and church in Ji'nan, it would no longer apply. Consequently, in 1652 Ibáñez returned to Anhai to obtain the vestments and chalices and on his journey received assistance from the Jesuit houses through which he passed.[19]

When Ibáñez arrived at Anhai in January 1653, he found that another Franciscan, the lay brother Cristobal de San Diego (Christophorus a S. Didaco), had arrived from Manila without bringing a subsidy, so Ibáñez was forced to wait in Anhai for the subsidy. (This brother Cristobal would live only a short time, dying on October 31 of that year in Quanzhou.)[20] In the meanwhile, during the years 1653 and 1654, Caballero lived in misery and penury in Ji'nan.[21] He did not know how to speak Chinese, nor did he know how to go about learning it. Consequently, his contacts with Chinese were severely limited, and he could not engage in the ministry that was his purpose for coming there. On holy days he was alone in the house, without even a manservant for company. His Franciscan companions were not with him, and his lack of funds reduced him to the most meagre existence. Father Schall occasionally sent money from Beijing and tried to console him with letters. Finally, in January 1655 Ibáñez returned with part of the alms that had been sent from the provincial. Armed with funds and a growing facility in speaking Chinese, Caballero began making trips outside the walls of the city of Ji'nan into neighboring villages, where the missionaries were increasingly successful in performing baptisms.

Success brought criticism, and Caballero rebutted the accusation that the priests had paid the Chinese silver in order to baptize them by describing the extensive preparations of those Christians who would be baptized.[22] To begin with, all people seeking baptism were instructed in what they should believe and what they should deny themselves and renounce from the heart. This was followed by continuing instruction on confessing, receiving the Eucharist, works of mercy, precepts of the Decalogue, and the doctrines of the church. Every Sunday before the mass, the congregation recited, for two choruses on their knees, the rosary of the Virgin and all of the Christian doctrine *(la doctrina cristiana)*. This was followed by specific questions on the Apostles' Creed *(Credo)*, which were addressed individually to both adults and children. The mass was read, followed by a brief sermon appropriate to the time and season. It was rare that on a given Sunday no one would confess, and during Lent everyone—both men and women—confessed.

Compelling anecdotes were part of the missionary process, and Caballero told the story of a five-year-old whose father had been baptized. The boy became obsessed with repeating the holy names "Jesus, Mary" and repeated them even when playing with other children his own age. One day, the father was removing a large container of boiling water from the fire when the bottom fell out, mortally wounding the little boy.[23] The father held the boy, who was very agitated and clamoring that he wanted to go to his house and be with his father. When the boy insisted that he go to his own house, the father said, "Well, I do not wish you to leave," and the boy slapped his father for impeding him and died. His father then realized that his son wanted to go to the Heavenly Father's house. In 1652 Caballero visited a town twenty leagues from Ji'nan where a Christian community had been founded by the Jesuits, but it had been abandoned for six years and the people had apostatized. Caballero was able to reconvert them, to the amazement of the next Jesuit who visited there.

Schall asked Caballero to send some intriguing figure of a saint to give to the Shunzhi Emperor's mother. Even if she was not a Christian, Schall said, she was sympathetic and would help protect Christianity from the "priests of the idols" (i.e., Buddhists).[24] Schall said that the emperor's mother sent him alms and other things and that a brother of the emperor visited and dealt directly with him.[25] Schall conveyed news from the Jesuit vice-provincial, Manuel Dias the Younger (1574–1659). Dias said that although he supported Caballero's presence in Ji'nan, he could not authorize turning over the Jesuit residence in Ji'nan to Caballero without the approval of the Jesuit superior in Macau. Nursing a guilty conscience, Dias asked Schall to seek Caballero's forgiveness for his role in causing Caballero's kidnapping near Nanjing in 1634. In 1651 Schall sent Caballero books on the Chinese language and twelve taels of silver.

Problems: Women, Servants, Loneliness, and Lack of Money

The Christian priests' relations with women in Shandong were a particularly sensitive matter. In China at that time most women were secluded from public contact with men. This seclusion fostered suspicion over the contacts between the priests and women. It was in this atmosphere that Caballero was accused of touching and groping the female confirmands' breasts. However, Caballero explained the process by saying that the godmother removed a little of the collar of the adult women that hung below the chin so that he could apply a drop of oil directly on the throat with a feather from the chrismatory (silver vial of holy oil).[26] Caballero's explanation did not end the suspicion.

Caballero spoke of having to flee Ji'nan when the "Tartars" (Manchus) entered and destroyed some houses. Some villagers from outside Ji'nan came to ask Caballero to visit their villages, which had been without a priest's services since their baptism five or six years before. They had lapsed into old superstitions and idolatries, calling on both God and "Baal" (obviously a bibically generic term for a non-Christian god). Few people from the outside world cared about these humble Chinese, and they responded with enthusiasm to Caballero's concern. They listened attentively to his instruction and knelt before the altar praying in alternating chants, a practice still heard in Catholic churches in China today. On Sundays following the mass, they lined up in church, the men on one side and the women on the other, and sang the prayers of Christian doctrine. Caballero baptized over two hundred adults and children during two visits. Upon his departure, the men and women followed him to the outskirts of the village in a tearful, emotional farewell.

Caballero's relations with the Jesuits in China were mixed. With Schall in Beijing and De Ferrariis or Valat in Ji'nan, he worked positively, but there were other Jesuits who were not amicable. Caballero felt a debt to Schall for all his assistance but noted that other Jesuits criticized Schall for helping him and for leading him to Ji'nan.[27] Caballero's famous kidnapping in 1634 could be attributed to his appearing at a difficult time, but his conflicts with the Jesuits usually emerged from philosophical rather than personal differences. Whereas Caballero may have been strict in theological issues, in personal relationships he was genial and accommodating.

When Caballero returned to Ji'nan from his second visit to the Christians in the outlying villages, he met the Jesuit Father De Ferrariis who had until recently (1648) lived alone in Ji'nan.[28] De Ferrariis had been sent by the Jesuit vice-provincial, Manuel Dias the Younger, to evict Caballero, under the mistaken assumption that Caballero was still occupying the Jesuit residence. Dias was unaware that Caballero had vacated the Jesuit house six months before and had acquired a separate house for the Franciscans. Ironically, the Jesuit house was in such bad condition that Caballero invited De Ferrariis to stay in the Franciscan house, but he (with some embarrassment) declined the invitation.[29] However, Caballero and De Ferrariis established an amicable relationship. Caballero thought him quiet and peaceful, and neither troubled the other. De Ferrariis told Caballero that he disagreed with the quarreling among religious orders, and to show his sincerity, he read to Caballero what he was writing to his superior along these lines. De Ferrariis asked Caballero to relinquish to him the ministry to the flocks in the outlying villages, to which Caballero agreed. This was a reasonable request since the Jesuits had initiated the ministry in those villages; however, Caballero noted that De Ferrariis was not able to care for them properly.

Caballero wrote in January 1653 that although Christianity had been preached in China for more than seventy years, the fruits had been small.[30] He believed this was due to the fickleness of the Chinese, who commonly forgot their commitment a few months after being baptized. Others learned the catechism and yet remained unbaptized because of a certain listlessness and sloth toward things that were spiritual and unseen. In addition, it was particularly difficult to minister to the women.

As of January 1653, it was difficult for any of the Franciscans (Father Joseph de Casanova in Anhai and Caballero and Ibáñez in Ji'nan) to find and keep a manservant. Caballero wrote:

> [U]ntil now we have not been able to find nor to keep a manservant who is willing. I have had three here in succession, his salary being meals and four or five reals a month. No one is willing if he is not given some advance payment, and then the little service that there is, if one does not command it each day and each time, they do not wish to do it. If they do it, it is done as badly as if they had not done it. If they are told to do it, they do not obey; if they are scolded, they lose respect for the religious and suffer shame (loss of face), turning against him.[31]

Consequently, as of January 3, 1653, the Franciscan fathers in Ji'nan had been without a manservant for six months while Ibáñez did the cooking and Caballero the cleaning. When a Christian brought an eighteen-year-old to serve as a manservant, in the fifteen days that he worked at the residence, the youth stole the Chinese Christians' bedding and three garments from the priests.

At this point in the mission in Ji'nan, the priests still lived in great isolation. The Jesuit De Ferrariis had complained of the isolation in 1648, and Caballero noted in 1653 that when Ibáñez was gone, he was left alone in the house "without a single soul" with whom he could share even a meal. The isolation was due, in part, to the fathers' lack of facility in the Chinese language. What they learned was largely self-taught, and Caballero complained that "what one learns without a teacher in a week, one could learn with a teacher in an hour."[32] Nevertheless, Caballero toiled on in the belief that the difficulties were part of God's larger plan.

In a letter of January 3, 1653, to the Franciscan provincial in the Philippines, Father Sebastianus a Iesu de Moron, Caballero gave the impression that Ji'nan was merely a temporary mission assignment while he waited for permission to go to Korea. The Franciscan missionaries in Shandong were supported by an annual subsidy *(subsidio)* or assistance *(socorro)* from the provincial in the Philippines and by government support from the patronato. Caballero spoke of having no one to send to Anhai to receive the subsidy except Ibáñez. Because of the long distances involved and the difficulties in obtaining the subsidy, Caballero suggested that the provincial send the subsidy for three years rather than one year at a time.

Caballero was astounded at the Chinese people's lack of fear over the terrors of hell and their lack of desire for the glory of salvation.[33] (The notion of hell had been introduced to the Chinese by Buddhism in the second century A.D., and this notion was widely propagated by popular Buddhism and Daoism.)[34]

They appeared to be affected only by what was visible. Because of this and because European-style paintings of Christian themes had proven to be a dramatic way of conveying the Christian teaching to the Chinese, Caballero asked the provincial to send a painting of the Judgment or something serious, such as the horrors of hell, that would have the power to influence the Chinese in Shandong. He referred to a small canvas of the Judgment that stood in the convent of San Francisco or in the church at Santa Cruz in the Philippines.

In a letter of November 1653 to the Franciscan provincial in the Philippines, Caballero summarized the frustrating state of the China mission. The first Jesuits who entered China passed many years and endured numerous disappointments before attaining the fruits of conversions.[35] The Dominicans had been in China for twenty-three years (1632–1653) with scanty results. Caballero was the first Franciscan missionary in China, and he believed that God had guided him to Ji'nan, where he and the Jesuit Father De Ferrariis lived in harmony "as two brothers."[36]

At this time, Caballero and Ibáñez lived a hand-to-mouth existence in Ji'nan, which is well described in Caballero's own words:

> I get along here without assistance (the subsidy), except for the little that the brother Fr. Buenaventura [Ibáñez] brought for December in the year 1651. We got by with it, he and I and a manservant until September of 1652, at which time I sent him to Beijing, and there the son-in-law of a mandarin gave us fifty taels, which we owe, of silver. In January of 1653 Fr. Buenaventura departed for Anhai in order to fetch what might come from Manila. He took twenty taels on the road for 500 leagues, the distance from here to there. And in the journey, on account of it being indispensable, making the round trip on the road in twenty days [sic], and because of it being filled with bandits, with a manservant who was accompanying him, he expended another twenty taels more than was granted to him. I stay in the house for the whole of the present year. I do not know what comes from Manila and a mandarin gave me ten taels with which I may retile the roof of the house, that leaks everywhere. I passed time in such a way until the following April. A Manchu mandarin, twenty leagues distant from here, called me in order to baptize his wife, children and servants, although he is a non-believer, and they gave me eighteen taels of silver, with which I bought wheat and firewood, etc. for me and for a manservant, and I passed the time until August, then eating wild purslane [a low, trailing green plant with yellow flowers, used in salads and as a potherb] and a little bread. Fr. Johann Adam [Schall] sent me twenty taels from Beijing, without out me having done anything for him or making my need known to him. I bought wheat to last me until January.[37]

It was difficult for Caballero to give up the idea of going to Korea, and he underestimated the difficulties of getting there. He mistakenly believed that Korea was a province of China and later learned that it was a separate kingdom, but with the status of a tribute-bearing protectorate.[38] In December 1653 Caballero had still not abandoned his dream of establishing a mission in Korea. He appealed to the new provincial, Father Juan Pastor,[39] as he had to the previous provincial, for permission to move with his companions from Shandong province to Korea, "a province subject to this realm," and to the adjacent islands, including Japan.[40]

Caballero described to the new provincial how, on Sunday before the mass at the East Church in Ji'nan, the small number of Christians who attended gathered before the altar on their knees and, with Caballero leading them, prayed in two choruses the four prayers and commandments of God and the church in a loud voice. They continued their praying in two choruses to the crown of the Virgin and concluded with "Praise be to the Most High Sacrament and the Immaculate Conception."[41]

In apparent response to the provincial's wish that the Franciscans have less contact with the Jesuits, Caballero wrote that the Jesuits had shown considerable charity toward the Franciscans in Ji'nan, lending them money in their time of need.[42] Caballero noted that the Jesuits had done "a thousand deeds of kindness" for the financially strapped Franciscans in Shandong, lending them silver even when it was not solicited. In 1652 in Beijing, the Jesuit Father António Rodriguez lent them fifty taels.[43] In addition, the Jesuits lent Father Ibáñez twenty taels on his journey from Ji'nan to Anhai. Finally, Caballero himself owed the Jesuits fifteen taels. Their need had been aggravated by the fact that no subsidy had been received from the Philippines during the years 1652 and 1653.[44] There were three Franciscans in China in need of support: Caballero and Ibáñez in Ji'nan and Father José de Casanova in Anhai. Finally, the subsidy arrived in 1655 in the amount of two hundred pesos from the provincial and four hundred pesos in alms from the lord governor of the Philippines, Don Sabiniano.[45]

The distance from Ji'nan to Anhai, the port used by the Franciscans for communicating and receiving subsidies from the Philippines, was said to be five hundred leagues. Father Ibáñez had gone there with a manservant to retrieve the subsidy; halfway back, he fell seriously ill and was cared for by the Jesuits in Hangzhou.[46] After one month, Ibáñez was well enough to continue the journey back to Ji'nan in the company of his manservant and a Jesuit who was traveling to Beijing. Caballero felt the need to justify the expense of paying a manservant to accompany Ibáñez on his journey to Anhai.[47] The highways in China were unsafe, and even the Jesuits and Dominicans, with their long experience in China, did not travel without a native guide. The taverns and roads were filled with highwaymen who roamed in gangs armed with arrows, sabers, and swift horses. Caballero had himself once encountered them and received a deep wound in his forehead. Seventy pesos was expended in paying for the accompanying manservant: forty pesos for his travel expenses and thirty pesos for his labor.

Caballero had sent José de Casanova south by January 25, 1654, because the frigidity of the climate at Ji'nan aggravated his chest congestion and asthma. Because it was so cold and icy in Ji'nan, Caballero the previous January had requested the provincial to send coarse woolen cloth.[48] In 1655 Caballero dispatched a manservant (the same manservant who had accompanied Ibáñez) with letters to take to de Casanova, who was waiting in Anhai, commanding him to return to Manila because of his asthma.[49]

Travel between Ji'nan and Anhai was further complicated by Ming loyalists, who were fighting against the Manchus. Manchu soldiers detained the porter midway through his journey. Noting that he spoke with the accent of the rebellious Fujian region and finding on his person letters in foreign writing and foreign money, the Manchus suspected the porter of being a spy. Even though a Jesuit priest vouched for him and denied that he was a spy or a rebel, the governor of Nanjing sent him to Beijing. The porter was held in prison in Bejing until Schall intervened and explained that there was nothing in the letters that was contrary to either the emperor or the realm.[50] Finally, the porter was released and returned to Ji'nan in November 1655, but without the letters.[51]

In his December 6, 1655, letter to the provincial, Caballero once more expressed the wish to go to Korea because he believed the Koreans were more disposed to receive the gospel than the Chinese.[52] He still hoped that Schall, with all his contacts in Beijing, might obtain permission for him to go to Korea. However, there was a dawning recognition that the ease with which he came to Ji'nan and obtained a house there might have been a sign from God that he was meant to remain there. Furthermore, his relations with the Jesuit priest, De Ferrariis, who occupied the other church, were very amicable. Caballero had worked in harmony with this Jesuit "with the temperament of an angel" to serve the Christians there.

The Jesuits and Franciscans cooperated in Ji'nan in ways that led Caballero to propose that they extend this cooperation to reduce the cost of carrying the Franciscan subsidy from Anhai to Ji'nan.[53] It took more than two months to traverse the 500 leagues of dangerous roads from Ji'nan to Anhai and an additional two months to return. Caballero had been quite willing to share the Franciscan supply of holy oil with the Jesuits because their shipments from Europe had been disrupted by a dispute between the pope and Portuguese authorities. In this same spirit of cooperation, Caballero proposed that the Franciscan provincial send the subsidy of silver plus holy oil and letters for the Ji'nan mission to the Dominican Father Morales or to another Dominican who resided in the village of Luojia (in the Fuan district) in Fujian province. Morales could then forward the subsidy to Father António de Gouvea, S.J. (1592–1677), in Fuzhou, a distance that involved only four days of travel. Caballero proposed that Gouvea pick the subsidy up from Morales and send it to the Jesuit vice-provincial, Father da Cunha, in

Hangzhou (see map 1). To retrieve the subsidy from Hangzhou rather than Anhai would reduce the distance to be traveled from Ji'nan by half, from 500 to 250 leagues, and also reduce the related dangers of travel. Caballero had already received written agreement from both Morales and the Jesuit superior to this plan.

The great distance between Ji'nan and the seaport of Anhai, along with the high costs of supporting such a distant mission, brought complaints from the new Franciscan provincial in Manila, Father Alonso de San Francisco. Consequently, in a letter of June 18, 1656, Caballero explained at length to the new provincial why they had established a mission so far in the interior of China.[54] First of all, he was urged to enter further into China by the provincial of that time, the present Bishop Antonio de San Gregorio. Second, the Jesuit Father Pietro Canevari, who was based in Quanzhou, had urged Caballero to go elsewhere because the Jesuits already had established a base in that region of Fujian province. Caballero went on to give other reasons, but ultimately, he believed that it was "our Lord" *(nuestro Señor)* who opened the doors to Ji'nan while blocking his desire to go to Korea.[55] Whereas he received help from Schall in Beijing and from three literati in Ji'nan who contributed 130 taels to buy a building for a house and church that cost 150 taels, obstacles appeared to block his every attempt to go to Korea. In addition, the great harmony in Ji'nan between the Franciscans and Jesuits confirmed that Ji'nan was the right mission site.[56]

Between his arrival in Ji'nan in late October 1650 and June 18, 1656, Caballero baptized 738 people mostly from Ji'nan and others from nearby villages. He baptized 25 moribund children *(in articulo mortis)*. These children were born to non-Christian parents who had presumably abandoned them. Caballero revealed a growing affection for the Christians of Ji'nan, and he spoke of their enthusiasm and joy for the church. In accord with the Chinese custom that men and women not mingle publicly, Caballero conducted a mass on Saturday for the women and on Sunday for the men.[57] They were taught the fasts and festivals in accordance with the papal decrees that he and Father Juan Bañeza de Morales carried from Rome to Manila. After five and one-half years in Ji'nan, Caballero had not baptized a single literatus or person of wealth. Rather, all of his baptisms were of the poorest and most common people.[58] Caballero bemoaned the fact that his conversions in Ji'nan had been limited to the poorest people, and he believed the same thing was true of missionaries in Beijing and elsewhere in China.[59] He was reluctant to ask the Chinese Christians to financially support the church and its priests for two reasons. First, the Chinese converts were all poor; and, second, the other religious sects in China squeezed the people for money in a manner that he felt Christianity should avoid.

Caballero divided the Chinese into three categories, on the basis of his missionary experiences.[60] The first category was the literati, from which the officials were drawn. Caballero described them as learned men who were skilled in writing very good books displaying excellent method and style. However, their path to salvation was impeded by their ambition and sensuality. Although Caballero noted that there were a few Christian literati in China, they were limited not only in number but also in spiritual fervor. By March 7, 1659, Caballero and his fellow Franciscans in Ji'nan had baptized 1,552 people but not a single literatus, although the literati had devoted considerable time to listening to what he had to say and disputing the content of Christian teaching with him.[61] This was prior to his collaboration with the literatus Shang Huqing, which is described in the next chapter.

Most of the conversions Caballero and his confreres made were from a second category consisting of workers, soldiers, and *yamen* (local court) clerks who served the officials. These people were very poor and backward, which Caballero believed made them more receptive to baptism. Whereas sometimes in China whole families or villages were baptized together, Caballero spoke of his Christians being scattered among nonbelievers "as a rose among a bramble of thorns" *(como una rosa entre un zarzal de espinas).*[62] It was common for relatives and friends to curse them for becoming Christians. As missionaries it was necessary to travel among these humble people, sharing their meagre diet, which consisted mainly of vegetables and sometimes eggs, but rarely meat or fish.

The third category of Chinese consisted of merchants, contractors, and skilled workers. This group displayed neither admirable qualities, like the literati, nor faithfulness, like the poor. Rather they were obsessed with personal profit, and Caballero compared them to "grave diggers in their avarice and cheating" who had no interest in the gospel. Caballero justified the Franciscans' apostolate to the poor and humble and the lack of interest of the Chinese "nobles and rich people" by citing from the Bible: "It is easier for a camel to go through the eye of a needle than for a rich man to enter the kingdom of God" (Matthew 19:24, Mark 10:25, Luke 18:25).[63]

Although the previous provincial, Father Juan Pastor, required that the Franciscan confreres periodically visit Manila, Caballero explained that he had been unable to abandon the Christians there in Ji'nan.[64] Now he was even less able to do so because his Jesuit colleague in Ji'nan, De Ferrariis, was preparing to depart for Macau, where he had been called by his superior.[65] Caballero wrote that for him to leave Ji'nan would be like leaving a vineyard without harvesting the grapes that were ripe.

Frustration

In the 1650s, the Franciscans suffered from great isolation in Ji'nan, though this situation was alleviated when they later established a Franciscan base in Canton

(Guangzhou). Then instead of going through Anhai in Fujian or the nettlesome Portuguese authorities in Macau, they could communicate with the provincial in the Philippines by sending letters on the well-traveled Ambassador's Route (see map 1) to Canton. In two letters (written on March 7 and 8, 1659) to the newly appointed provincial of the Province of San Gregorio of the Philippines, Father J. de Capistrano, Caballero echoed a familiar theme. No aid had been received from the provincial since 1655, when six hundred pesos had arrived. Since then only a few letters with little in the form of financial aid had reached Caballero.

The missionaries in Ji'nan lacked even sufficient clothing to keep warm against the bitter cold and snow of the winters there.[66] The Franciscan head of the convent in Macau, Father Cristobal de la Magdalene, had sent nineteen taels, which amounted to twenty-five pesos, a small amount. For the third time Caballero was writing to the provincial and to Father Sebastian Rodriguez, O.F.M., without knowing whether the letters reached their destinations in the Philippines. The Franciscans were unable to legally send letters directly to Macau, which was seven hundred leagues south of Ji'nan, and so sent them first to the Jesuits in Beijing, which was only a hundred leagues to the north. The Jesuits then did the courtesy of sending the letters south eight hundred leagues to Macau. Some holy oil and silver were sent from Macau with the help of the Jesuits. Here and elsewhere Caballero said that it was unnecessary to send wine. The attacks by thieves on the couriers sometimes caused everything to be lost.[67] In his letter to the Franciscan provincial of March 1659, Caballero said that he felt abandoned by his Franciscan brothers, who not only had not sent them sufficient aid but who also criticized the mission in Ji'nan as a waste of time.[68]

In contrast to the beautiful South Church in Beijing built by Schall and frequented by the Shunzhi Emperor (r. 1644–1661), the two churches in Ji'nan were "very poor and ungraceful in appearance" *(muy pobres y deslucidas en el edificio).*[69] Nevertheless, after the French-born Jesuit Jean Valat (Wang Ruwang) (1614–1696) arrived, he and Caballero worked in loving harmony, "as if we were brothers" *(como si fueramos hermanos),* Caballero said. The Franciscan church was a bit better off than the Jesuit church, but part of it was falling down, with no one to repair it. Both Ibáñez and Caballero were in fairly good health in March 1659, although Caballero described himself as "already old, with a cane and sickly" *(yo ya viejo, cano y achacoso).*

The long-awaited aid from the province in the Philippines finally arrived in 1659, but to retrieve it, Caballero had to travel from Ji'nan to Lanxi, a district in Zhejiang province three hundred leagues south of Ji'nan. After arriving in Lanxi, he wrote a letter of acknowledgment on September 20 to the former deputy provincial, Father Francisco de San Diego (Franciscus a S. Didaco), who had been an intermediary in the transfer.[70] (Over two years had elapsed since the provincial had sent five hundred pesos and a letter from Panguil, in the province of Laguna in the Philippines, on July 27, 1657.) The transfer had to pass through several hands. The Dominican Father Victorio Riccio[71] received the letter and the funds in the Philippines and sent them with Father Luo Wenzao (Gregorio Lopez) to the Dominican Father Francisco Varo in Fuan.[72] Varo forwarded them to the Jesuit church in Lanxi.

To receive the aid, Caballero and two Christian menservants departed from Ji'nan on July 15 and, after a two-month journey, arrived in Lanxi on September 15.[73] It was a long, difficult journey, filled with obstacles. Caballero estimated the distance as "more than 200 leagues."[74] In an unnamed city along the way, he was detained for fifteen days because of a threat from gangs of bandits. During that time, he was lodged in the house of a Manchu official who was a Christian and whose mother was very devout. The mother, son, and other Christians made their confession to Caballero. The next night, they all had to flee the city in the middle of the night because of the attacking bandits.[75] The mandarin and his family fled on horses, but Caballero and his two menservants had to walk with their bundles on their backs. In the chaos, Caballero lost his sleeping blankets, but they eventually were able to rent some donkeys to ride. In another city, Caballero lodged in the house of a non-Christian official.

Upon arriving in Lanxi, Caballero received the news of the election of a new Franciscan provincial in Manila, Father Juan de Capistrano. Caballero wrote on September 21, 1659, to congratulate him on his election.[76] Caballero again shared his frustration that none of their fellow Franciscans in the Philippines-based province, except Father Sebastian Rodriguez, held the China mission in high regard.[77] In spite of the lack of converts, Caballero argued that the China mission should not be judged a failure because God's wisdom was inscrutable. He used several plant metaphors to make this point. First, he compared the Chinese people to a tree in which some of the branches (comparable to provinces) are filled with greenery and yield ripe fruit while other branches appear to be desiccated.[78] He compared the emerging Christians in China to "roses among millions and millions of thorns" *(rosas entre millones y millones de espinas)*. At present, the ears of corn appeared to be very far from ripeness, but with the attention of missionaries, they could be brought to harvest.

In the appendix to a letter to Father San Diego dated September 5, 1659, at Lanxi, Caballero wrote that in the past in Ji'nan, he and Ibáñez made wine that, although small in amount, had sufficed.[79] In the Shandong site where he was proposing that a new church be established, it would not be possible to make wine because the grapes were too frail and thin. Consequently, he asked that if two new missionaries should be sent, they should bring two pots of wine with them and two units of wax candles because wax candles were very expensive in China.

Christmas of 1659 in Ji'nan was celebrated by the small circle of Christians as a major event. Three weeks before Christmas, they began to prepare themselves, arranging their offerings and coming to be confessed, first the women and then the men, so that they might receive communion.[80] On Christmas Eve, Christians came from the small villages outside Ji'nan to the East Church. While Caballero worked from sundown through the middle of the night in a small adjacent room confessing them, the men filled the church, singing praises to the Lord Jesus and to his holy mother, Mary, praying in chorus in a high voice, first the rosary of the Virgin and then her litany, the fifteen mysteries. After finishing with the confessions, Caballero preached a sermon on the mystery then said mass and gave communion to those who had not received it in the preceding days. At four o'clock in the morning, Father Ibáñez said three masses; at dawn, he said two more masses for those who arrived late and also for some who stayed the entire night. Finally, the parishioners trooped home.[81] Meanwhile, the Jesuit Father Valat of the West Church was traveling twenty leagues to celebrate Christmas with small Christian communities, who joyously celebrated with flutes and other instruments and candles.

Caballero concluded his letter of January 12, 1660, to the Franciscan provincial with effusive praise for two Jesuits, Fathers Schall and Valat, for their great assistance to the Franciscans. In return for Schall's support of money, clothes, and candles, Caballero suggested that the provincial write a letter of gratitude and include as a gift a white surplice. The Beijing Jesuits favored white sacristy robes, but the cloth was not made in China, so the material had to be shipped from Macau. Caballero called Valat "an angel" who "loves us greatly and does many good works for us," although he too lived under conditions of poverty there in Ji'nan.[82]

Caballero sometimes passed on commercial information. In his letter of June 18, 1656, he wrote that the Dutch from their bases in Formosa and Jakarta were again petitioning the emperor for permission to establish a trading factory in Canton.[83] Although their previous petition had been rejected by Beijing, they were again pressing their case with gifts and asking this time not only for a factory in Canton but also for permission to send an embassy to the emperor. They were said to be requesting permission to purchase the city or port of Macau, in return for which they would double the contribution paid by the Portuguese to the Chinese throne. In the same letter, Caballero added that an embassy with a large train of about one hundred Muscovites plus many animals and horses arrived at Beijing in February 1656 after a five-month journey from the grand duke's court in Moscow.[84] Caballero added that the Muscovites were Christians but schismatics (cismaticos) who all wore crosses around their necks and crossed themselves from right to left rather than from left to right in the Roman manner. They did not understand Latin. (These characteristics identify them as Russian Orthodox.)

While most of Caballero's correspondence was directed at fellow missionaries, there was also some contact with the Spanish governor general of the Philippines, Manrique Francisco de Lara Sabiniano, who had sent four hundred pesos to the Ji'nan mission in 1654, which arrived in 1655.[85] On January 12, 1660, Caballero wrote a long letter to Don Sabiniano in which he conveyed information about pirates on the Chinese coast and their relations with the Chinese government. He described how Zheng Chenggong (Koxinga) in 1659 had sailed up the Yangzi River with three thousand well-armed boats and attacked the city of Nanjing.[86] He also described how a large number of Manchu horsemen came south from Beijing and forced Zheng's forces to retreat. Caballero also explained Zheng's background by referring to his father, Zheng Zhilong (1604–1661), whose coastal piracy was altered in 1630 when an agreement was concluded with the Ming government of the Chongzhen Emperor (r. 1628–1644), to whom he became a loyal vassal. Later, when the Manchus conquered the Ming, Zheng agreed to transfer his loyalty to the conquerors, but his son rejected the agreement and continued his opposition to the Manchus from the sea.[87] Caballero ended his letter to the governor by recommending that he conclude contracts of commerce and friendship with the Manchus at Canton.[88] The Manchu ruler, the Shunzhi Emperor, although young, was very careful in governing and upright. Caballero prayed that he might be converted.

Hope

Caballero expressed the hope that before he died, the province might send two young missionaries so that he might oversee their training in the language and in missionary methods. With enough aid, Caballero hoped to open another mission church in Shandong. If two new missionaries were provided, one would stay with Caballero and the other would assist Ibáñez at the new church.

There was some question over what route such missionaries might follow in traveling from the Philippines to Ji'nan. Caballero tentatively suggested that they might come by way of Macau, although he recognized that the past friendliness of the Jesuits toward the Franciscans in Ji'nan might not extend to the arrival of two more Franciscans in Macau. The sea routes had been closed because of the many maritime pirates in rebellion against the Manchus.[89] The Manchu campaign against Zheng Chenggong (Koxinga) along the southeastern coast of China had disrupted the former route of communication through Anhai. The old entry ports of Amoy or Anhai had become so dominated by anti-Manchu pirate rebels that any association with them might taint these missionaries.[90] Instead, Caballero proposed that they enter at Fuan district, where the Dominicans could meet them and guide them to the Jesuit house at Lanxi. He could then travel from Ji'nan to Lanxi to meet them. Caballero asked that each of the new missionaries bring his own vestments needed for the mass along with linen cover, missals, wafflelike irons for making communion wafers, and chrism.[91]

In addition to two Franciscan missionaries, Caballero asked that the provincial send two adolescent boys (fourteen to fifteen years old) of mixed breed drawn from the Chinese trading families in the Philippines who might serve at mass and as menservants.[92] These boys might be from families of Chinese traders in the Philippines or Indians from the "Camarines."[93] In another letter he asked for "two little Indians from the Camarines" *(dos buenos indizuelos de Camarines)* because he and Ibáñez were suffering terribly from the Chinese menservants who were expensive and troublesome and did not provide good service.[94] The fathers had no one to cook for them and those servants who had cooked for them cooked badly, in spite of the missionaries' efforts to teach them how to cook properly. It is quite possible that what the missionaries found objectionable was the Chinese style of cooking rather than the quality of the cooking per se. In any case, the Chinese menservants resisted learning the style of cooking taught by the missionaries. The problems were similar with other household duties. When the Spanish priests shouted at them in emotional frustration, the menservants responded by speaking nonsense and at times were even disrespectful toward the Christian religion. Caballero lamented the fact that they were unable to make use of a whip *(azote)* to discipline the menservants, but such a means of discipline would have provoked gossip and brought undesirable attention to the mission.

In his letter of January 4, 1660, to the provincial, Caballero extended his request list to include, in addition to the two new missionaries and two menservants, a lay brother who might oversee the household and the menservants and "do the work of Martha" so that the priests would be free to preach and minister without domestic distractions. (Caballero was referring to the story of Martha in Luke 10:40 and to the division of domestic and ministerial duties made by the New Testament church in Acts 6:2–4.)[95] Before Ibáñez joined him in Ji'nan, when Caballero had to leave the house for ministerial duties or to study the language, his menservants twice broke the lock on his bedroom door and carried off his bedding and most of his clothes, not stealing any silver because there was none.[96] Caballero also proposed to use a lay brother like the Jesuits, who sent lay brothers in the company of Christian menservants to obtain the subsidies.

The presence of a lay brother would free Caballero from making journeys like the strenuous four-hundred-plus-league (elsewhere he wrote three-hundred-league) journey to Lanxi that he recently made to secure the subsidy (see map 1). (Although Caballero did at times travel in a sedan chair, such travel would have been limited to the local area.)[97] That journey involved many unknown features, and he undertook it with the help of a map from the Dominicans. He had to travel through the rains and flooded land that was being invaded by a hundred thousand pirates in their assault on Nanjing. The highways were filled with thieves and "tigers and other ferocious beasts," whose footprints and claw marks he saw in the mud alongside the road.

In his letter to Father Rodriguez of September 26, 1659, Caballero asked that the two new Franciscan companions be "learned and strong" *(litteris et virtute)* and competent to learn this difficult Chinese language.[98] However, Caballero was not thinking simply in terms of learning Chinese or surviving the harsh conditions of a missionary's life in Ji'nan. In his letter to the father provincial of January 4, 1660, Caballero explained that the new missionaries should be "solid in strength and learning" *(en maciza virtud y letras)* for two reasons:[99] first, to match the abilities of the Jesuit and Dominican missionaries in China; and, second, because learning was held in such high regard in China. He wrote that the Chinese literati spoke well and wrote good books in moral philosophy. Some of them were leaders of sects with whom it was necessary for the missionaries to debate effectively. Caballero described other literati as babbling on about things that were chimerical, absurd, and contrary to reason.

In 1660 Caballero celebrated his fifty-eighth birthday, and there were signs of nostalgia in his letters. Thirty-one years after arriving in the Philippines, he had not forgotten the nuns. In his letter to Rodriguez of December 25, 1660, he sent special greetings to Mother Juana, the mother abbess; Mother Clara of San Francisco; and Mother Magdalena of the Conception.[100] Earlier, on January 13, 1660, Caballero had written a nostalgic letter to his old superior, Antonio de San Gregorio, bishop of Caceres.[101] This letter differs from most of his other correspondence, which focused on the needs of the Shandong mission. Bishop San Gregorio had been the provincial when Caballero entered China for the second time, and Caballero had written to him from the entry port of Anhai on August 9, 1649.[102] Now, over ten years later, Caballero was informing him of the situation in Shandong and revealing personal details that had no strategic relevance to the mission. His hair had turned very gray, especially his beard, and if he were to enter through the bishop's gate wearing his Manchu clothing, he doubted that the bishop would be able to recognize him.[103] It was not only in appearance that he had changed. He wore Manchu clothes and spoke Chinese with such fluency that recently when he visited a Dominican and spoke Chinese, the other priest did not recognize him until he spoke Spanish. He concluded by saying that he did not want to be long-winded with the bishop but wished only that he not be forgotten in the bishop's masses and prayers as his young son of many years before. It was almost as if he were saying goodbye to his old mentor, whom he sensed would be dead within a year.

Life as a missionary in Shandong involved many hardships. This is why Caballero requested that young missionaries be sent to Shandong.[104] When Caballero arrived in 1649, he was forty-seven years old but had already acquired some knowledge of the spoken and written languages from his earlier stay in China. In addition, there were many physical discomforts, including extreme cold and heat, poor food, uncomfortable housing, and a life of poverty. In response to hearing the gospel, rather then being receptive, the humble people of Shandong tended to react in a coarse, churlish manner and resisted his message. In addition, it was necessary for the missionaries to spend much time traveling. Writing on December 25, 1660, Caballero was getting ready to depart by horse (or donkey) on the following day, the feast of Saint John the Evangelist, to perform some baptisms.[105] One can only imagine how many times he prepared for such a journey during his years in Shandong.

Persecution

In 1663, the governor of Shandong publicly posted edicts against certain subversive sects, among which was listed the "holy law of God" *(la santa ley de Dios)*, or Christianity.[106] Caballero believed that the inclusion of Christianity on the list was due to the activity of certain Buddhist monks and sectarians at the court, because the governor of Shandong appeared to be favorably disposed toward the Christians in Ji'nan. Moreover, on the same day that the edicts were posted, Father Valat began to erect a façade on the West Church with a cross at the peak that was visible for some distance. He was able to complete this very visible structure without anyone bringing the edict to his attention. In June of the following year (1664), Caballero built a similar façade on the East Church; the three spikes of the cross at the peak appeared silver in the sunlight. Thousands of people came from neighboring towns to see it, and according to Caballero, the governor and other mandarins who passed admired and praised the façade.

One wonders if Caballero may have misinterpreted all the attention that this cross received. There were numerous instances of negative reactions to the cross and crucifix in China, particularly when placed on the outside of buildings where they were believed by many Chinese to have a disruptive effect on geomantic forces *(fengshui)*. The fact that Caballero included this information in his 1667 report on the persecution of 1664–1669 indicates that he believed there was some connection between the construction of the façades with crosses and anti-Christian feeling.

Caballero's description of the instigator of the persecution was scathing. Although he does not mention Yang Guangxian (1597–1669) by name, Caballero clearly had him in mind when he described a "wicked old man, a Chinese literatus in his manner, a despicable and seditious man" *(un malvado viejo, letrado sinico a su modo, hombre bajo y sediçioso)*.[107] Caballero described him as an atheist, "of which there are many of these diabolical sects among the Chinese literati of this realm" *(que ay muchos desta diabolica secta en letrados sinicos deste reyno)* who was "so blasphemous against our good Christ and his most pure Mother, who printed two diabolical books against son and mother." Caballero claimed that in these books Yang portrayed Christ as the head of a band of thieves, claiming that he was born not of a virgin but rather of an adulterous and evil woman and that his doctrine then being preached by missionaries in China promoted rebellion and sedition.

On January 20, 1665, Valat and Caballero were called before a magistrate in Ji'nan, who asked them what teaching and law they professed. In standard Chinese fashion, kneeling before the magistrate, they answered that they professed "the holy law of God, the creator of all" *(la santa ley de Dios criador de todo)*.[108] When the magistrate asked if they wished to go to Beijing, they answered that they had no business there, but that they would go freely if they were ordered to do so. They were then ordered to return to their houses. Two days later, the magistrate sent several officials to each of the churches. To intimidate the fathers, three executioners were included who were well known for administering lashings and decapitations. On one afternoon a few months before, the executioners had decapitated over eighty men connected with some rebellion. Upon arriving at the churches, they tied the menservants by the neck and led them with Father Caballero, along with Father Valat and his two menservants, to the yamen, or local court. They formed a procession through the streets with the four tied menservants in front, followed by Valat and Caballero and then the executioners and finally a mob of people. The targets of the proceeding were recognized to be the fathers because it was well known that the binding of one's menservants reflected disgrace upon the employers rather than the servants. The missionaries were obliged to wait at the magistrate's court without seeing the magistrate, and when night fell, the fathers were forced to spend the entire night there under guard.

Early the next morning they were brought again to the magistrate's court. The fathers refused to pay the bribe to their jailers to avoid being chained by the neck. At the court, they passed the time in the cold, surrounded by a growing number of Christians who had come to show support. Finally, at midday, the priests were sent on to another tribunal. There appears to have been either confusion about jurisdiction or an unwillingness to handle the case, because after this second magistrate attempted to pass the fathers on to a higher-level magistrate, he refused to accept them and returned the fathers to the second magistrate.[109] After being marched through the streets in disgrace from tribunal to tribunal for a period of five days, they were sent to the most infamous prison in Ji'nan, notorious for housing thieves, highwaymen, murderers, and other criminals who were subject to capital punishment. Caballero's mentality and the spiritual source of his strength are revealed in the repeated comparisons he made between this experience and that of Jesus in the Passion.

While they were incarcerated, the two churches were searched. All the European and Chinese books and manuscripts were removed and burned. The searchers took a few religious ornaments and then sealed the doors of the churches, leaving one or two menservants to watch over the residences. Meanwhile the fathers were in jail, at night sleeping "so squeezed together and close as if sardines in a basket" *(tan estrechos y apretados entre si como sardinas en canasta)*. Not a single Christian was allowed to visit the fathers in jail, only a literatus whose official standing was ambiguous. He visited them and paid for their two meals each day and arranged with the jailers to give them a better sleeping place. Refusing to pay the bribes that were customary in Chinese society, the fathers were kept in this prison for five days and then returned to the first magistrate.

The first magistrate ordered that they be sent to Beijing, but meanwhile he allowed them to be placed under house arrest in one of the two church residences.[110] Among their house guards was one of the executioners. The fathers conversed with him about Christianity, and he was later baptized. After fifteen days of house arrest, they were called back to the first magistrate just prior to the Chinese New Year. Because this was the major holiday of the year in China, many assumed that some good news would be forthcoming, but instead on February 13 the magistrate ordered them immediately remanded to another jail that was also notorious.

This jail was not for criminals scheduled for execution but rather for prisoners who were to be punished with whipping and other forms of corporal punishment and with exile. This prison was even more crowded than the first; even when standing, the twenty to thirty prisoners were pressed against each other like sheep in a narrow sheepfold.[111] To go from one part of the room to another, it was necessary to climb over the other prisoners. When the fathers first entered the jail, there was no floor space, except for an area adjacent to the door. During the day this door was opened, giving access to an enclosed area surrounded by walls; however, at night it was closed. During the first night, those men needing to urinate had to pass over the fathers to use a hole in the cell door and to urinate over Caballero's head, which was next to the door. When dawn arrived, the fathers found that they were sitting in a stream of urine that had flowed back inside. Yet rather than being discouraged by these disgusting conditions, Caballero was energized by them. Although Caballero was humiliated by incidents like the stream of urine, he also received something intensely stimulating from the incident, in the energizing manner of Christian martyrdom.

One of the jailers was a Christian, and he arranged to have a monk be given a ducat of silver in exchange for vacating his space for the two fathers, who crowded themselves into the space for one man. Caballero then came down with a stomach upset and diarrhea, which lasted for five days. During the nights when he was most afflicted, it was extremely difficult under the restrictions of priestly modesty to defecate without getting fecal matter on others when there was not even enough room to spit *(escupir)*.

The jail was usually filled with loud and clamorous activity that would not cease until the middle of the night. Singing, grumbling, faultfinding, and punching filled the night. Some prisoners became drunk and began screaming. Some gambled with cards and dice until dawn. The night preceding the first day of the Chinese New Year was particularly tumultuous, and Caballero described it as a "bacchanal" (drunken orgy). Some prisoners were rejoicing, others were cursing. Some were singing, and others were attacking their fellow prisoners like rabid dogs. Some were laughing, while others were moaning. Many of the prisoners were completely naked, and some sodomized others.[112] It was "a living portrait of hell" *(un vivo retrato de infierno)* that even emulated the smoldering atmosphere of hell with smoke from the small cooking stoves. In the midst of all this chaos, the priests slept.

Although the Chinese Christians were the poorest of people, they managed to bring the fathers food and occasionally bribed the guards to gain entrance to the jail cell. In the cell were eight or ten children aged four to eight years whose parents had died in captivity or else were simply paupers. The children were kept alive by the leftovers from other prisoners, and when the fathers ate, these small children gathered around them, watching them eat and waiting for some small bits of food that the priests gave to them. When the Christians heard of the children, they doubled the amount of food brought to the priests.

After the fathers had been incarcerated in this jail for fifteen days, the magistrate asked for some taels of silver in return for their release, but the fathers refused. Finally, after twenty-three days of confinement, they were delivered to guards who would take them to Beijing. To cover the expense of the journey, it was necessary to melt down two small silver Communion chalices to be used as money. The Christians helped them as much as their poverty allowed and accompanied them on their way for a good distance outside of the city.[113] In this emotional scene, the Christians threw themselves on the ground in a row along the road, weeping. Even before their departure, the fathers had noticed that the authorities were imprisoning the Christians, both men and women. Caballero felt that he and Valat were leaving them as sheep without a pastor before hungry wolves and no doubt had Matthew 10:16 and Luke 10:3 in mind.[114]

They departed from Ji'nan on March 11, accompanied by four Christians who refused to desert them and two guards. One of the guards was the executioner mentioned earlier, who received religious instruction during the journey. They covered the distance of ninety-five leagues in eight days (perhaps part of it was by boat on the Grand Canal) and arrived in Beijing on March 18. The persecution instigated by Yang Guangxian was in full swing. Caballero and Valat along with most of the other missionaries were deported on September 13 and arrived in Canton on March 25, 1666.[115] Caballero never returned to Shandong but died at Canton on May 13, 1669, and was buried outside the city walls on Henan Island at Baogang.[116]

2

The Attempt to Blend Confucianism and Christianity

中

The Collaboration between Caballero and Shang Huqing

The attempt of missionaries to communicate with the Chinese literati was far more characteristic of the Jesuits than the Franciscans. This difference was due, in part, to the greater intellectual tendencies and training of the Jesuits and, in part, to the location of Franciscan missionaries in the less urban areas of China, where fewer literati were to be found. The Franciscan apostolate was aimed at uneducated and less sophisticated classes. However, Caballero was an unusual Franciscan missionary because by 1653 he had written drafts of three works in Chinese.

In November 1653 he described these works to the Franciscan provincial with the following words:

In this year of 1653 I have composed three books, written in the usage of the country, in Chinese letters. The first contains the general foundations, taken from the Chinese books, in order to recognize the Creator and the Lord of heaven and earth, to whom one should alone worship and make sacrifices, and not to any other. The second [book], with the fundamentals of their Chinese books, shows them with evidence the vanity of idols and of all the idolatry there is in the world.[1]
. . . Then I call on the natural law, expressing the Ten Commandments of the Decalogue in the explanation of each commandment, and the works of mercy where, as an example, one had the honor of attending to the deceased with true piety toward the interred, relinquishing their vain superstitions and vain sacrifices. The third book contains the explanation of the three virtues: faith, hope, and charity, and examples, with the fundamental principles taken from their books, to show the obligation that they have to believe the truth that I preach to them, even though they have not seen it nor come with the knowledge. Explaining the mystery of the Three and One with accommodating examples, and I call the exposition of all the Creed, and the meaning of heaven and hell, with examples appropriate to the capacity of this people.[2]

Caballero wrote these three Chinese works in collaboration with a Chinese literatus in 1653. He wrote to the provincial that he had paid an unnamed "Chinese literatus" *(letrado chino)* four taels of silver for making a rough draft of these three works.[3]

This literatus could not have been Caballero's most serious Chinese collaborator, Shang Huqing, because Shang did not meet Caballero in Ji'nan until after 1659. Shang Huqing (styled Wei Tang; postbaptismal pen name Shiji) was baptized several years before Caballero met him. He was born in 1619 in Shanyang (also called Huaian prefecture), located on the Grand Canal in northern Jiangsu province (see map 1).[4] He was baptized by the Jesuit Father Francesco Sambiasi at a relatively early age, probably before he was twenty-five years old.[5] At the age of forty, Shang attained the *juren* degree in the sixteenth year of the reign of the Shunzhi Emperor (1659).[6] The juren degree was based on a provincial-level examination and was secondary only to the *jinshi*-degree examination administered every three years at the capital.

In 1659, Shang was appointed magistrate of the Wei district of Laizhou prefecture in eastern Shandong but was dismissed within less than a year, apparently for some dereliction of duty.[7] After being discharged from his post, he "drifted like duckweed" to Ji'nan.[8] There he met Fathers Caballero and Valat and spent many hours "from morning until night" discussing Christianity with both of them. He sought to understand the similarities and differences between the Literati Teaching (Confucianism) and Christianity. After extensive discussions with Caballero and Valat about the Lord of Heaven Teaching (Christianity), Shang had written drafts of *Bu Ru wengao (A Warning to Repair the Deficiencies of the Literati)* and *Zhengxue liu shi (The Touchstone of True Knowledge)* and was proposing to correct these and to have his friends edit them.[9]

Then one day Caballero showed Shang a volume containing an explanation of the Four Books of Confucius and said: "Being a foreigner, I do not dare to write a commentary on the Classics. I have merely assembled several points of similarity between them and the Heavenly Teaching and I have explained them in my fashion. What do you think?"[10] Although Shang did not elaborate, it appears that he revised Caballero's draft, which became the *Tian Ru yin (Imprints of the Heavenly Teaching and the Literati Teaching).* Whereas the original idea belonged to Caballero, it is difficult to know how much was revised by Shang. What one can say with certainty is that they were collaborators. The authorship of *Imprints* belongs at least as much to Shang Huqing as to Caballero, because Caballero would have been incapable of writing a book that demanded such a substantial knowledge of the Chinese classics. On the other hand, since Shang's understanding of Christian theology was insufficient for writing such a book, it required a collaborative effort.

However, I have found no specific acknowledgment of this collaboration in Caballero's extensive correspondence. On the contrary, Caballero emphasized that he had not converted a single literatus and that he did not have close relations with them. He made some critical statements that the literati like to debate the points of similarity and difference between the Literati Teaching and the Heavenly Teaching (Christianity), but they did not accept the Heavenly Teaching. Yet Caballero was collaborating extensively with Shang. Could it be that they had some sort of disagreement that caused Caballero not to mention him? Or did Caballero avoid mentioning him for the same reason that the Jesuits minimized references to literati, namely, in order to avoid criticism and the possible accusation of heterodoxy from their confreres and other Europeans?

Imprints of the Heavenly Teaching and the Literati Teaching

Imprints of the Heavenly Teaching and the Literati Teaching (Tian Ru yin) is the briefest of Shang's works.[11] The text of approximately 7,500 characters has a very simple structure that divides into thirty-seven sections, each of which is based upon one or more passages from the Four Books. Most of the cited passages (twenty-three) come from the *Analects,* while fifteen come from the *Mean,* five from the *Mencius,* and three from the introduction of the *Great Learning.*[12]

The title *Imprints* (i.e., manifestations) *of the Heavenly Teaching and the Literati Teaching* was apparently chosen by Shang rather than Caballero and is explained in Shang's 1664 preface. In it he referred to the *Book of History,* "Announcement of Tang," which speaks of God giving mankind a moral sense.[13] This imprint of a moral sense was received by Confucius, and Shang asks how, if the origins or source of this imprint are not investigated, can printed documents be understood? Shang compared the Lord of Heaven's creation of things to the imprint of a vermilion seal or the imprint made by a mulberry paper stamp upon mulberry paper.[14] The original imprint of Heaven gave its imprint to all things. Sages continually arise, and this imprint of Heaven is the source of their virtue. He quotes from the *Book of Rites (Li ji):* "The son of Heaven has goodness which is caused by the virtue in Heaven."[15] Shang chose the title *Tian Ru yin* in order to convey the aim of reconciling the differences between Christianity and Confucianism and to show their underlying unity. He wrote: "They say that the Four Books are imprints of the original imprint, and from that one can entitle this book 'The Imprints of the Heavenly and Literati Teachings.'"[16]

Long after the original composition of the *Imprints* in 1664, Shang's son, Run Wangbi, wrote a brief preface in which he listed the other collaborators as follows:

The Christian Shang Huqing, styled Zhangtang, has explained the meaning.

Du Tingfen [magistrate of Ji'nan, 1647–1648] from Liangxi [on the Grand Canal in Wu district in Suzhou], styled Yiling, has proofread [the text].

The inferior learners, Taiyuan and Mingwu of Wulin [i.e., Hangzhou], recorded [the text].[17]

Although Run's preface is undated, one could conclude that it was written several years after 1664 because Run speaks of first reading a copy of *Imprints* when he was a youth who was "not yet old enough to make the ritualistic morning and evening inquiries about the health of his parents."[18]

Run does not mention Caballero by name but refers in vague terms to a "Western gentleman who came from Europe" and who, after three years of persevering through storms, arrived on the shores of China.[19] This may be a reference to Caballero, or it could also be read as a plural reference to missionaries as a group. Run states that this missionary taught about the Lord who creates everything, but the literati were smug in their response and said: "Although the Heavenly and Literati Teachings are not very different, one may say that the Literati Teaching is sufficient." Run compares the two teachings by referring to the Literati's *xing zhi li* (rational nature) and the Christian *chao xing* (transcendent nature). While our rational nature appears to be sufficient for the daily needs of human relations, it is our transcendent nature that enables us to recognize "our Great Lord and Great Father" *(wu Dajun Dafu)* and revere him. In traditional Chinese culture, one cannot be a true son without showing filial piety toward one's father. In the same way, one who does not demonstrate loyalty toward one's lord cannot be a true subject. Extending this same principle, Run asks: if one does not show filial piety toward the Great Father and loyalty toward the Great Lord, how then can one be truly human?[20] Run then briefly refers to fundamental Christian concepts, including human creation from God, the return to God after death and burial, prayer to the Trinity, redemption through grace, the indestructibility of the soul, preparation for death, judgment, heaven, and hell.

In addition, Run quotes Confucius (*Analects* 14:37), who said: "I study things on the lower level but my understanding penetrates the higher level (i.e., matters of heaven). It is Heaven that knows me."[21] Run uses this quote to argue that human nature should attain a transcendent nature. He also uses a metaphor *hegui* (on the same track), which is reminiscent of the phrase *gai xian yi zhe* (to tune the string, to get out of the old rut) used by the Christian literatus Zhang Xingyao (1633–after 1715) of Hangzhou.[22] The mentality of Shang Huqing and Run Wangbi is remarkable in that they are so open to adopting new ideas promoted by foreigners. But this was a two-way process that made demands upon both sides. While Chinese literati had to accept that their culture was deficient in developing certain truths of this foreign teaching, Europeans had to recognize that certain aspects of Christianity that they held dear were, in fact, European cultural accretions and not part of the essential core of Christian teaching.

One of the prefaces of the *Imprints* was written by a prominent Chinese literatus. It was typical of literati to participate in a network of literati friendships based on shared regional origins or common interests. This network probably explains how one of the prefaces in the 1664 edition of the *Imprints* was written by Wei Xuequ (pen name Qingcheng). Wei had attained the juren degree under the Shunzhi Emperor.[23] He was a native of Jiashan district in Jiaxing prefecture in northeastern Zhejiang province, just to the east of the Grand Canal.[24] He was a noted poet, writer, and calligrapher, and he served as a *daotai* (circuit intendant) in western Zhili province. Unlike Shang Huqing, he gave no sign of being a Christian, though an older cousin, Wei Xuelian, a jinshi degree holder, had converted by 1642.[25]

Wei Xuequ's father, Wei Dazhong (original name Tinggeng, styled Kongshi, pen name Kuoyuan), had attained fame as a courageous opponent of the notorious eunuch Wei Zhongxian (1568–1627). His father was a jinshi of 1616 and a Hanlin scholar. A member of the controversial Donglin party, he was imprisoned on false charges of taking bribes, suffered cruel beatings in prison, and was eventually put to death in 1625 as part of a group who became immortalized as the Six Heroes *(Liu Junzi)*.[26] Wei Xuequ was probably asked by Shang or a mutual literatus friend to write a preface because of his family's prestige. Wei wrote of having seen his cousin Wei Xuelian together with the European missionaries "before my hair had withered," that is, sometime before 1644, when Wei Xuelian died. Although Wei Xuequ mentions Caballero by name, there is no evidence that they had met.[27] The short preface of approximately 250 characters was dated the summer of 1664.

Wei believed that the Heavenly and Literati Teachings were in harmony. Whereas many scholars of that time had become superficial and had "lost the direction of Confucius and Mencius," Wei argued that the common features of these two teachings could be revealed by studying the Four Books.[28] By twice making emphatic reference to the Song dynasty Neo-Confucians Zhou Dunyi, the Cheng brothers (Cheng Hao and Cheng Yi), Zhang Zai, and Zhu Xi, Wei implied that the Heavenly Teaching was in harmony with the teachings of the Song Neo-Confucians as presented in their commentary on the Four Books. Wei praised Caballero's commentary on the Four Books and its attempt to show the harmony of the Heavenly and Literati Teachings as part of an East–West movement. The Literati Teaching was carried to the West while the Western missionaries in China explained the harmony of the two teachings. Wei referred to this with the oft-quoted Confucian phrase, "What is inside and outside of the Four Seas is the same."[29] Finally, he found symbolic significance in the physical fact that Caballero's residence in China (Ji'nan) was close to the former residence of Confucius in Qufu. What is so fascinating about Wei's preface, which is so sympathetic to Christianity, is that it was written at the very time that a harsh anti-Christian campaign was being initiated by Yang Guangxian.

The Touchstone of True Knowledge

The Touchstone of True Knowledge (Zhengxue liu shi) at approximately 27,500 characters is a longer work than the *Imprints* but considerably shorter than *A Warning*. It is divided into seven chapters, each of which explains the differences *(bian)* between fundamental Christian and Literati concepts. These include explaining the differences between the Lord of Heaven *(Tianzhu)* and the Neo-Confucian Supreme Ultimate *(Taiji);* between the Christian Lord of Heaven and the ancient Chinese Lord Above *(Shangdi);* between the Lord of Heaven and the physical form of heaven; between the Supreme Ultimate, principle *(li)* and ether *(qi);* between Heaven and Earth and living things; between the Western and the Literati teachings on the creation of mankind; between sacrificing to ghosts and to spirits; and between Christian life and death and the Chinese conception of souls *(hun po)*.

The Touchstone is attributed to Caballero, but it appears upon analysis to be more the work of Shang.[30] In fact, in his preface of 1664 to the *Imprints,* Shang claims *The Touchstone* and *A Warning* as his works.[31] Shang's son, Run Wangbi, made a similar claim.[32] So how was the work attributed to Caballero? While the *Imprints* and *The Touchstone* were both collaborative efforts between Caballero and Shang, the degree of collaboration differed. Whereas Caballero was the the initiator in the sense of writing a draft of *Imprints* that Shang then edited, Shang was the major author of *The Touchstone.*

Although Shang claimed *The Touchstone* was written in 1664, the extant copies of it were printed in 1698. Caballero had died in 1669, but Shang was still alive and wrote a preface for the 1698 printing. The misleading basis for claiming that Caballero was the author is the 1698 printed title page, which states: "written by Li Andang [i.e., Caballero], a member of the Society of Saint Francis from the Far West."[33] The title page does not mention Shang. Four Franciscans are listed as "Franciscan co-revisors" of this edition. They were Fathers Fernández-Oliver, Bañeza, Incarnatione, and Nieto-Díaz, all of whom are discussed in later chapters.

But by the early eighteenth century, the Chinese Rites Controversy had created a less accommodating atmosphere, and other Franciscans had second thoughts about the orthodoxy of *The Touchstone*. In 1704, six years after signing as one of the coeditors, Bañeza, now Franciscan provincial commissioner in Canton, wrote to Fernández-Oliver and his other former confreres in Shandong to say that the work should be withdrawn. It had been discovered that "some propositions were found which did not conform to the truth of our holy faith, which was attributable to negligence in making an accurate translation from its original and to a lack of care at the time of the printing."[34] It was ordered that the woodblocks be locked up and that no further printing or dissemination of *The Touchstone* be permitted until the errors were corrected. Bañeza indicated that he had consulted on this matter with the elected assistants, Father Navarro, who was minister of the church in Shunde district, seven leagues from Canton; and Father Tarín, minister of the church of the Blessed Virgin Mary of Portiuncula within the walls of Canton city. Their bases near Canton and lack of significant experience in the interior of China reinforced the European patterns in their thinking and made them less receptive to the processes of inculturation in which Caballero and Shang Huqing had been involved.

In his *Touchstone* preface, Shang dealt with the fundamental problem of reconciling the Heavenly and Literati Teachings. He followed orthodox Confucian positions in attacking the extremists Yang Zhu and Mo Di (ca. 420 B.C.) and like-minded heterodoxies (*yiduan*), false teachings (*xieshuo*), and Buddhism and Daoism (*Er Shi*). This was standard Confucian terminology for referring to the enemies of truth. What was new about Shang's approach was that he was trying to enlarge the Confucian point of view by claiming that universal truth embraced not only the Literati Teaching but also the Heavenly Teaching. He argued for the enlargement on two grounds: First, the scholars (missionaries) from the West were not barbarians (i.e., ignorant of the truth). Second, those sages capable of discovering the truth were not limited to a single place or nation but were universal in extent, in the same way that truth was universal.

To support this argument, Shang cited two passages from *Mencius*.[35] He first cited the passage that said that Chinese converted barbarians but were not converted by barbarians (*Mencius* IIIa.4). This idea was crucial, because if the European missionaries were regarded as barbarians, then the Classics could justify rejecting them. Shang went on to cite *Mencius* IVb.1 on how the legendary ruler Shun and the later Zhou dynasty founder King Wen, although born far apart and in different ages, really grasped the same truths. Of equal significance was the fact that while Shun was born among the "eastern barbarians," King Wen was born among the "western barbarians." So although they were said to have been born among barbarians, they did not embody the mentality of barbarians. Shang attempted to legitimize the teaching of the European missionaries using a similar logic.

Shang made no explicit reference to Jesus in this preface; however, he did refer to the biblical prophets as "wise men of antiquity" *(zhe ren)* who revealed this teaching and established a religion.[36] This allusion would have had echoes of affinity with the Chinese sages of antiquity, and it indicated that Shang was addressing, not Christian converts, but a broader group of literati and attempting to open their minds to a consideration of the Lord of Heaven Teaching. The term "wise men of antiquity" (zhe ren) appears in the *Book of History (Shujing)* and the *Book of Odes (Shijing)*, though not with great frequency. A few lines later, Shang made several references to "sages" *(sheng ren)*, a term that occurs with frequency in the Classics. It referred to the legendary sages Yao, Shun, and Yu; to King Tang, who founded the Shang dynasty; to Kings Wen and Wu, who founded the Zhou dynasty; to the Duke of Zhou; and to Confucius.

Shang believed that Heaven, human nature, and the Way *(Dao)* were linked in a harmonious relationship. He wrote: "The Way follows one's natural disposition and one's natural disposition is decreed by Heaven" *(Dao shuai yu xing; xing ming yu Tian).*[37] Shang said that the Literati spoke of Heaven, but they did not understand Heaven. Consequently, how could the Way emerge, and how could one's natural disposition be revealed? On the contrary, one's natural disposition was obscured and the Dao was confused. Shang compared the situation in China to that of a mortally ill person. Although the "most benevolent and most compassionate Lord of Heaven had great pity for the people who were drowning in China," the Lord of Heaven was unable to govern China and unable to teach the Chinese.[38] Shang wrote that the goodness of the Lord of Heaven's great wisdom and great ability had been secretly revealed by the missionaries, who carried this revelation all the way from the West *(Xitu)* to the Middle Kingdom (China) by means of a great effort to save the world and to save his ignorant people by teaching them to base themselves in the path of the Way. If they did so, they would understand that the Lord of Heaven was the basis of one's inherent nature and the source of the Way, and they would grasp "true knowledge" *(zhengxue).*

Shang's Magnum Opus: *A Warning*

A Warning to Repair the Deficiencies of the Literati (Bu Ru wengao) was composed by Shang Huqing in 1664.[39] The table of contents of *A Warning* lists five chapters *(juan)*, each of which has six sections *(pian)*. However, the fifth chapter is missing, and it is uncertain whether it was ever composed.[40] *A Warning* is a work of substantial length (approximately 166,500 characters, not counting the marginal comments of an obscure figure named Gan Lichuan). After the introduction (3,400 characters), the four chapters follow in varying length (42,000, 31,200, 38,800, and 51,100 characters).[41] The text follows a traditional Literati form of question and answer. The questions are posed sometimes merely for the sake of obtaining information about the Heavenly Teaching and at other times to provide Shang with an opportunity to respond to criticism of the Heavenly Teaching.

The contents of the work have no discernible organization. While the five chapters have no headings, the thirty sections do. Although the sections are not organized into a particular structure, three main themes recur. One theme explains basic Christian concepts. A second theme deals with the relationship between the Literati Teaching and Christianity. A third theme involves a disparagement of Buddhist and Daoist concepts and other superstitious practices, such as magical arts, transmigration, the prohibition on killing animals, and the Daoist cultivation of immortality.

The origins of *A Warning* date from a meeting between Shang and his friend Gan Lichuan in the fall of 1663 at Lisha, an ancient literary name for Ji'nan.[42] The name was derived from Ji'nan's location at the foot of Li Mountain (Lishan), which was five *li* (less than two miles) south of Ji'nan (see figure 2.1).[43] At that meeting they resolved to collaborate by having Gan correct the work that Shang would write. The result was the marginal notations by Gan that are found interspersed throughout *A Warning*. The Jesuit missionaries in China also made a contribution to the text, although it is very difficult to determine in what form. Two of the four chapters (1 and 3) have the following notation at the beginning: "written by a scholar (or scholars) of the Society of Jesus from the Far West" *(Taixi Yesuhui shi zhe)*.[44] One concludes that the work was a collaboration but written primarily by Shang.

The role that Shang believed the Heavenly Teaching could play in China was captured in the phrase "*bu Ru*" (to supplement or repair the Literati Teaching). The term "bu" does not occur frequently in the Confucian Classics. The earliest occurrence is in the *Book of Odes,* the ode Zheng Min (Mao number 260). Both Bernhard Karlgren and Arthur Waley translate "bu" in this ode as meaning to "mend," in the sense of mending a hole in the embroidered fabric of a royal robe.[45] The term "bu" appears four times in one passage from the *Zuo Commentary (Zuochuan)* to the *Spring and Autumn Annals,* which quotes the above-cited ode from the *Book of Odes.* Legge translated the term twice as to "mend" errors and twice as to "repair" defects or faults.[46] "Bu" occurs six times in the *Mencius,* meaning either to "supply a deficiency" of seed, "supplement the short," or "mend."[47]

It is typical of literary works in traditional China to build upon earlier works, and the phrase "bu Ru" is no exception. It is derived from the phrases *"bu Ru pi Fo"* (supplement the Literati and criticize the Buddhists) and *"bu Ru yi Fo"* (supplement the Literati and displace the Buddhists) by the famous Christian scholar–official Xu Wending (Guangqi) (1562–1633).[48] Xu also used the variant

Fig. 2.1. A map of Licheng district that includes the Shandong provincial capital, Ji'nan, portrayed as a walled city (near the center), from an 1840 gazetteer. Li Mountain (Li Shan) is located five li (less than two miles) south of the South Gate of Ji'nan. It was at the base of this mountain near the city Lisha (the literary name for Ji'nan) in 1663 that the Christian literatus Shang Huqing met with his friend Gan Lichuan to plan the work *Bu Ru wengao (A Warning to Repair the Deficiencies of the Literati)*. This map appears in *Ji'nan fuzhi*. Edited by Wang Zengfang et al. Compiled by Cheng Guan et al. 1840 80 *ce*. 1:27b–28a. Courtesy of the Shandong Sheng Tushuguan (Shandong Provincial Library).

phrase *"jue Fo bu Ru"* (discontinue Buddhism and supplement the Literati Teaching). Xu's ideas influenced later Christian literati, and he appears to have become the founding teacher of a Confucian–Christian tradition. The Christian literati Shang Huqing and Zhang Xingyao (1633–after 1715) of Hangzhou were both influenced by Xu's formula, which combined a sympathetic correction of Confucianism with harsh criticism of Buddhism. Whereas Zhang urged the Literati to overcome their "negligence" (*shulue*), Shang urged them to overcome their "imbalance" (*pian*). A variation on Xu's phrase was attributed to the eminent scholar–official Qian Shisheng (1575–1652). Qian came from a venerable and wealthy clan in Jiashan in northeastern Zhejiang province and served as grand secretary under the last Ming emperor during the years 1633–1636.[49] He had worked quietly to defend Donglin members accused of trumped-up crimes by the notorious eunuch Wei Zhongxian. Qian said that the Heavenly

Teaching "suffices for our Literati Teaching to repair what is lost" *(zu wei wu Ru bu wang).*[50] Little is known of his relationship to Christianity, but this phrase reflects a very sympathetic attitude.[51]

Repairing the Deficiencies of the Literati

Shang criticized the Literati for being imbalanced in discussing humans without sufficient regard for Heaven, in discussing life without sufficient regard for death, in discussing the present life without sufficient regard for the afterlife, and in discussing material forms without sufficient regard for immaterial forms. In a marginal notation, Gan Lichuan compared Shang's supplementing of true learning to a medicine.[52] Shang wrote that the Heavenly Learning did not change the Literati's aim of attaining enlightenment, but the Literati's "errors" *(bai que)* were very numerous. These errors had created an imbalance (one-sidedness) in the Literati that the Heavenly Teaching could repair.[53]

The term "pian" (imbalanced) would have been very familiar to Literati from the famous commentary on the Four Books by the Song Neo-Confucian philosopher, Zhu Xi (1230–1300). The first page of Zhu's introduction to the *Doctrine of the Mean (Zhongyong)* quotes Cheng Yi (1033–1108) to explain the fundamental term *zhong* (the Mean) as meaning "not imbalanced" *(bu pian).*[54] This shows how much Shang saw his interpretation at least partly in harmony with the Literati tradition that included Zhu Xi. On the other hand, Shang's criticism of the Song Neo-Confucians is reflected in Gan's marginal notation on this passage: "People of today still consume the mere spittle *(tuoyu)* of the Song Literati teaching but they are unwilling to think of correcting the deficiencies [of the Song Literati] and so they are unable to be transformed by the teaching." Yet it seems that the criticism here is aimed not merely at the Song Neo-Confucians but also at contemporary Literati who were uncritically accepting whatever the Song Literati said as truth without doing their own thinking. This would be close to Shang's own thinking, and presumably Shang and Gan were in fundamental agreement on the main issues.

The meaning of "bu" as supplementing what is deficient in the Literati Teaching is brought out at the beginning of chapter 1. The questioner asked, since the Literati Teaching was a complete teaching in that the sages cultivated themselves internally and pursued the "kingly way" *(wang dao)* externally, how was it that the Heavenly Teaching could be called greater than the Literati Teaching?[55] Shang replied by saying that while the Literati Teaching focused on studying our material nature *(yinxing xing),* the Heavenly Teaching focused on our transcendent nature *(chaoxing xing).* He called the study of the former "Human Knowledge" *(ren xue).* However, since it focused exclusively on human beings, it was limited and needed to be supplemented by the Heavenly Teaching. Because of this exclusive emphasis on Human Knowledge the Literati were utterly without understanding in regard to the great matter of life and death.

Shang believed that, in their overwhelming concern with developing their moral nature *(de xing),* the Literati had neglected other important matters of both an immanent and a transcendent nature. Shang appears to have been criticizing the Literati for an inward turning toward introspection that occurred in the late Ming and early Qing. His criticism was prompted by his contact with an external influence supplied by the European missionaries. Shang believed that this inward turning was an aberration from the Literati tradition and, in support of borrowing from the new teaching from Europe, he alluded to Confucius's statement in *Analects* 2:11: "He who by reanimating the Old can gain knowledge of the New is fit to be a teacher."[56]

A Warning discussed some of the Literati's most fundamental forms of resistance to Christianity. One of these was their ambivalence toward the afterlife. Shang criticized the Literati for adopting a mocking attitude and for refusing to think seriously about ultimate concerns. Shang claimed that the Literati's reaction to the afterlife was contradictory. Although they mocked the Christian notion of an afterlife with rewards in heaven and punishments in hell, they accepted Buddhist notions of transmigration and rebirth in the six forms of sentient beings (humans, animals, hungry ghosts, malevolent nature spirits, existence in heaven, and existence in hell).[57] Shang wrote that the Literati were skeptical of notions of the immortality of the soul and of rewards and punishments in the afterlife in the form of eternal punishment in hell and eternal joy in heaven. Furthermore, they did not believe in the Incarnation (of God in the human form of Jesus). They preferred rather to believe in the merit to be achieved through the Buddhist practices of burning fake paper money for the deceased, offering fake silver ingots for ancestors, and breaking open the gates of hell by chants and incantations for the release of departed spirits.

Confucius's reticence on spirits and matters of life of death is often epitomized by the passage from *Analects* 11:11: "Jilu (Zilu) asked about serving the spiritual beings. Confucius said, 'If we are not yet able to serve man, how can we serve spiritual beings?' 'I venture to ask about death.' Confucius said, 'If we do not yet know about life, how can we know about death?'"[58] Yet the exact meaning of Confucius's statement and his degree of agnosticism remain debatable. Shang did not believe that Confucius was agnostic, and he interpreted this passage simply to refer to a lack of explicit discussion of spirits and of life and death; that is, a deficiency that could be supplemented by the Heavenly Teaching.[59] Shang compared the Literati's attitude to an irrevocable decision, such as losing one's way on a path (i.e., a life) that cannot be retraced: "Once one goes down a path, one cannot come back again; once one has made a mistake, one cannot correct it."[60]

Mainstreaming Christianity as Part of Chinese Orthodoxy

Shang's receptivity to new and foreign ideas is the sort of openness that is applauded by many people in our own age as tolerant and the antithesis of chauvinism. However, the widespread hostility to Christianity found among many multiculturalists in the West today complicates the task of giving Shang's ideas an objective evaluation. Nevertheless, Shang's works, especially his lengthy *Warning* represents a thoughtful attempt to follow Confucius's dictum to study old knowledge in order to learn new knowledge.

Shang was filled with tremendous admiration for the European missionaries and impressed by their devotion to God. He wrote:

> These itinerant scholars from the West crossed the cold seas for three years and overcame many forms of death to reach the Middle Kingdom (China). Why should they do this? They serve and honor the Lord of Heaven as the highest Truth. They wish to assist as messengers in explaining this teaching to the people. They act like sons in regard to the Great Parent (Father–Mother). Their worldly recompense is like a drop or mere piece of grain and they have very few worldly possessions. Therefore they abandon family, disregard their personal concerns and neither borrow nor lend money.[61]

This laudatory view of European missionaries did not fit all of the missionaries. Certain Jesuits were accused of practicing usury, and others lived in a comfortable style at the court in Beijing. But Shang's contacts with missionaries were largely limited to those who lived in poor provincial areas like Ji'nan, such as Caballero and Valat, who lived lives of poverty and self-sacrifice. However, it was neither Caballero nor Valat who baptized Shang, but rather the Jesuit Father Francesco Sambiasi (Bi Fangji; styled Jinliang) (1582–1649).[62] Sambiasi arrived in Macau in 1610 and was in Beijing from 1613 until 1616, when he was forced to leave because of the negative effects of the anti-Christian movement in Nanjing.[63]

Sambiasi returned to Beijing before the end of the anti-Christian movement and was secretly lodged in the house of Xu Guangqi. He left Beijing for Shanghai in 1622 and over the next twenty-three years was active in visiting towns in east central China in the provinces of Henan, Shanxi, Shandong, and Nanjing (present-day Anhui and Jiangsu). In these towns he baptized many Chinese, including Shang. Sambiasi had a charismatic personality and impressed many Chinese with his knowledge of mathematics and astronomy as well as theology. He was articulate and had a kind, friendly manner that was both modest and impressive. One young literatus was converted by Sambiasi because his mother dreamt that she saw a venerable man with a long beard and the clothing of a literatus who told her to desist from worshipping false gods for worship of the true God.[64] When this young literatus met Sambiasi in Nanjing, the description seemed to fit Sambiasi so well that he was baptized. Shang states that it was while Sambiasi was traveling back and forth between Beijing and Ji'nan that the priest baptized him. Sambiasi was known to have been working in the provinces of Shandong and Nanjing in the years 1631–1643.[65] Given that Shang's birth date was around 1619, it appears that he was baptized at a youthful age and before he was twenty-five. However, his commitment to Christianity appears to have deepened after his crisis in 1659, when he was dismissed as magistrate of Wei district.

Shang presented the essential events contained in the Bible, applying the traditional Chinese term for heterodoxy (falsehood), yiduan, to the worship of false gods. He spoke of the first human beings, Adam and Eve, and original sin, which led them and their descendants to commit acts of evil.[66] Abraham and Isaac were described as great sages of antiquity who had foreknowledge of the Incarnation of the Lord who would save the world. Shang described the sage Moses as transforming a stick into a snake and honoring the Lord's command by leading the enslaved Judean people (a hundred thousand in number) out of Egypt and back to their homeland. The persistent desire of humans for evil continued and was punished by the Lord, for whom the people had little genuine feeling, down to the time of the sage–emperor (sheng huang) David. After the rule of Solomon (961–922 B.C.),[67] the Western Assyrians (i.e., Babylonians) usurped the throne (in 722 B.C.), and the people of Judea were despondent for seventy years (i.e., the Babylonian captivity, 597–538 B.C.) and from that time onward participated extensively in heterodoxies, or yiduan.

Continuing his presentation, without noting any break between Old and New Testament events, Shang wrote that in the reign of Herod Antipas a prophecy circulated that there would be born a "perfect human being" or "sage" (zhi ren) who would save the world.[68] An angel announced a pregnancy in Bethlehem (tianshen bao shen bailengyun) to a virgin descended from sages (zhennü shengyi). When he was born of this Holy Mother (Sheng Mu), a new star appeared.[69] The Magi (Sheng Wang) and shepherds came to pay their respects and then fled from Herod.[70] When this sage, whom Shang called "God the Son" (Tianzhu zi), attained thirty years of age, he left his mother and went to Judea, where in various towns he taught people the truth. He fulfilled a prior prophecy that someone would be incarnated among mankind who would redeem others and perform wondrous acts (jiushu deng shi xian dasheng ji). He saved the lame, the blind, the deaf, and the dead by causing them to walk, to see, to hear, and to be raised from the dead (jiu yishi zhi pi long xumu zhong ren. Shi zhi bulü shi ting sishi fuhuo).

Unlike a number of Christian literati, Shang was explicit in presenting the Crucifixion of Jesus. He described Satan (Mo) as a great enemy who belonged to an evil faction (xie dang) that harmed the truth and caused Jesus to be crucified.

Through the sacrifice of his holy body and holy blood, Jesus redeemed all of mankind from their sins and leads people to heaven. Shang wrote that those who did not avail themselves of this redemption will suffer.

Shang explained the Crucifixion of Jesus as a result of the Pharisees *(Falisaie)* coming under the influence of Satan. He wrote that "the Lord of Heaven Jesus was the great ruler–father of the myriad people" *(Tianzhu Yesu wan min zhi da junfu),* but the people's reverence for him produced jealousy and hatred.[71] Although the common people were sometimes doubtful, it was the Pharisees who took the lead in developing a scheme to kill Jesus. The Pharisees' pride and jealousy poisoned the thinking of the masses. After they had killed Jesus, the people did not realize how close they had been to the Savior. Shang criticized the Pharisees of Judea for their elitism, love of reputation, and obsession with the details of deportment. This criticism seems to also apply, mutatis mutandis, to many of the literati in Shang's own day.

Shang as a Prophet in China

Although the missionaries had traveled the eighty thousand to ninety thousand li (twenty-seven thousand to thirty thousand miles) to come to China and convey the Lord of Heaven Teaching, it was being rejected by the Chinese people.[72] This caused the Western scholars (i.e., the missionaries) to weep bitterly with flowing tears. Consequently, Shang felt that he needed to take on the role of shaking like an ancient bell or crowing like a rooster, which are classical allusions (*Analects* 3:24). He felt obliged to write this book in order to warn the people, hence the term *gaowen* (written warning) in the title. Shang believed that the literati of his day needed to be repaired (bu). The meaning of the term "bu" is elaborated throughout *A Warning*. In the introduction, Shang presented bu as "supplementing" in the sense of broadening a narrow-mindedness in the literati. He criticized the literati for clinging to a partial rather than a universal view of truth and for concentrating too much on poetry and compositions and failing to see that this focus on nonessentials was part of an illness.[73] The Literati had erred by departing from orthodox teaching and being influenced by Buddhism. Shang's attack on Buddhism echoes the views of numerous other Christian literati, including Xu Guangqi and Zhang Xingyao.

Although Gan Lichuan's marginal comments are his own and not Shang's, one can assume that he and Shang had considerable discussion over the meaning of the title and that Gan would have had a clear sense of Shang's meaning. On the opening page of part 1, Gan commented that the blending of the Literati Teaching of man with the Heavenly Teaching would enable the deficiencies of the Literati *(Ru que)* to be "repaired" (bu).[74] Elsewhere Gan related the phrase "bu Ru" (supplement the Literati) to the manifestation of true teachings in history.[75] Shang's text deals with the difficult problem of why the Heavenly Teaching was not included among the ancient sage teachings of China. Shang argued that the Heavenly Teaching was present and that Heaven conveyed the truth to the people through a process of "universal transmission" *(gong chuan)*.[76] Prior to the end of the three ancient dynasties (Xia, Shang, and Zhou), the Dao (the Way or truth) was transmitted by the ancient emperors to later kings, while the early sages conveyed it to later worthies. However, as time went on, the positions of prince, minister, teacher, and literatus became divided, and heterodoxies in the form of Yang Zhu's egoism and Mozi's indiscriminate love arose. Shang stated that "down to the present, the Heavenly Teaching and the Literati Teaching have been on the same track" *(zhi jin wei Tian Ru he che)*.[77] He cited numerous passages from the Classics, predominantly from the *History* and the *Analects* but also from the *Odes* and *Mencius*, to support his view. One of these citations is from the *Analects* 20:1, in which the legendary emperor Yao, in his charge to his successor Shun, orders him to hold fast to the Mean *(zhi qi zhong)*. Shang contrasted the concern of the Heavenly Teaching to hold fast to the Mean with the heterodoxies of the extremist philosophies of Yang Zhu and Mozi.

Yang Zhu and Mozi belonged to antiquity and had few adherents in Shang's day. However, Yang Zhu and Mozi had become metonyms or generic terms for a heterodox type of thinking that diverged from the truth into extreme and false viewpoints. The most prominent heterodoxies in Shang's day were Buddhism and Daoism, and his attack upon them was relentless. Gan's commentary on this passage included the phrase "criticize the Buddhists and supplement the Literati" *(pi Fo bu Ru)*. What Shang found so unforgivable in the Buddhists and Daoists was their pluralism, which rejected a single universal notion of truth. In contrast, the Literati Teaching and the Heavenly Teaching sought universal truth. Shang quoted Confucius (*Analects* 4:10): "A gentleman in his dealings with the world inclines his mind neither for nor against things but rather seeks what is right."[78]

Shang went on to say that "what is right" *(yi zhe)* is given to humans by the Lord-on-High and is developed through their spiritual nature *(ling xing)*. He compared this spiritual nature to a scale *(hengshi)* for weighing truth and a universal teacher *(gongshi)* of mankind. Shang emphasized the universal nature of the search for truth by saying: "Men of the Eastern Sea and Western Sea live in different lands, but under the same Heaven. They have different cultures, but the same truths." The world was filled with contradictory doctrines, but Shang argued that, unlike the Buddhists and Daoists who accept pluralistic forms of truth, the Literati and Heavenly Teachings are committed to finding universal truth, which would produce harmony. This was the ideal of the Chinese ancients, and this was the ideal of the European missionaries.

Shang stated that while China was filled with Buddhists and Daoists, there were very few genuine seekers of the Way of the sages Yao, Shun, Confucius, and Mencius.[79] While the Buddhists and Daoists were destructive in their logic and investigated abstractions, the school of the Song Neo-Confucians *(Ru li)* dealt merely with the dregs and sediment from which urgent and valuable matters were absent. What was needed was a scale to measure value and a "touchstone" *(liushi)* to distinguish what was important from what was unimportant. The "Western worthies" *(Xi xian)* could provide this through the Heavenly Teaching. Shang explained this using the metaphor of gold that was not limited to one place and could be traded (i.e., transferred) to others. Gan's commentary on this passage distinguished between the different ways in which the two schools of Buddhism and Daoism versus the Literati Teaching should be handled. Because the Buddhists and Daoists were completely cunning in evaluating what was important, they must be severely criticized *(pi)*. Moreover, the Song Neo-Confucians dealt with complete abstractions that needed to be supplemented (bu) by the Heavenly Teaching. Gan believed that a process of alternately criticizing and supplementing the basic meaning of Song Neo-Confucianism could reveal the teaching of the Four Sages *(Si Ju)*: Yao, Shun, Confucius, and Mencius.

The echoes of ideas and phrases among several generations of Christian literati makes some degree of contact between them likely. Both Shang and Zhang Xingyao were influenced by Xu Guangqi. Zhang also appears to have been influenced by Shang. Likewise, Zhang spoke of the universal basis of truth toward which both the Literati and the Christians strove: "Sages arise in both the East and the West, but their minds are the same."[80]

Separating Orthodoxy from Heterodoxy:
Neo-Confucianism and Buddhism

While Shang relentlessly criticized Buddhists and Daoists, his attitude toward the Song Literati (Neo-Confucians) was much more complicated. Because Shang was a believer in the tradition of the Transmission of the Way *(Daotong)*, it would have been extreme for him to have rejected the Song Literati teachings of Zhou Dunyi, Zhang Zai, the Cheng brothers, and Zhu Xi. These literati were widely recognized to be orthodox transmitters of truth from the ancients. On the other hand, Song Neo-Confucian cosmology provided some of the strongest intellectual arguments against Christianity in China. As a result, Shang was forced to criticize certain interpretations of the Song Literati that were contradictory to the Heavenly Teaching. The most basic element of Neo-Confucian cosmology was the *Taiji* (Supreme Ultimate), which explained the generation and corruption of the world in cyclical terms and without reference to biblical creation from nothingness (ex nihilo) and without a divine guiding force. Neo-Confucian cosmology reduced the world to two basic elements: qi (ether, or the material component) and li (principle).

Shang used a metaphor from the construction of a building to show the incomplete nature of this cosmology and to show why it needed to be supplemented by the Heavenly Teaching. He compared qi to the wood and bricks in a house and li to the pattern that penetrated the house. However, Shang believed that something was missing. There was no "engineer" *(gongshi)* who would "act to determine what is the front of the house and what is the sleeping quarters in the rear, to determine where the kitchen, bathroom, gates, and walls are, to determine the types of wood in the rafters."[81] He also referred to the need for an "artisan" *(gongjiang)*.[82] Shang believed that the Heavenly Teaching could supplement this deficiency in the Song cosmology. Gan's commentary added that Taiji, along with li and qi, represented a partial form of metaphysics. These two elements needed a *zhuzai* (lord, controlling force) in order to be complete. This missing element was provided by the God of the Heavenly Teaching. This was another example of how the Literati Teaching was imbalanced (pian) and needed to be repaired (bu).

While Song cosmology provided an intellectual basis for Literati criticisms of the Heavenly Teaching, the foreign origins of Christianity made it vulnerable to attack. Shang presented this chauvinism through the mouth of an anonymous scholar who noted that since antiquity, "emperors, kings, worthies and sages" *(di wang xian sheng)* had all spoken of Heaven and serving the Lord.[83] Since the Heavenly Teaching was presented in the principles of the Literati, this scholar asked, why was there a need to depend on the Western scholars? This view represented the ethnocentric argument of Chinese self-sufficiency, namely, that the teachings of China were complete and required nothing from foreign cultures.

Shang went on to present a second and more blatantly chauvinistic, even xenophobic, argument, namely, that foreign teachings by their very nature were inferior to Chinese teachings. This argument had been used to attack Buddhism. While the Buddha Dharma began in the countries bordering on the west of China, the Heavenly Teaching came from the Far West. It was brought to China by Western people (missionaries) who attacked other Western people in the same way that the tyrannical state of Yan was attacked by another state that was equally tyrannical *(Mencius* IIb.8) and had no moral basis to do so. On these grounds, the questioner asked how Buddhism and Daoism could be regarded as false and yet the Heavenly Teaching be regarded as true.

Shang responded that such criticisms of the Heavenly Teaching were based on superficial associations.[84] A more fundamental basis of criticism would be the content of their respective teachings. By such an examination, one would see that "the Buddha and Laozi base their teachings on the void and emptiness" *(Fo Lao yi kongji xuwu wei jiao),* and they regard the Heavenly Teaching as something completely different and unreconcilable. The Literati agreed with the Buddhists in that they saw the Heavenly Teaching as something different and unreconcilable. Gan's commentary on this passage explained that the Heavenly Teaching sufficed to "supplement" or "repair" (bu) the deficiencies of the Literati Teaching by criticizing those who followed the errors of the Buddhists and by rectifying these errors. Gan explained that the Literati had an incomplete grasp of what caused things. Their understanding was based on principles of a purely causative (cause-and-effect) nature *(yin xing),* but they had not yet attained the deeper understanding of a transcendent nature *(chao xing).* Gan added that the purpose of *A Warning* was to develop this deeper spiritual understanding.

Reinterpreting the Creation of the World in China

Unlike Judeo-Christian culture, China lacked a highly developed notion of creation. Chinese creation myths lacked a creator whose divine will ordained the act of creation.[85] The cosmology later developed by the Song Literati merely reinforced this lack of creation by providing it with cosmological underpinnings. The famous "Diagram of the Supreme Ultimate" *(Taiji tu)* of Zhou Dunyi (1017–1073) presented a cyclical view of creation that conflicted with the Judeo-Christian notion of creation ex nihilo depicted in the book of Genesis. However, the lack of a highly developed creation myth in Chinese culture could be traced to Chinese legendary history. Shang stated that both logic and the ancient texts of many lands confirmed that there was a creation of the world and mankind.[86] In China, the ancient texts referred to the creation myth of Pan Gu at a time when there were no humans. The records of the Far West were more complete on creation and spoke of the creation that occurred before Adam when there were no humans.

Drawing upon chronologies based on the Bible, Shang wrote that the period from Creation until his own day had not yet been 7,000 years.[87] Gan's commentary was more specific, saying that from Creation until 1664 amounted to 6,862 years whereas the period from the Incarnation of the Lord of Heaven (Jesus) until 1664 amounted to 1,664 years.[88] Shang stated that the Chinese almanacs *(lishu)* were not continuous because of the destruction of records (the Legalist burning of the books in 213 B.C.) during the Qin dynasty. As a result, the exact number of years down to the Han dynasty could not be computed precisely using Chinese records. Shang claimed that when Confucius edited the Six Classics, he deleted uncertain materials. Consequently, the literati were left with texts that made numerous references to Chinese antiquity but about which there was ambiguity, such as the Great Commentary of the *Book of Changes (Yi da chuan),* which referred to Fu Xi, Shen Nong, the Yellow Emperor, Yao, and

Shun. Shang noted that the *Book of History* also contained incoherent words in the discussion of Yao and Shun.

Shang cited comments from several historians. Nan Xuan (1515–1596), in his *Zizhi tongjian gangmu qianbian* (An abridged view of the period before the Comprehensive Mirror History), spoke of events prior to Yao and Shun and said that history should begin with Fu Xi. The Grand Historian Sima Qian (ca. 165–ca. 85 B.C.) wrote in his *Shiji* (Historical records) that the Chinese had no knowledge of events prior to Shen Nong. Wang Shizhen (1526–1590) in *Gangjian huizuan* stated that, on the basis of the classical texts (which are more reliable than the commentaries), the period from Emperor Yao to the Shunzhi Emperor (r. 1644–1661) amounted to just four thousand years. But before Yao there was a period of countless years.

In regard to Chinese antiquity, Shang distinguished two categories. The first category involved fantastic myths that defied logic, while the second involved more realistic events, which he believed were based on historical records. Shang included in the first category the myth of Nü Gua (Wa) to explain how the Heavenly Teaching repaired this deficiency. According to legend, when heaven was damaged by a battle between the legendary ruler Zhuan Xu and Gong Gong, the latter struck his head against the Puzhou Mountain, causing it to tumble down. This damaged the pillars of heaven and destroyed the supports at the four corners of the earth. Nü Gua, said to have been a sister/wife of Fu Xi, repaired the damage by melting a five-colored stone and cutting off a turtle's feet to hold up the earth at its four corners. Nü repaired (bu) or supplemented the light and warmth of heaven by burning a mineral substance (five-colored stone). Scholars today date the Nü Gua myth from the Zhou dynasty (ca. 1050–221 B.C.), but it was first fully developed in Han texts, such as the *Huainanzi, Liezi,* and *Shanhai jing* (Mountain and Sea Classic).[89] A later myth, not mentioned by Shang, depicted Nü Gua as the creatrix of humans. This myth was incorporated into the opening lines of the famous novel *The Story of the Stone (Shitouji),* also known as *Dream of the Red Chamber (Honglou meng).*[90]

Fu Xi and Nü Gua were depicted in the stone reliefs of Wu Liang offering shrines (ca. A.D. 150) as having upper bodies that were human and snakelike lower bodies.[91] However Shang wrote that only those who were deficient in reasoning would believe that Fu Xi had a human head and a snake's body. Likewise, they would not believe that there were countless years without a beginning prior to Yao, that is, a world without creation.

In the second category of more realistic events of antiquity, Shang referred to Sui Ren, who first taught people to cook food with fire; You Chao, who first taught people to live in houses; and Shen Nong, who first taught people agriculture. Shang regarded these events as verified by historical records. Furthermore, the creation of heaven and earth and people and things, in Shang's eyes, was due to some cause, and this cause was provided by the Lord of Heaven. Shang referred to *en* (grace) as being part of this process, and Gan's commentary clarified that this meant "the Lord's grace" *(Zhu en).*

For many teachings, truth is inseparable from the idea of transmission. Through transmission, truth is not newly discovered by each generation but rather is handed down from antiquity by teachers and prophets. Transmission is a fundamental part of both Confucianism and Christianity. In Christianity, it is expressed biblically by the covenant between the monotheistic God, Yahweh, and the descendants of Abraham. In Jesus, both a descendant of Abraham and the Son of God, the transmission became based more on belief than on blood, and yet it remained a teaching whose truth was transmitted in history. The Catholic notion of apostolic succession also reflected a transmission of authority from Jesus to Peter to (as of the year 2001) 261 papal successors. In Confucianism, transmission is expressed by the word *chuan* and is found in the term *Daochuan* (Transmission of the Way), which is equivalent in meaning to Daotong.[92] The Way (i.e., Truth) was transmitted from the sages of antiquity to later generations. The process was captured by Confucius in his claim that he was a transmitter and not a creator *(Analects* 7:1) of the teaching. Shang used the term "gong chuan" (universal transmission) to refer to this process, but with this difference: he believed that the truths of the Literati Teaching and the truths of the Lord of Heaven Teaching were in harmony. Shang also referred to the "Orthodox Transmission" *(Zheng Chuan).*[93] It appears to have been similar in meaning to Daochuan or Daotong (The Transmission of the Truth).

One of the many problems that Shang faced in arguing that the Literati and Lord of Heaven Teachings were in harmony was the fact that the Chinese Classics did not refer explicitly to the Heavenly Teaching. Confucius himself said that Heaven did not speak *(Analects* 17:19), and his disciple Zigong said that Confucius's explanations of "human nature and the way of Heaven cannot be heard" *(Analects* 5:12). The *Doctrine of the Mean* is claimed to have been edited by Confucius's grandson Zisi. Shang noted that Zisi said that Confucius was the first to link the renewal of the Heavenly Mandate *(Tian Ming)* with the passage from the *Book of Odes:* "The operations of Heaven have neither sound nor smell."[94] Shang said that the meaning of this phrase was very deep. It did not refer to nothingness in the Buddhist sense but rather referred to something that could not be seen or heard. In his commentary on the opening passage of *Doctrine of the Mean,* Zhu Xi used the term *chuan,* which is translated by Legge as "handed down from a teacher" and by Wing-tsit Chan as "transmission."[95] Shang used the term to mean God's revelation of his will to mankind.

Shang used the term "gong chuan" (universal transmission) of the Sage Teaching *(Sheng Jiao).* While most literati saw the Sage Teaching as being synonymous with the Literati Teaching, Shang saw it as embracing both the Literati Teaching and the Lord of Heaven Teaching. Whereas the specifics of the Lord of Heaven Teaching were not explicitly discussed in the Classics, the evidence of the heavenly commands was found in principles in these Classics. These principles could clearly manifest the Heavenly Teaching, whose clarity in antiquity had been lost in modern times.

How the Collaboration of Caballero and Shang Sinified the Christian Message

Wanwu benmo yueyan (A Brief Summary of the Beginning and End of All Things) is a short work of 2,640 characters printed in the late 1600s at the Fuyin Tang (Gospel Church) in the western suburbs of Canton.[96] This work is also attributed to Caballero, but its tone is completely unlike his other works in Chinese. The difference appears to be due to the absence of Shang Huqing as a collaborator. The revisor *(ding)* who prepared the text for printing was Father Bonaventura Ibáñez. Ibáñez had been with Caballero during the founding of the Franciscan mission in Ji'nan in the early 1650s, but he soon left Ji'nan. In 1662 Caballero sent Ibáñez to Rome to secure reinforcements. He returned by way of Cadiz, Honduras, Acapulco, and the Philippines, arriving in Macau in May 1672 with four recruits. Ibáñez later became commissioner of the Franciscan mission in China based in Canton. Since Caballero had died at Canton in 1669, the two never met again, although Ibáñez was buried beside Caballero at Baogang on Henan Island outside of Canton.

The difference between *A Summary* and Caballero's previous works is apparent in the choice of vocabulary. Instead of referring to Christianity in terms like "Lord of Heaven Teaching" *(Tianzhu Jiao)* that emerge out of Chinese traditions, Christianity is referred to as the "New Teaching" *(Xin Jiao)* in contrast to the "Old Teaching" *(Gu Jiao)*. The preface states: "The sacrificial rites of the Old Teaching foreshadow the image of the sacrificial rites of the New Teaching."[97] The phrasing was drawn from Christian tradition, which distinguishes between the Old and New Testaments, but it is alien to the literati tradition of China. This approach is found not only in the preface to *A Summary* but also in the text, which places heavy emphasis on biblical Creation and on the Trinity, which were Christian concepts difficult to reconcile with the Confucian tradition.[98]

All of the basic doctrines of Christianity are introduced in the text of *A Summary*, including good and evil spirits, the Lord of Heaven as a great father, God's creation of human beings in the form of Adam and Eve, the temptation by Satan, the fall of the human race, original sin, the Ten Commandments, the Incarnation of God in the human form of Jesus, the immaculate conception and virgin birth; the life of Jesus, the Crucifixion, the Resurrection, the Ascension, the doctrine of grace, the Last Judgment, and eternal damnation in hell and eternal bliss in heaven.

The emphasis throughout the work is that the Western scholars have come from afar to bring a new teaching to China.[99] There is very little attempt to relate this new teaching of Christianity to traditional Chinese teachings, probably because when Caballero wrote this work in 1653, he had very little knowledge of those teachings. It is doubtful that Ibáñez ever acquired such a knowledge. The cosmological underpinnings of *A Summary* are completely Western. For example, the placement of hell at the center of the universe is a thoroughly Ptolemaic–Aristotelian conception, which was given metaphorical elaboration in literary works such as Dante's *Divine Comedy.*[100] The Aristotelian Four Elements (earth, air, fire, and water) are mentioned rather than the Chinese Five Forces (earth, fire, water, metal, and wood). Only in the reference to the Five Human Relationships *(Wu Lun)* and possibly in the repeated references to ancestors are there attempts to relate Christianity to the Chinese context.[101]

The contents of this work appear to fit Caballero's description of the second of the three books in Chinese that he composed in 1653, when Ibáñez was with him in Ji'nan. He wrote:

> The second [book], with the fundamentals of their Chinese books, shows them with evidence the vanity of idols and of all the idolatry there is in the world. . . . Then I call on the natural law, expressing the Ten Commandments of the Decalogue in the explanation of each commandment, and the works of mercy, where as an example one had the honor of attending to the deceased with true piety of the interred, relinquishing their vain superstitions and vain sacrifices.[102]

Caballero certainly lacked the ability to express himself in polished literary Chinese, and the Chinese text of *A Summary* was quite possibly formulated by the "Chinese literatus" *(letrado chino)* whom Caballero paid to make a rough draft of these works six or seven years before meeting Shang.[103] Unlike Shang, who was a true collaborator with Caballero, this Chinese literatus appears to have simply served in the editorial role of helping Caballero express his thoughts in grammatical and fluent literary Chinese.

The other two works Caballero described writing in 1653 do not appear to correspond to his other Chinese works, *Imprints* and *The Touchstone,* probably because they underwent considerable revision through Caballero's contact with Shang Huqing. By contrast, *A Summary* remained in its original form, except for some editing overseen by Ibáñez. The work is said to have been printed, along with *Imprints,* in 1664, when the mission finances at Ji'nan permitted.[104] However, no copy of this edition has been found. The extant copy of this work was printed at the Gospel Church in western Canton. Since Ibáñez also printed a catechism that was written at this church, it is likely that Ibáñez, rather than

Caballero, was responsible for this printing. It was probably printed sometime between Ibáñez's return to China in 1672 and his death in 1691.[105]

A Summary is significant because it reveals the crucial role that Shang Huqing played in Caballero's other, more important writings. While A Summary is in Chinese, apart from translating Christian teachings into Chinese, there is very little inculturation of Christianity into Chinese culture. The Christian ideas are presented as they were taught in a European context and without sensitivity to those parts that might have required more explanation or been more controversial. While there had been collaboration on the level of translation into Chinese and this probably raised a number of questions that had to be answered for the translator, the collaboration did not carry to a very deep level. By contrast, Caballero and Shang working together represent one of the most important collaborative efforts of the seventeenth century. Theirs was not the first such effort—Ricci had collaborated with Xu Guangqi in writing Tianzhu shiyi (The True Meaning of the Lord of Heaven)—but given the austere conditions under which Caballero and Shang worked in Ji'nan, it was every bit as remarkable.

3

The Return to Shandong after the Anti-Christian Persecution of 1664–1669

The Arrival of Augustinus a S. Paschale, O.F.M., in Shandong

In the minds of Spanish Franciscans, Father Caballero became a model whose success the Franciscans were eager to emulate. However, the anti-Christian persecution of 1664–1669 delayed their return to Shandong. The first to retrace Caballero's path was Augustin de San Pasqual, more commonly known by his Latin name, Augustinus a Sancti Paschale (Li [Gu] Anding, Weizhi) (1637–1697). Father Paschale was born in the village of Marabella in the province of Malaga in 1637 and entered the Franciscan order in 1656 in Valencia.[1] He departed from Spain in 1665 and arrived in the company of twenty-eight confreres in Manila in 1666.[2] There he served in the province of San Gregorio.

Finally, on January 10, 1670, Paschale boarded a ship in Manila owned by Armenian merchants.[3] He and his companion, Father Juan a Camara, landed in Timor and finally at Batavia on the island of Java on October 22, 1670. While they were living in the company of Christians in Batavia for seven or eight months, the news arrived that the anti-Christian persecution in China was ending and that the priests expelled to Canton would soon be allowed to return to their mission bases in China. Paschale and Camara arrived in Macau in June or July 1671. Paschale went to Canton, determined to return to Caballero's old mission site in Ji'nan. However, the Jesuit Father Andreas Lubelli, under orders from his superior, refused to admit Paschale to the Jesuit residence in Canton until the Dominican Father Francisco Varo intervened on Paschale's behalf.[4] Paschale remained in Canton for eight months and then, with the intention of going ultimately to Shandong, departed for Fujian on September 22, 1672. In Fujian he lived with the Dominicans for five years.[5]

Meanwhile additional Franciscans were being sent from the Philippines. On August 23, 1676, Fathers Petrus de la Piñuela and Michael Flores arrived in Luojia (in the Fuan district), where they were welcomed by Paschale. Flores went to

Muyang for language study, while Paschale and Piñuela went to Ningde district, a coastal city in northern Fujian province (see map 1). However, because of the coastal pirates who supported the Ming cause against the Manchu monarchy, government officials were extremely sensitive to potentially subversive elements in this region. Paschale criticized the Chinese of Ningde for being cowardly in their anxiety over the potential for revolt from three Europeans living together, but he also appears to have been expressing some frustration at the lack of missionary success in Ningde. He dreamt of the Franciscans returning to the mission field of Caballero's success in Shandong.[6] Paschale also felt a sense of urgency about the situation because he was afraid that the Manchu soldiers might occupy the empty church in Ji'nan and make it impossible for the Franciscans to retrieve it. This had happened to the Dominicans' church in Fuzhou.

Paschale and Flores departed from Ningde on September 9, 1677, and on November 5 reached Taian, twenty-four leagues (two days' travel) south of Ji'nan (see map 2), becoming the first Franciscans in Shandong since the departure of Caballero over twenty-two years earlier, in 1665. In the area around Taian they found four Christian churches in four small villages.[7] The eight hundred Christians of these churches were simple country people who claimed to be members of the Confraternity of the Virgin. They explained that Father Valat was away from Ji'nan on a one-and-a-half-month trip to serve the ten thousand Christians in Zhili (now Hebei) province. He was in Zhengding prefecture, which was nine days' distance from Taian.[8] They were not expecting him to return until after Christmas. They cautioned the Franciscans not to enter Ji'nan until Valat returned because there was a scholar–official in Ji'nan who was hostile to Christianity. This official had engaged Valat in a dispute over the occupation of the church that Caballero had formerly occupied.[9]

When word of the Franciscans' presence reached Ji'nan, two Christians from there came to Taian to visit Paschale. Eventually Valat wrote, explaining that he had previously arranged with the mandarins that Paschale would be able to occupy the church on the very Chinese grounds that he was a younger brother of Li Andang (Caballero), who had owned the church. For this reason, Valat advised that Paschale change his Chinese surname from Gu to Li, using the same character as Caballero.[10] Valat said that he had been residing at the Franciscan church (the East Church). but that upon Paschale's arrival, he would move to the Jesuit church (the West Church). There would, however, be some difficulty in accounting for Flores's presence, and Valat advised Paschale to present Flores as his secretary rather than a priest.

Leaving Flores behind in Taian, Paschale traveled to Ji'nan. He arrived there on December 16, 1677, and moved into the East Church. On the very next day, an official came to visit, pressing him with questions about his surname and whether he was, in fact, a younger brother of Caballero. This official was a close friend of Valat and a subordinate to the anti-Christian official in Ji'nan, to whom he was obliged to report on Paschale's arrival.[11] Several days later at two o'clock in the afternoon, the anti-Christian official himself suddenly arrived at the church, accompanied by a hundred men. This official, whose rank in the province was the second highest, just below the governor *(xunfu)*, held the office of provincial administration commissioner *(buzhengshi)*, who acted as a lieutenant governor with heavy fiscal duties, including tax collection.[12] This official was polite and stayed until nightfall, listening carefully to what Paschale said. Paschale took this as a sign of his interest in Christianity, but it is more likely to have been the attention of one gathering information and listening for incriminating comments. Paschale attempted to explain some basic Christian theology and took particular joy in refuting certain Buddhist teachings. After listening attentively without interruption, the official said, "Master, you are right in all that you say, but we Chinese are interested only in money and women."[13] This is a surprising comment from a literatus, unless he was speaking tongue-in-cheek and Paschale took his ironic comment literally.

Valat returned to Ji'nan on Christmas Eve 1677. He welcomed Paschale and returned to his own church on the second day after Christmas. Flores arrived in Ji'nan after Epiphany (January 6). It had been nearly thirteen years since Caballero had been forcibly removed from these premises in March 1665. What remained were a small table, a few implements for saying mass, and some books in manuscript in Chinese.[14] The East Church had been subdivided into apartments, one of which had been used by Valat and into which Christians squeezed to hear mass. Paschale had the room partitions removed and timbers placed where necessary to shore up the sadly neglected building. Once cleared of room dividers, the sanctuary measured approximately 47½ feet in length and 19½ feet in width. Through minor repairs and painting, Paschale had the church put into usable condition. However, it was in need of major repairs and had many leaks. Paschale had already spent 60 taels of silver (the equivalent of 80 pesos) for the repairs and for winter clothing for himself and Flores. Three hundred more pesos (225 taels of silver) would be needed to completely repair the church.

Finances were always a problem for the missionaries in Shandong, and their letters to religious superiors are filled with accountings of expenses and pleas for more funds. Paschale stated that he and Flores departed from Fujian with 350 to 400 pesos.[15] He spent 97 pesos on the journey, 80 pesos on preparing the church and purchasing winter clothing, and 53 pesos on food and servants over a seven-and-a-half-month period, leaving a balance of 120 pesos. Paschale complained that living expenses, particularly firewood, were greater in Shandong than in Fujian and a recent drought had made the situation even worse. He feared that the remaining 120 pesos would be insufficient for a year.[16] The food in Shandong is said to have cost twice as much as in Fujian, that is, 100 pesos instead of 50 pesos for one year.[17]

Paschale found Shandong a difficult mission field. He noted that more fervor was required than in Fujian, which had proved very fertile territory for propagating the gospel. In his first eight months in Shandong, Paschale baptized approximately seventy persons, the most prominent of whom was a literatus from Henan province who was the brother of a minor official charged with tax collection in Ji'nan. This literatus had learned about Christianity from reading a book, and he accompanied his brother to Ji'nan because he wished to be baptized in the Christian church there.

Paschale visited other sites in Shandong where Caballero had established churches. In northern Shandong there were three district seats, Xincheng, Boxing, and Putai (see map 2), where Caballero had baptized 1,500 people prior to the persecution of 1664–1665. In these places, Paschale found only 150 people who would identify themselves as Christians. In the nearby district seat of Qingcheng, some Christians remained, but in Yanshen (Yanshenzhen) the church had been razed to the ground. There the Christians, except for one deaf man, were too afraid of the mandarin to invite the priest to their home or to be confessed. A group of ten or twelve women made indirect contact, but they were afraid to come to the inn where Paschale was staying or to invite him to their homes because of their husbands. Eventually, a cooperative husband permitted the priest to come to his house and allowed his wife and other Christians to be confessed. Paschale baptized four adult women there but was unable to say mass.[18] When he visited these towns, he was accompanied by a catechist and a servant.[19] They would take four donkeys, one for each of them plus a fourth to carry the mass utensils and the bedding. Paschale would send the catechist ahead of him to preach and to stir up the people in preparation for his arrival.

As of November 1678, there were 400 Christians in Ji'nan who were ministered to by Valat and Paschale without distinction. In addition they ministered to 150 Christians in two towns (Xincheng and Boxing?) that were two days' distance from Ji'nan.[20] Other Christians in outlying areas were cared for by an unnamed Jesuit. In one year and twenty days since his arrival in Ji'nan, Paschale had baptized a total of 90 infants and adults.

Paschale found the winter weather in Shandong as cold as the reception from the populace. He complained that the frigid temperatures were intolerable *("el frio es insufrible")*.[21] This was a common complaint of many Spanish missionaries, who were accustomed to the warmer climates of Spain, Mexico, and the Philippines. The structure that housed the church and the parsonage was in need of such extensive repair that Paschale wanted to demolish it, but he was afraid the mandarins would refuse to give him another site.[22]

Not only were expenses in Shandong greater than in Fujian, but in the southern province Paschale had managed with two servants while in Shandong he needed three servants plus a boy.[23] One of the servants was needed to accompany him on his many trips. In his absence, the church and residence had to be constantly guarded against thieves. The servants were each paid one peso and two reals each month (one peso was worth eight reals). The boy was paid with clothing. Paschale referred twice to a Chinese manservant named Domingo, who appears to have been one of Paschale's servants in Ji'nan.[24] In Shandong, unlike in Fujian, rice was expensive, though wheat could be obtained cheaply. Whereas firewood had been inexpensive in Fujian, it was so costly in Ji'nan that cooking was done with charcoal. Charcoal braziers were used to heat rooms against the harsh cold from November until mid-April. And, unlike Fujian, where their residence in Ningde had been close to the sea, Ji'nan was far from the ocean and he was unable to obtain decent fish to eat. The inhospitable atmosphere of Shandong led Paschale to propose that the Franciscans abandon their missionary efforts in both Shandong and Fujian and concentrate their ten missionaries in Guandong province, which happened to have a warmer climate than Shandong.

Paschale's letters in 1678 and 1679 are filled with anxiety about financial difficulties and the high costs of doing missionary work in Ji'nan. For the Spanish priests based in Manila (unlike their Portuguese counterparts in Macau), it was much more difficult to transport the financial aid to Shandong than to Canton and Fujian. Aid to Shandong had to be carried to the church of the Dominican fathers in Lanxi district, which was in Zhejiang province, southwest of Hangzhou. Paschale claimed that the distance from Ji'nan to Lanxi was 380 leagues.[25]

On November 8, 1679, Paschale received Ibáñez's letters of July 30 and September 14 along with a letter from the Jesuit vice-provincial, Father F. Verbiest, inside of which was a *huipiao* (a reply from a superior to an inquiry), that is, a letter from Venerable Liu of Ji'nan, indicating that one hundred taels of silver were to be remitted to Paschale on the twentieth day of the tenth lunar month (November 22) 1679.[26] This silver had apparently come from Fujian to Hangzhou and then, through Valat's intercession, Verbiest had arranged for it to be transmitted to Paschale in Ji'nan by way of Liu. Paschale stated that this hundred taels plus the sixty taels that Ibáñez had sent earlier would be more than sufficient to provision the mission with wheat and *xiaomi* (yellow millet) for 1680 and 1681.[27]

Paschale and Valat attempted to revive the cooperative relationship that had existed between Caballero and Valat. The baptized Christians who lived to the west and south of Ji'nan were cared for by Valat, while those in the east and north of Ji'nan were cared for by Paschale. If one priest was absent or ill, the other assumed his duties.[28]

Personal Tensions between Missionaries

Hostility between missionaries of the same nationality and even the same religious order surfaced in Shandong. Tension between Paschale and Flores caused Flores to depart in the autumn of 1678, less than a year after arriving in Ji'nan. Flores went to Canton, where he allied with Father Ibáñez against Paschale.[29] Paschale had a quarrelsome personality. In 1679 he criticized the purchase of a house by his fellow Franciscans in Canton, and he criticized the provincial commissioner in Canton, Father Ibáñez, for being ignorant of Chinese customs in spite of having lived in China for fourteen years.[30] Paschale was not necessarily wrong in his criticism, but it was delivered in a tactless way that had negative results. Because the house purchased in Canton was outside the city walls, Paschale said that it was in greater danger from both the violence of war and the pillaging of thieves. He also criticized the house as being overly large. In Ji'nan, he had been forced to sublet some side rooms connected to the East Church to some officials. The church's proximity to the site of the official examinations apparently increased the demand for it, which became so great that more than one scholar–official asked to use it, one of those being the provincial administrative commissioner.[31] Paschale believed that if the Canton Franciscans had a large residence, they would be subject to similar sorts of demands from officials. Finally, Paschale criticized the cost of their house. A thousand taels of silver (1,333 pesos) was, in his view, extravagant, considering that he lacked a mere 100 taels to buy a mission house in Jining, thirty leagues south of Ji'nan.[32]

In December 1679 there were two Franciscans in Fujian (Incarnatione and Piñuela), one in Shandong (Paschale), and six in Guangdong (Juan Marti, Jaime Tarin, Francisco Nieto-Díaz, M. Florez, Blas Garcia, and B. Ibáñez).[33] There appears to have been more interchange of Franciscans between Shandong and Fujian than between Shandong and Canton. In fact, given the greater manpower and the meagre historical results in Canton, one may question whether Canton was really a productive mission site and whether the large contingent of missionaries based there might not have been more effective in places like Fujian and Shandong. Seen in this light, Paschale's charge that the missionaries in Canton were out of touch with Chinese customs had merit, but his proposal that the Franciscan mission in Shandong be shifted to Guangdong and Fujian did not. Ibáñez responded to Paschale that although the Franciscans had founded four new churches (two in Canton, one in Dongguan, and one in Ningde), there was an official mandate against founding new churches. Since the Franciscan church in Ji'nan was the only one that had received official sanction, it would be unwise to relinquish it.[34]

Paschale sent a manservant to Ningde in search of Father Pedro de la Piñuela (Shi Duolu, Zhenduo) (1650–1704).[35] The servant found him, not in Ningde, but in Jiangle, with a Jesuit, Father Simão Rodrigues (Li Shouqian) (1645–1682) (see map 1). Piñuela and Rodrigues, although of different religious orders, were both Spanish and had entered Fujian by way of the Philippines. However, the Chinese manservant had a far more favorable impression of Rodrigues than of Piñuela. In contrast to Rodrigues's composure and humble words, which followed Chinese custom, the servant found Piñuela discomposed, flushed, and loud-voiced (*gaosheng*), which the Chinese found offensive. In addition, Piñuela was wearing colored shoes, which the manservant regarded as presumptuous because in Jiangle only the literati wore colored shoes.[36] Paschale, while noting that the Chinese tended to be hypercritical, passed along this criticism of Piñuela to Ibáñez in a thoughtless manner. Clearly, Piñuela was either not sensitive to or had not yet mastered Chinese customs, and this was a telling deficiency on his part. Yet Paschale's comments also revealed a tactlessness that made the criticism appear petty. This explains, in part, Ibáñez's negative reaction to Paschale.

Ibáñez was very critical of Paschale and referred to him as a "rooster" (*gallo*), that is, an aggressive personality, who needed an amenable "capon" as a companion.[37] Whereas Flores was too aggressive to get along with Paschale, Father Incarnatione was thought to be accommodating enough. Consequently, when Incarnatione wrote from Ningde of his unhappiness and his desire to join Paschale in Ji'nan, Ibáñez gave his permission. Paschale and Incarnatione had been on friendly terms in Manila, and Paschale's isolation could be alleviated by Incarnatione's presence.

Drawing from descriptions by Flores and others who knew Paschale, Ibáñez described him as very religious but too controlling. After Flores's departure, Paschale wrote that no one wanted to join him in Ji'nan because word had gotten around that he was domineering and bullied his companion. In a theatrical gesture, Paschale promised to subordinate himself to any brother who joined him in Ji'nan, or, if Ibáñez wished, he was willing to go to a remote mission site, like Dingzhou or Jining, and work alone.[38] Ibáñez believed that Paschale suffered from melancholia, a neurotic condition marked by depression and mistrust of others. This may indeed have been true, but Paschale's situation in Ji'nan was far more difficult than Ibáñez's in Canton, and Ibáñez betrayed a defensiveness that indicates his disagreement was at least partly personal. For his part, Paschale claimed that Flores left Ji'nan because he had mishandled the Chinese demands to sublet the side rooms in the East Church. He described Flores as someone whose impatience and inability to adapt himself to Chinese customs caused bad relations with Chinese Christians and led to his departure from Ji'nan.[39]

In 1679 Father Incarnatione traveled from Manila to Ningde to deliver the aid to Father Piñuela. Incarnatione carried not only the 450 pesos from the procurator but also contributions given to him by devout Christians in Manila, which amounted to an additional 450 taels of silver.[40] Ibáñez criticized Incarnatione for going from Ningde to Jiangle in Fujian, where the Jesuits already had a parish. In Jiangle, without consulting with the Jesuit priest, Incarnatione baptized thirty Christians whom the catechists there had already instructed. In addition, he bought a house for 110 taels and opened a church in it. Ibáñez also criticized Incarnatione for not obtaining permission from the Chinese officials to do these things. The implication was that Incarnatione was reckless.

Ibáñez noted that Fujian province had more Christians than all the rest of China.[41] He conceded that the Jesuits had converted far greater numbers of Chinese but believed that the quality of the Franciscan converts was greater. For every Chinese that the Franciscans and Dominicans baptized, the Jesuits baptized four to six. From the time of their entry into China in 1632 until 1680 when Ibáñez wrote this letter, the Dominicans had converted two thousand Chinese. Over a period of fifteen years in Shandong (1650–1665), while the great Franciscan pioneer, Caballero, baptized four thousand Christians, his Jesuit counterpart in Shandong, Valat, baptized ten thousand Chinese. And yet Ibáñez claimed that Valat did this while remaining largely in Ji'nan without making many trips or expending much labor. Ibáñez claimed that the Franciscans and Dominicans could duplicate the Jesuit success but chose not to because the Jesuit converts were of a lesser quality. He then used a parable to explain the difference between these converts: There are two fields of equal size and fertility, and one is planted to yield many grapes and the other is cultivated to yield grapes that will produce a better wine.[42] Although the grapes from the first field will be greater in number, the grapes from the second will produce a better quality of wine, that is, metaphorically speaking, more committed Christians who are less likely to backslide and apostatize in times of trouble.

Many missionaries had forceful personalities, and although this frequently engendered disputes, it also had its benefits. Between January 1 and July 23, 1681, Paschale baptized nine hundred souls.[43] One town that he visited had been filled with Christians who had apostatized because no priest had visited them for twenty years (ca. 1661–1681). They were initially reluctant to welcome Paschale and made excuses. When they said no house was available to lodge him, Paschale said he would sleep in the street. Eventually, his persistence paid off, and the whole town was converted. This appears to have been a small town filled with kinsmen, which often accounted for the conversion of entire families and extended families.

The Arrival of Father Incarnatione in Ji'nan

Bernardus ab Incarnatione, O.F.M. (Bernardo de la Encarnación) (Guo Nabi) (ca. 1630–1719), was born in the village of Alamanza in the province of León in

Spain. He entered the Franciscan order in the religious province of San Pablo and, after completing his studies, arrived in the Philippines in 1663. He worked there for sixteen years. In 1678, he boarded a ship with Pedro de Alarcón, O.P., and three Jesuits; they landed on the south China coastal island of Amoy on June 24.[44] He was forced to remain in Amoy for two months because of hostilities between the Manchus and the pirate Zheng Jing, also known as Zheng Shifan (d. 1681). Zheng was the eldest son of Zheng Chenggong, the Ming loyalist and pirate who conducted a naval war against the Manchus from a base in Taiwan. Finally, in September, Incarnatione and his Dominican companion were able to continue on to Fuan in Fujian province.[45] Incarnatione was met by Father Piñuela in the village of Muyang, where they remained for three months in a Dominican mission while Incarnatione acquired the rudiments of Chinese. He and Piñuela then proceeded to the mission at Ningde in December 1678, where he served for over a year.

In July of 1680 Incarnatione left Ningde and went to Ji'nan, where he would remain for the next twenty-nine years serving the mission in Shandong. Paschale left him to found a mission at Nanjing in 1681, and two years later (1683) Paschale departed from Shandong forever, leaving Incarnatione to care for all eighteen churches in Shandong for two years. In May 1685 Father Emmanuel de la Bañeza, O.F.M., arrived in Jining and then came to Ji'nan to visit with Incarnatione.[46] After receiving instruction in Chinese, Bañeza returned to Jining to care for the Christians there. Incarnatione, with the approval of the magistrate in Putai, constructed a new church there. However, in the priest's absence, trouble broke out and the magistrate withdrew his support for the church. The trouble was quieted by the intervention of Father Verbiest from the capital in Beijing.

On July 20, 1686, in the midst of a drought and the pillaging of marauding thieves, the governor of Shandong called Incarnatione to his yamen (local court) in Ji'nan to consult on ending the difficulties. Incarnatione spoke of the need to cultivate the true God in order to placate his anger and obtain mercy. The next day Incarnatione set out for the city of Linqu (see map 2), apparently the center of the drought and turmoil, where the magistrate was a Christian named He Ruling.[47] When he arrived on July 23, abundant rain fell, which the magistrate ascribed to divine blessing. Incarnatione's preaching was favorably received, and he was given a house in Linqu by the magistrate, and a number of catechumens were instructed daily for two months. He returned after a two-month absence and baptized seven hundred neophytes, then returned to Ji'nan for the Easter celebration of 1687. After his departure, the new, small mission in Linqu was afflicted by grave calamity. Violent bandits entered the city, killed several neophytes, and stole the money from the church treasury. When news of this tragedy reached Incarnatione, he immediately returned to Linqu to strengthen the vacillating faithful and baptized an additional two hundred people.

Incarnatione then founded a small church in the neighboring city of Qingzhou, where the more important magistrates resided. On February 10, 1688, he quietly occupied the house in Linqu and said mass. However, opponents sprang up, particularly among the Muslims in Linqu. After Father Joseph Osca arrived in Ji'nan and was suitably trained, Incarnatione relinquished his duties there to him and moved his residence to Qingzhou. For ten years, Incarnatione cared for the Christians of this region in central Shandong, particularly Linqu. When difficulties arose, he turned to the Jesuits at the court in Beijing and to the Jesuit vice-provincial, Father Tomé Pereira, S.J. (Xu Risheng) (1645–1708), for assistance in obtaining the local magistrates' favor. Then, Incarnatione was transferred to care for the Christians in Taian and around 1703 was assigned responsibility for the Christians in Yizhou. A river flood nearly destroyed the house, and the ill treatment of Christians increased. Incarnatione was in Taian and encountered the Kangxi Emperor on his fourth Southern Tour (January 16–March 14, 1703).

After his disastrous visit with the Kangxi Emperor at Beijing, the papal legate, Carolus Thomas Maillard de Tournon, returned to Canton by way of the Grand Canal.[48] Along the way, in response to the legate's invitation, Incarnatione hastened to meet him at Jining on November 3, 1706. He visited with the legate until November 8 and on the sixth presented, along with Fathers Nieto-Díaz and Fernández-Oliver, a statement under oath on the core of the Chinese teaching. Later, at the invitation of Bishop Della Chiesa, Incarnatione traveled with his confreres Fathers Francisco a Conceptione Nieto-Díaz, Martino Alemán, Francisco a S. Ioseph, and Antonio Pacecco to Linqing to be examined on March 9 and 10, 1707, and again on June 12, so that they might obtain the imperial *piao* (permission) needed to continue to function as missionaries in China.[49] With the help of the Jesuits, this permission was granted.

Incarnatione was residing in Ji'nan in 1708 when violence broke out against the Christians in Taian, and one of Incarnatione's menservants was arrested and led in chains into the public square. Another outbreak against Christians occurred in Taian in 1709, and in spite of constant trips to and fro between Ji'-nan and Taian, Incarnatione was able to do little to alleviate the suffering of the Christians. Leaving the churches of Ji'nan and Taian in the hands of Father Bañeza, Incarnatione and the other fathers departed for the province of Jiangxi, arriving in Nan'an district in June 1709.[50]

Father Osca

Joseph de Osca, O.F.M. (Ke Ruose, Yilin) (1659–1735), was born in the poor village of Alacuás in the diocese of Valencia, Spain.[51] Around 1676 he was ordained in the Franciscan order in the religious province of Saint John the Baptist in Valencia. He was sent to the Philippines in 1682–1684, arrived in Macau April 20, 1686, and in May went to join the Franciscans at their residence outside the walls of Canton. In late August or early September he was sent to the Franciscan residence in Huizhou prefecture, where he studied the Chinese language and customs. It was decided that he would go to Ji'nan, where he arrived late in 1687 and was trained under Father Incarnatione.[52]

For the missionaries in the provinces of China, some of their most momentous experiences were the Southern Tours by the Kangxi Emperor. When the emperor made his first Southern Tour (November 5, 1684–January 3, 1685), the missionaries based in Ji'nan were absent. Incarnatione was visiting in Jining, and Valat was in Nanjing.[53] On this tour the emperor entered Ji'nan on November 8 by the West Gate, passed through the main street riding on a white horse surrounded by numerous guards, and exited by the South Gate (see figures 3.1 and 3.2).[54] The vast crowds knelt when the emperor passed with his entourage. However, the first tour was the most abbreviated of the six Southern Tours, lasting only sixty days.

It was the second Southern Tour that established the style of imperial grandeur that characterized the remaining tours.[55] Covering a daily distance of fifteen miles on land or thirty miles on water, the emperor and his enormous entourage traveled two thousand miles in a seventy-day period (January 28–April 8, 1689). The tour enabled him to inspect the countryside while solidifying his position as a Manchu ruler over the Chinese people. It was required by a 1675 law that all officials stationed within one hundred li (thirty-three miles) of an emperor's route travel to greet him.[56] In return for the lavish demonstrations of hospitality by people along the route, the emperor granted remissions of taxes and grain tribute and made contributions to local schools and temples. In addition, he held audiences with a wide range of people, including dignitaries and commoners. He was very much interested in meeting with the foreign missionaries. After leaving Ji'nan, he proceeded to Mount Tai, one of the sacred mountains of China, where he performed a traditional ritual.

The Kangxi Emperor decided to have the second Southern Tour commemorated in what would be the first major painting project sponsored by a Qing emperor.[57] To execute this painting, the court chose a group of orthodox literati artists who followed the stylistic principles of the famous Ming literati artist, Dong Qichang (1555–1636).[58] The best-known orthodox painter of that time, Wang Hui (1632–1717), arrived in Beijing early in 1691 to undertake this imperial commission. Wang gave overall direction to a number of painting assistants, the most prominent of whom was Song Junye (d. 1713). Song had not only studied under Wang but also had accompanied the emperor on the second Southern Tour. Probably Song and one or two assistants made preliminary

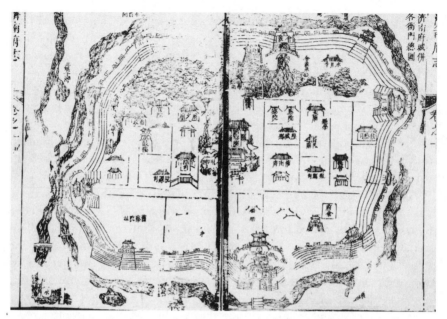

Fig. 3.1. A map of Ji'nan prefecture from a 1692 gazetteer, depicting the city wall and moat along with the traditional four gates. The Jesuit West Church was located only a short distance from the West Gate (shown on the left side). The exact location of the Franciscan East Church is unknown. This map appears in *Ji'nan fuzhi*. Compiled by Tang Menglai. Edited by Jiang Jun. (1692) 20 *ce.* 54 *juan,* juan 1: 2b–3a. Courtesy of the Beijing Tushuguan (National Library of China–Beijing).

sketches of the tour, based on personal observations.[59] From these rough drafts of ink on paper, final drafts emerged, which, in turn, evolved into the final version of ink and mineral color on silk. This work was done during the years 1692–1695. The result was contained in twelve long hand scrolls measuring over seven hundred feet in total length, which were collectively titled *Nanxuntu* (Picture of the Southern Tour). The second of these twelve scrolls depicts the emperor's journey through northern Shandong to Ji'nan and gives us some remarkable illustrations of Ji'nan (see figures 3.3 and 3.4).

As the emperor's entourage approached Ji'nan in February 1689, Osca was at a loss as to what he should do. Having been in Ji'nan for only one year, he was considerably less than fluent in Mandarin, and he felt insecure in speaking with the emperor. He considered absenting himself from the city and spoke with the Christians of Ji'nan about the advisability of doing so.[60] They urged him not to leave the city, particularly since no priest had been present at either of the two Christian churches when the emperor had last passed through four years before. In this respect, the Chinese Christians appeared more sensitive than Osca to the

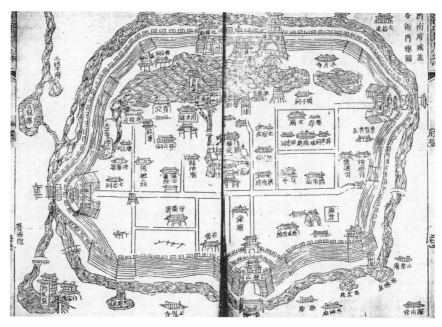

Fig. 3.2. A map of Ji'nan prefecture from an 1840 gazetteer. Gazetteers were often based upon earlier works and there are great similarities between the 1692 and 1840 edition gazetteer maps of Jinan. The sites that the Kangxi Emperor visited during his Southern Tour of 1689 are shown on this map. These include the Fountain Springs (Baotuquan) in the lower left corner, the residence of the provincial governor (in the middle), and the tower near the North Gate (top middle). The emperor departed through the South Gate (bottom middle). This map appears in *Ji'nan fuzhi*. Edited by Wang Zengfang et al. Compiled by Cheng Guan et al. (1840) 80 *ce*. 1: 25b–26a. Courtesy of the Shandong Sheng Tushuguan (Shandong Provincial Library).

danger that a foreign priest might be suspected of sedition.

On the morning of February 4, Osca joined a number of townsmen in riding on horseback some ten li (three and a third miles) outside the city walls of Ji'nan to receive the emperor. As the Kangxi Emperor passed, he caught sight of Osca's notably foreign appearance and commanded him to come closer.[61] Because of the circumstances and the mass of courtiers, Osca became confused and went toward the prince instead of the emperor.[62] A member of the imperial entourage grabbed him by the right arm and brought him before the emperor. The emperor, with a cheerful and smiling countenance, took Osca by the left arm, leading him six or seven steps and asking him his surname, given name, how long he had been in China, whether he understood mathematics and astronomy, and whether he had been to the court in Beijing.[63] The emperor had to ask Osca his name twice before hearing the answer Ke or, more fully, Ke

Ruose. Osca said that he had arrived in China two years before and had not been to the court in Beijing because he did not know mathematics and astronomy and he had not known Chinese well enough to make the journey. The emperor ordered him to return to his church and said that his senior bodyguard *(shiwei)*, Zhao Chang (also known as Pursai), might visit the church in a short while.

The emperor spent two hours visiting sites in Ji'nan, including the Fountain Springs, known as Baotuquan, which were located just outside the city wall on the southwestern side of the city and not far from the gates Pulimen and Shen-shunmen (see figure 3.2).[64] In addition, he visited the residence of the provincial governor in the center of the city and the tower near the North Gate. The emperor left Ji'nan through the South Gate to rest in the southern suburbs *(nanguan-li)* before departing for a site eight leagues south of Ji'nan where he would spend the night.

After eating, Osca departed at about noon to gather from his house some gifts for the emperor, including two bottles of grape wine, a glass bottle or cup, a pair of linen handkerchiefs with point lace, two candles of white wax, and some incense.[65] Although these things might strike us as insubstantial, their European origins would have given them an exotic flavor in China. When Osca arrived at the church, he found two of the emperor's courtiers, Zhao Chang (Pursai) and the Venerable Wu, already there. Zhao and Wu performed the ceremonial *koutou,* in which they struck their heads nine times before the altar of the Lord of Heaven. In addition, they contributed twenty taels of silver bundled in a yellow cloth with the emperor's official seal.[66]

However, the purpose of this visit was clearly to gather information, and Zhao and Wu proceeded to question Osca on a number of matters. Essentially, they were following up and expanding upon the line of questioning initiated by the emperor. They asked how and when Osca had come to China. He answered that he had arrived two years before at the time when Father P. Grimaldi (Min Ming-wo) had left Beijing for Siam and Europe in September or November 1686. In response to questions about which missionaries he had visited in China, Osca answered that he had not yet visited the missionaries in Beijing but that he had visited Father Ioannes Dominicus Gabiani, S.J. (Bi Jia), who was based in Nanjing. They asked various questions about the Ottoman Turks and the conflict with the Austrian Empire that was then taking place. They asked about Osca's country of origin. He answered that it was Spain, which was also the home country (i.e., the Iberian peninsula) of the Portuguese missionary, Tomé Pereira, S.J., of Beijing, whom they knew and praised.[67]

On this Southern Tour the Kangxi Emperor used the same approach with missionaries in Ji'nan, Nanjing, Hangzhou, and Jining. Personal contact was often made during the emperor's procession, in which the foreign priest's appearance caused him to stand out from the rest of the crowd. (Perhaps the emperor's

Fig. 3.3. A section of the scroll painting depicting the Kangxi Emperor's second Southern Inspection Tour (*Nanx-untu*). This section depicts the emperor's entrance into Ji'nan at the West Gate on February 4, 1689. Father Joseph de Osca encountered the emperor shortly before he reached this point. This scroll is the second of twelve long hand scrolls measuring over seven hundred feet in total length and painted in 1691–1695 by a team of artists under the direction of Wang Hui. Ink and mineral colors on silk. Musée Guimet Paris. ©R.M.N.

Fig. 3.4. A section of the scroll painting depicting the Kangxi Emperor's second Southern Inspection Tour (*Nanxuntu*). This section depicts the imperial entourage moving through the streets of Ji'nan on February 4, 1689. Wang Hui and assistants. Musée Guimet Paris, © R.M.N.

assistants were looking for such foreigners.) This led to a personal meeting with the emperor, which was typically followed by a visit to the church–residence by the emperor's trusted Manchu assistant, Zhao Chang, along with the Venerable Wu and an imperial escort. The same two courtiers visited each of the churches and presented the same gifts of twenty taels of silver and sometimes fruit from Manchuria. In Nanjing the emperor encountered two Jesuits, Fathers Gabiani and de Fontaney; in Hangzhou, Fathers Intorcetta and Posateri, also Jesuits; and in Jining the Franciscan Father Manuel de S. Juan.[68] While this was an overwhelming experience and a mark of approval for the Christian fathers, it was also a clever form of surveillance by the emperor and his staff. Foreigners were potentially a source of trouble. A good emperor kept track of their movements and activities, and the Kangxi Emperor was a very good emperor. These visits permitted him to gather intelligence on the activities of these foreigners in China in a manner that flattered the missionaries with imperial attention. It was all very civilized.

In 1693 Osca went to Taian to restore the church there. At the end of 1694 he was assigned to the Christian church in Zhaozhou prefecture in Guangdong province. He probably left Shandong early in 1695, because he was recorded as being in Nanjing in April and in Zhaozhou in October of that year.

Father Bañeza

Manuel de San Juan Bautista de la Bañeza, O.F.M. (Emmanuel a S. Ioanne Baptista) (Li Anning, Weiji) (1656–1711), was born at La Bañeza in the diocese of Austuricensis in Spain.[69] He entered the Franciscan order in the religious province of Saint Joseph and in 1682 enlisted in the Philippine mission, arriving there on July 9, 1684. In October he traveled to Macau with a group of Spanish Franciscans and remained there for two and a half months. Bañeza was delayed in joining his Franciscan confreres in Canton because of a dispute over swearing to an oath (possibly the piao required by the Chinese authorities), which was resisted by the vicar apostolic, Bishop François Pallu and, later, Bishop Della Chiesa.

Eventually Bañeza was assigned to the province of Shandong, where he was to join Father Incarnatione. He departed from Macau on January 21, 1685, and went to Canton, where he spent a few days at the Franciscan residence outside the walls.[70] On February 13, he departed from Canton by boat, taking the Ambassador's Route (see map 1) northward to the Yangzi River, eastward to the Grand Canal, and then northward to Shandong. After Bañeza had acquired a minimal fluency in Chinese, Incarnatione turned over the church at Jining to him and went to Ji'nan.

Bañeza toiled in isolation in Shandong until he was plucked out of obscurity by a memorable event that occurred on March 31, 1689.[71] On that day the Kangxi Emperor with his enormous entourage was passing on the Grand Canal through Jining on his second Southern Tour. Bañeza went to Shifozha on the canal, one league away from the city of Jining. The emperor saw Bañeza and wanted to speak with him. However, because Bañeza's small boat could not keep up with the emperor's, he was given a horse to accompany the emperor's boat from the bank of the canal. When the procession arrived at Tianjingzha, Bañeza stood waiting on the roadside until the emperor saw him. After a meeting in which they spoke for three hours, the emperor gave Bañeza fruits from the imperial table, a standard mark of honor. Bañeza's encounter with the Kangxi Emperor followed the typical pattern in meetings between the emperor and European missionaries on these Southern Tours. After the emperor's assistants visited his church, Bañeza hurried back to the emperor to present gifts in return, and, after showing some reluctance, the emperor accepted from among the gifts two glass fruits.

Most of the missionaries in Shandong who came after Paschale's departure in the autumn of 1683 had a more optimistic view of the mission there. However, Paschale's negative impressions remained with him, and when he was elected commissary of the Franciscan China mission on November 22, 1685 (a capacity in which he served until 1690), he revived the proposal for abandoning Shandong that he had first made in 1678.[72] In response to the proposal that the Franciscans exchange their missions in Shandong with Jesuit missions in Fujian, Bañeza gave eleven reasons why this would be unwise.[73]

First, Bañeza argued that the churches of Ji'nan and Jining had the license and permission of the Kangxi Emperor's decree of January 7, 1671, which permitted missionaries to return to already existing missions. Second, whereas these two churches had more than three thousand members, the two Jesuit churches in Fujian did not exceed three hundred. Third, it would be wrong to abandon the effort begun with so much effort by Caballero. Fourth, churches closer to the imperial court experienced less persecution from officials than those farther away. Fifth, the linguistic demands were less in Shandong, where Mandarin was spoken both by the officials and the people, than in Fujian, where the people spoke a different dialect. The remaining six reasons touched upon preserving the missionary legacy of Caballero and the fact that Paschale was also at odds with the other Shandong missionaries in promoting this plan.

Bañeza voiced the familiar complaint of missionary isolation in a letter written from Jining to Tomé Pereira in Beijing on March 14, 1690.[74] He wrote that because of his lack of contact with Ji'nan, he had not received much news of the Beijing fathers. However, the location of Jining near the Grand Canal sometimes produced visitors with news, such as the time the servant of the Beijing fathers,

Vitus Yeun [Yuen?], gave him the news that Fathers Pereira and Gerbillon had returned from the borderlands of Russia, where they had participated in the negotiations of the Treaty of Nerchinsk (1689).

Anti-Christian Persecution Reemerges

Francisco de San José Palencia, O.F.M. (Ba Lianren) (1666–1733), served in Linqu in October 1702 and in Dongchang in 1707, before establishing residency at Ji'nan in 1709.[75] He instituted some confraternities in Boxing sometime before November 28, 1712.[76] On January 20, 1709, in Ji'nan Father Palencia wrote a letter to Father Dominique Parrenin, S.J., of Beijing about a recent persecution in Taian and Mengyin in central Shandong. In Taian the disturbance was caused by the district magistrate *(zhixian)* surnamed Wu, who used the occasion of an edict from the emperor to undertake a campaign against certain sects, among whom he included Christians.[77] In the campaign, several Christians were subjected to lashings.[78] When Father Incarnatione of Ji'nan attempted to intervene on the Christians' behalf, the magistrate was unmoved. When one of the Christians presented the magistrate with books explaining Christianity and an imperial edict *(shangyu)* in the form of a piao, or official permit, to preach in China that had been granted since December 30, 1706, the magistrate and his assistant tore them into pieces and had the offending Christian whipped. The magistrate further threatened to have him and the other Christians whipped to death if they did not apostatize their Christian faith.

The Taian magistrate had a close friendship with the district magistrate at Mengyin, whom he convinced to undertake a persecution of Christians.[79] First, several Christian kinsmen were arrested and released after the payment of silver. Then the official began destroying a church under construction and burning a holy image in the street. The laborers in the church were subjected to twenty lashes with a whip. All the Christians were also whipped, except for three whom the magistrate pardoned because of old age, illness, and literati status. After being beaten, some of them were placed in cangues (wooden collars confining the neck and hands) or were abused in other ways. Finally, he ordered them all to abandon the Christian faith. He was particularly concerned that the literatus apostatize; if he did not, the magistrate threatened to take away his degree. The literatus communicated all of this to Incarnatione.

Father Palencia made a trip to Taian and confirmed all that had been reported. He then went to Mengyin and found the church destroyed and the holy image of God burned and confirmed that the Christians had indeed been whipped and abused. The magistrate in Mengyin soon learned of his arrival and sent a guard *(charen)* to order Palencia to report to him immediately, upon pain of expulsion from the town.[80] In addition, the magistrate forbade the innkeeper to provide the father with lodgings. Consequently, Palencia departed from Mengyin before sunset, although conditions were cold and inconvenient.

In a letter of May 3, 1709, to the Franciscan minister provincial in Manila, Cristobal de Jesús de Montánchez, O.F.M., Palencia described the desperate state of the Shandong mission: "Today, dearest father, this poor mission is the most destroyed and devastated that is imaginable, for the ministers are outcast, the temples devastated, the Christians without a pastor, held tight in the hands of wolves, and every day the hardships, persecutions, hatefulness of the emperor and the important mandarins grow."[81] One is struck by the fire in Palencia's words, which contrasts with the victimized state of the church he describes. Here we see a mentality that, rather than being cast into despair by devastating events, is energized by them. To refer to this merely as a martyr's mentality would be to saddle the idea with the negative associations of today's world. This mentality also had an extremely positive side that drew upon its spiritual resources to endure periods of great hardship and suffering.

Palencia was filled with admiration for the work of Father Nieto-Díaz and for his conversion of fifteen hundred people within fifteen days near Dongping. Palencia was oblivious to the fact that the sectarian and seditious nature of some of his converts may have been the cause of Nieto-Díaz's being jailed for fifteen days in Dongping. He saw the Chinese people's timidity overcome by an infusion of strength received through the Christian gospel. He took joy in the fact that "although the Christians have been so maltreated, vituperated, insulted, destroyed in property, whipped, exiled, no one had backslid, thanks to God."[82] Palencia was familiar with these anti-Christian persecutions because for over a year prior to May 1709, he had worked outside his church base in Ji'nan, caring for several small Christian communities.[83]

In 1709, the situation of Christianity in Shandong became grim. Officials in many areas were taking actions against Christians. Palencia showed little subtlety in interpreting why these actions were being taken and saw the hand of Satan in it all. On May 7 he was in Ji'nan and wrote to Father Franchi that the magistrate in Yanzhou prefecture was "very evil, the superiors of this city [the provincial capital Ji'nan] all are deferring to him, and if God does not take a hand, the business will be very bad."[84] Palencia's relations with the Jesuits appear to have been amicable, because Franchi facilitated Palencia's contact with the Jesuit visitor of China and Japan from 1708 to 1714, Father Giovanni Paolo Gozani, S.J., of Piedmont (1659–1732), who was based at Kaifeng. Palencia wrote to the Jesuit visitor also on May 7, 1709, that the situation in Dongping was "very bad, and many times over bad."[85] The officials believed the subprefectural magistrate (*zhizhou*) of Dongping rather than the "Europeans" (*europeos*). Palencia claimed that the officials disregarded the imperial edicts (shangyu), the written communications *(tongxin)* of the Board of Rites in Beijing, and the imperial permission (piao).

In the same letter, Palencia noted that several officials were gathering in Ji'nan to discuss this affair. They included the governor of Shandong, Jiang Chenxi (1653–1721); the provincial administrative commissioner; the surveillance commissioner *(anchasi);* and the magistrate of Dongping.[86] They had sent a runner *(bao)* to the military official to obtain soldiers from Dongping prefecture to apprehend Nieto-Díaz, who was expected to arrive in Ji'nan in three days. Palencia requested Father Gozani's assistance "so that the demon (Satan) may not get away with what he seeks."[87] In spite of demonizing the opposition, Palencia was practical enough to note that the respect previously shown to the missionaries by the Chinese common people had been based, in part, upon the official sanction that the missionaries had received. If that sanction were to be withdrawn, then the popular respect for the missionaries might turn into "hatred against God and his servants" *(odio contra Dios y sus siervos).*

On May 22, from Ji'nan, Nieto-Díaz sent a copy of the accusation *(chengzi)* filed under his name that had been placed in the Board of Rites. Nieto-Díaz was apparently incarcerated at that point, although it is not clear whether the deposition was his. When Palencia wrote to Gozani on June 1, 1709, Nieto-Díaz was still in jail.[88]

4

To Kiss the Image of the Crucified Jesus and to Feel the Whip upon One's Flesh

中

Venerability versus Youth

Father Michael Fernández-Oliver (Nan Huaide) (1665–1726) was born in Villena in the province of Alicante in Spain.[1] He enrolled in the Order of the Friars Minor in the religious province of San Pedro in 1681. He was recruited for the China mission by Father Michael Sánchez, who traveled to Spain in 1685 as procurator.[2] Departing from Seville in 1689 on the ship *Sancta Cruz,* Fernández-Oliver crossed both the Atlantic and Pacific Oceans, reaching Manila in 1691, where he was affiliated with the Discalced Franciscans. Finally, he arrived in Canton in October 1692.[3] He was sent to Nanjing, where Bishop Della Chiesa was then located, to study Chinese. Then he was appointed to go to Shandong and replace Father Osca, who was being transferred to Guangdong province.

When Fernández-Oliver arrived in Ji'nan early in 1695, he was immediately confronted with a situation that youthful zeal sometimes finds difficult to handle. Whereas Fernández-Oliver was only twenty-nine or thirty years old, Father Valat was eighty. Given the reverence for age in China at that time, Valat had venerable status. Moreover, he had lived in Shandong from 1652 until 1665 and then, after the persecution, had returned to Ji'nan in 1673 and lived there for most of the following twenty-two years. Consequently, his experience and associations in Ji'nan might easily have been intimidating to the newly arrived Fernández-Oliver. Valat's famously benign disposition had enabled him to get along with a number of Franciscan missionaries, including the amicable Caballero and the quarrelsome Paschale. However, his advanced age and the fact that he was nearing the end of his life (he died on October 7, 1696) might have made him irascible. Whatever the reason, he was critical of Fernández-Oliver, particularly for dining in the homes of parishioners.

In 1696, Valat and Fernández-Oliver had a confrontation in the house of Ling Iucunda, a parishioner of the Franciscan East Church. The next day, Fernández-

Oliver wrote a long letter in response to Valat's criticism.[4] He said he had chosen to write a letter rather than speak in person in part because Valat had
expressed difficulty in understanding his Castilian dialect and in part because
Fernández-Oliver took this criticism seriously enough to respond in writing.[5]
One also suspects that he was intimidated by Valat and that a letter was for that
reason preferable to another personal confrontation. Valat apparently had strong
views on this matter, because he not only was vehement in his criticism of Fernández-Oliver but also criticized another priest for entering the house of a Chinese Christian, calling it disgraceful.

Fernández-Oliver's letter was filled with strong emotions. He felt that Valat
did not respect him as a priest and complained that even though Valat was superior in age, he was not superior in priestly rank. His comment that "God does
not reward age but rather merit" (y no está Dios a premiar canas, sino es a los méri-
tos) shows how unacclimatized to Chinese culture Fernández-Oliver was at this
point.[6] Valat, after spending forty-four years in China (1651–1696), would have
known better and have understood that age was a powerful basis for respect
among the Chinese.

Fernández-Oliver defended his right to eat in the houses of Christians and
noted that, in addition to eating with Ling Iucunda, he had also eaten several
times in the homes of the catechist (xianggong), Wei, and the parish leader
(huizhang), Dong.[7] This he justified by claiming that a worker deserved his
wages. This was a biblical allusion to Luke 10:7—"Stay in that one house, sharing their food and drink; for the worker earns his pay" (New English Bible)—
and 1 Timothy 5:17–18.[8] Furthermore, Fernández-Oliver noted that while the
parishioners sustained him with material food, he would repay it with spiritual
food. He could not resist repeating the comments of others who "say of Your
Fathership that he is envious and that I [am] a little long-suffering" (como ya lo
hacen de decir de V.P. es envidioso y yo poco sufrido). Fernández-Oliver pointed out
the inconsistency of Valat's criticism. On one hand, Valat opposed Fernández-
Oliver's distribution of food to parishioners prior to a festival.[9] And yet just
before Valat celebrated the rite of confirmation at the Holy Mother of God
Church (Sheng Mu Tang), the women's chapel of the West Church, Valat had
distributed rice and flour for the women to use to prepare food.

There was also a disagreement over the expansion of the East Church. Before
leaving Ji'nan in 1686, Osca purchased a house.[10] When it became known that
the Christians wished to open a church for women in that house, Valat was not
supportive, supposedly because there was a court of law on the same street,
which Valat felt would impede the church's activities. While the Jesuit West
Church had its Holy Mother of God Church for women, there was now an
attempt to establish a women's church as part of the East Church (Dong Tang)
or East Lord of Heaven Church (Dong Tianzhu Tang). As was typical of women's

churches in China, it was dedicated to the Virgin Mary and called the Church of the Queen Mother of the Angels (Zhong Tianshen zhi Muhuang Tang) or slight variations thereof.

When the church opened, Valat asked several women whether they would attend this new East Church or whether they would attend his West Church. According to Maria Chang, a Christian woman of Ji'nan, he said: "Well, Venerable Valat does not like the East Holy Mother of God Church." Fernández-Oliver implied that Valat was guilty of petty jealousy over many things. He accused him of being hostile to their founding of an Archconfraternity of the Rope of Saint Francis (Sheng Fangjige Shengsu Hui).[11] He also accused Valat of being hostile when some festivity was held at a parishioner's home and of being peevish when he heard that Osca had visited with the Kangxi Emperor.

The Chinese Christians tended to criticize European priests who were unfamiliar with Chinese customs. As a newly arrived priest in Ji'nan, Fernández-Oliver probably made many mistakes that invited such criticism. Much of this criticism was conveyed to Valat, who apparently was eager to hear it. Fernández-Oliver asked why Valat believed these "thousand slanders" *(mil calumnias)*.[12] Some of Fernández-Oliver's complaints dealt with minor matters, but he believed that there was a pattern in Valat's criticism that reflected ill will, and he was puzzled by the hostility. Why, for example, although the Christians of Ji'nan celebrated the day of the Jesuit founder, Saint Ignatius (July 31), did Valat order them not to take communion on the day of Porciúncula (the Franciscan jubilee of August 2)? Why was he opposed to Fernández-Oliver inviting the parish leaders to eat with him on this day of Porciúncula? Why did Valat criticize him for establishing a women's church in Taian so that the men and women could celebrate mass separately in accord with Chinese custom? (On this most sensitive of issues involving contact with Chinese women, foreign priests were often suspected of inappropriate touching in administering the sacraments to women.) At a meeting of missionaries in Canton in 1668, it was decided that where it was not possible for the men and women to meet in separate churches, their meetings in the same church should be separated by an interval of time. On the other hand, Valat felt that Fernández-Oliver did not sufficiently support the Society of Mercy (Aijin Hui) that Valat had founded.[13]

Self-Flagellation in the Confraternity of the Passion

Confraternities, or religious brotherhoods, were largely voluntary associations of people, mostly laymen, organized under certain rules.[14] Although these fraternal associations were designed to prepare members for the afterlife, they were deeply involved in the life of their communities, whether in organizing funerals, orphanages, hospitals, or Sunday schools or engaging in other works of charity. They provided dowries, escorted condemned men to the scaffold, patronized the arts, and pursued as well as protected heretics. In China, they went out into the streets to gather abandoned and sickly children to baptize them before their death. There was an expansion in Europe of confraternities during the Catholic Reformation and Counter-Reformation, when confraternites came increasingly under clerical control.[15]

One of Fernández-Oliver's greatest achievements during his thirty-year apostolate (1695–1725) in Shandong was in organizing lay societies of Chinese Christians, such as the Confraternity of the Passion (Ku Hui). The progenitor of this confraternity was the Confraternity of the Passion of Christ (Yesu Ku Hui), first founded in China by the Jesuit Francesco Brancati (Pan Guoguang) (1607–1671). It was established by Father Brancati as one of six confraternities (also called congregations), each dedicated to a different constituency. In addition to the Confraternity for the Passion of Christ, which was for men, Brancati founded the Confraternity of the Holy Mother (Sheng Mu Hui) for women, the Confraternity of Holy Angels (Tianshen Hui) for children, the Confraternity of Saint Louis de Gonzaga (Sheng Leisi Hui) for students, the Confraternity of Saint Ignatius (Sheng Yi'najue Hui) for literati, and the Confraternity of Saint Francis Xavier (Sheng Fangjige Hui) for catechists.[16] In addition to confraternities, Chinese Christians founded benevolent societies. Many of these were modeled on Chinese benevolent societies, which were quite prominent in the late Ming and Qing periods.[17]

The Confraternity of the Passion consisted of the most fervent of Christians, who would gather to meditate on the sufferings of Christ at the time of his Crucifixion and to engage in penitential practices. These practices included fasting, wearing constraining fetters on the shoulders and arms, and the "discipline" (self-flagellation).[18] In Ji'nan, Fernández-Oliver held the meetings of the Confraternity of the Passion on Fridays after mass in the new East Church. The European-style windows were closed and a dark and quiet atmosphere created so that the discipline could be practiced with appropriate modesty. The setting betrayed a siege mentality. Each member of the confraternity came forward to kiss the image of the crucified Lord Jesus *(a besar la s. imagen de N. Señor crucificado)*— a striking act of tender intimacy that contrasted with the threat of physical violence from hostile outsiders. The practice in Ji'nan of kissing the image of the crucified Jesus was traced to Caballero, but for Fernández-Oliver, it was no coincidence that the Confraternity of the Passion was instituted in Ji'nan on the very day that the latest anti-Christian persecution arose in March 1700 in Cochin China.[19] On the contrary, Fernández-Oliver stated that the Lord wished to emphasize the contrast between the holy ceremony of tenderly kissing the image of the crucified Jesus and the violence occurring against him elsewhere.

The threat of physical violence from hostile outsiders evoked the flagellation of Christ, described in the Gospels of Matthew (27:26) and Mark (15:15). Scourging or whipping had been used as a punishment for delinquent clerics in the Christian Church since the fourth century. However, by the mid-eleventh century, flagellation had evolved into a form of voluntary penance in which the penitent imitated the sufferings of Christ.[20] It was part of an effort to expiate sin and impose self-discipline as well as a means of receiving divine grace in conformity with the Passion of Christ. Because it emerged out of monastic discipline, voluntary flagellation was referred to by the term "discipline" *(disciplina)*. Its practice was incorporated into nearly all religious orders from the sixteenth to the eighteenth centuries. In some orders, the flagellation was administered by a superior, but in other orders it was self-administered.[21] Generally, the discipline was practiced during the reading of the Psalms, especially the Fifty-first Psalm, known as the penitential psalm or *Miserere* ("Have mercy on me, O God, according to they steadfast love; according to thy abundant mercy blot out my transgressions. Wash me thoroughly from my iniquity, and cleanse me from my sin!" [Revised Standard Version]) Confraternities of *disciplinati* under the control of the Catholic Church arose in Europe, especially in Italy, from around 1350 and lasted into the nineteenth century. They were encouraged by Jesuit and Franciscan missionaries in mission regions in Asia and Latin America.

Although the practice of Christian self-flagellation is often viewed as a distinctly Western notion, recent studies have seen parallels between the ascetic practices of Europe and those of China. Specifically, there is a parallel between the outward signs of repentance in Christian self-flagellation and the Daoist practice *zibo* (self-slapping) and Buddhist *zipu* (self-beating) found in China beginning in the late Han period (second century A.D.).[22] The Chinese scholar Yang Liansheng claims that although the practitioners of zibo and zipu did not use whips, their intention was similar to the European flagellants who used the whip to draw blood as a means of washing the soul clean of its sins.[23] There is a strong possibility that the practice of self-beating was influenced by the ascetic practices of northern India. The term "zipu" is found in the *Yiqiejing yinyi*, a seventh-century work by the monk Xuan Ying that explains the sound and meaning of Buddhist terms translated from Sanskrit. Such practices were widespread in northern India at that time. More recently, Jonathan Chaves has explained self-mutilation as a sign of filial piety *(xiao)*, chastity *(zhen)*, and purity *(jie)* in the poetry of Wu Jiaji (1618–1684).[24] This means an indigenous ascetic discipline was practiced in Jiangsu province, the province directly to the south of Shandong, at the time when Christianity was being introduced in Shandong.

Tertiaries (Third Orders) in Shandong

Third orders are Christian groups that stand between the laity and clerics in religious life. Their members, called tertiaries, strive after Christian goals, following papal rules and being guided by religious orders. Third orders commonly consist of confraternities and archconfraternities, which are lay associations under religious authority whose members follow a spiritual regimen or perform some charitable or apostolic work. Whereas confraternities are limited to being local associations, archconfraternities can create an affiliation with confraternities of the same type.[25] "Sodality" is an alternate name for a confraternity, though it is usually associated with the Virgin Mary.

Confraternities were established among the Chinese very early in the history of the mission; Caballero was one of the first to introduce these associations. Tertiaries were obliged to wear a religious habit (usually a scapular and cord) beneath their outer clothing. According to Caballero, the first Chinese to wear the habit of the Archconfraternity of the Rope of Saint Francis in China was a daughter of an official of Anhai in Fujian. She was married to a Portuguese named Antonio Rodríguez. The couple; Rodríguez's father, Manuel Bello; and his mother were the first four people in China to wear the habit of a Tertiary order.[26] The habit had been given to them by Caballero in 1649. When Caballero moved on to Shandong the next year, he founded a chapter of the Archconfraternity of the Rope in Ji'nan. It is believed that Father Incarnatione founded a congregation of the third order in the town of Boxing in the years 1680–1707. Father Francisco de San José is said to have also instituted some confraternities in Boxing sometime before November 28, 1712.[27]

Some sense of the activity of the third orders in Ji'nan is shown in their accumulation of sufficient revenues to purchase a house and piece of property for church use without Fernández-Oliver's permission. When Fernández-Oliver informed his Franciscan superiors of this purchase, they defended clerical authority by sending a written protest against the purchase. The protest, dated January 12, 1719, was signed by the Franciscan provincial commissary, Father Juan Fernández Serrano and his assistants, Fathers Jaime Tarin and Martin Alemán.[28] This document was translated into idiomatic Chinese and read before all the religious of the third order in Ji'nan, insisting that the tertiaries accede to the wishes of their religious superior. Clearly this was a sign of growing (and not surprising) tension between the Chinese church and its European hierarchy. Some sense of the numbers of Chinese tertiaries in Ji'nan can be gleaned from a letter by Father Matías Alcazar de Santa Teresa dated October 2, 1759. He stated that within his mission were 1,276 confessing persons with baptisms of 170 children and 21 adults during the past year.[29] The Congregation of the Third

Order consisted of 178 persons of both sexes, both novices and full members. The Archconfraternity of the Rope numbered 330. Confraternities in Ji'nan also were responsible for printing religious literature. For example, in 1699 the Confraternity of the Cross (Aijing Shizijia Hui) oversaw the printing of *Moxiang shengong* (The pious exercise of meditation).

Fernández-Oliver's youthful zeal served the mission in Shandong very well. Although based in Ji'nan, he also ministered to Christians in nearby Xincheng, Gaoyuan, Linqing, Jiyang, and Lingxian (see map 2).[30] He was also needed in the more remote churches in Taian, Laiwu, and Yanshenzhen. Because of a feeling that previous Christians in Shandong had not been well instructed, Fernández-Oliver founded a number of confraternities to improve religious instruction. The Congregation of the Sacred Guardian Angels had already been established in Ji'nan. Around 1696 Fernández-Oliver founded the first Confraternity of Saint Francis in Ji'nan. The Confraternity of the Passion had already been established there by Caballero, but was founded for a second time by Fernández-Oliver in 1700.[31]

In 1701 Fernández-Oliver founded a third order of a confraternity of penitence for women. On September 1, 1703, he reported to the provincial commissioner, Father Emmanuel de la Bañeza, that during the past year in Ji'nan and surrounding villages, he had baptized 213 people.[32] He wrote that there were 26 tertiaries in the third order of penitence that he had instituted in the Church of the Blessed Virgin Mary, Queen of the Angels, on October 19, 1701, with the consent of the provincial commissioner. Fernández-Oliver noted that the women in this third order continued with fervor, although with some disagreements. It was augmented by the Congregation of the Sacred Guardian Angels (Congregatio SS. Angelorum Custodium).[33]

Fernández-Oliver accompanied Tournon, the papal legate, from Ji'nan to Jining, where, on November 5, 1706, Tournon confirmed the neophyte Liu Ru or Liu Ruowang of Fushan in Shandong.[34] Fernández-Oliver returned to Ji'nan with Liu on November 8, but Liu later died at Dengzhou.[35] It is possible that Liu accompanied Fernández-Oliver to Ji'nan to receive Tournon's confirmation on November 5, 1706, of the rules of the Confraternity of the Third Order of Penitence of Saint Francis.[36] The confirmation was written in Latin in Fernández-Oliver's hand in two pages on a folio sheet with Tournon's decree at the bottom of the page and was dated October 22, 1706. In June of the following year, the rules of the Third Order of Penitence of the Church of the Blessed Virgin Mary, Queen of the Angels (Zhong Tianshen zhi Muhuang ben hui Tang) of Ji'nan were printed in Ji'nan. The Chinese text had been made by Father Basilio Brollo de Gemona, O.F.M. (Ye Zunxiao) (1648–1704), in 1701 and was printed at the Church of the Imperial Road (Tianqu Tang), which was another name for the East Church.[37]

Fernández-Oliver on the Chinese Rites

Fernández-Oliver took a more accommodating position toward the Chinese rites than did most Franciscans. In a 1702 letter to two Franciscan confreres in Shandong, Fernández-Oliver expressed very accommodating views and showed how a missionary facing practical problems in the field might be more flexible than theologians far away in Europe.[38] Unlike those who prohibited the tablet "*jing Tian*" (revere Heaven) in the church because it referred to a pagan view of God, Fernández-Oliver allowed it on the grounds that the presence of the holy image emphasized that the tablet referred to God. Contrary to those who believed that the Chinese terms *Tian* (Heaven) and *Shangdi* (Lord-on-High) should not be used because they referred to a pre-Christian pagan deity, he argued they could be used in accordance with the explanations of the Society of Jesus, particularly of Fathers Ricci and Aleni.[39] Unlike those who said that the traditional Chinese rites to the dead should not be allowed because they were superstitious, he believed that they could be used, including the terms *shenwei* (spiritual seat) and *lingwei* (animal seat). When superstition or even a scent of it was present, he believed that the Chinese Christians should assist the nonbelievers with explanations of why such superstitious elements should be omitted.

In regard to the rites to Confucius, it was the custom among literati in China upon the day that they obtained an academic degree to pay reverence to Confucius. Some priests opposed this practice on the grounds that it revered Confucius as a deity, or idol, but Fernández-Oliver disagreed and said that the literati regarded Confucius as a teacher rather than a deity and that these ceremonies to Confucius and lesser teachers were merely a mark of their gratitude. The cultic sacrifices *(ji)* and ceremonies devoted to Confucius were permissible on the same grounds.[40] Whereas some Christians argued that the ancient Chinese notions of Tian (Heaven) and Shangdi (Lord-on-High) had not enabled the Chinese to know the monotheistic God of the Judeo-Christian tradition, Fernández-Oliver responded that it was "rash and a little unmerciful" *(temeraria y poco piadosa)* to say that the Chinese did not know God. He felt that such a position alienated the Chinese, who were intellectually proud, and prevented them from coming closer to the light of Christianity.[41]

Fernández-Oliver strongly opposed the prohibitions on using these traditional Chinese terms and rituals because these prohibitions created great obstacles to the spread of the gospel. They had evoked hostility from many Chinese in the form of anti-Christian satires that ridiculed the Christian refusal to allow Chinese mourners to bury paper money at the graveside of a loved one. They attacked Christianity for not cultivating a sufficiently pious affection for one's ancestors. Fernández-Oliver's concern was a pastoral one; he believed that all these prohibitions would place the neophytes in danger of apostatizing their faith

because of pressure from their relatives. He cited the example of a young catechist surnamed Yu whom he had baptized. When Yu refused to perform certain
familial rites because of the Christian prohibitions, his father forced him to apostatize, and Yu blamed the missionaries for causing this situation.

Fernández-Oliver Meets the Kangxi Emperor

The Kangxi Emperor's fourth Southern Tour (March 3–April 29, 1703) was
made in the forty-second year of his reign, when he was forty-nine years old (fifty
years by Chinese reckoning).[42] His visit to Ji'nan apparently happened on March
17 and was more abbreviated than in 1689, indicating the minor importance of
this provincial capital.[43] Instead of arriving in the morning, the imperial
entourage passed through Ji'nan in the middle of the day.[44] Fernández-Oliver
wrote that he and his Jesuit counterpart in Ji'nan, Father Antonio Faglia (Fa
Anduo, Shengxue) (1663–1706) of Brescia, were obliged to go out with many
residents of the city beyond the walls to greet the emperor. However, Faglia went
to visit a sick member of his flock and asked Fernández-Oliver to meet him at a
certain site.[45] Fernández-Oliver believed that this designated meeting place was
not on the emperor's itinerary; instead he went to the site where Father Osca in
1689 and Father Bañeza in 1696 had encountered the emperor on previous
Southern Tours. Fernández-Oliver's account of Faglia's actions betrays some irri-
tation, and he may have suspected that Faglia had other motives for not accompanying him. In any case, the emperor encountered Faglia first and gave him
thirty taels of silver.[46]

When the emperor later saw Fernández-Oliver, he ordered the porters to halt
the imperial sedan chair and asked why he had not come with the other European, Father Faglia. He proceeded to ask the standard set of questions: Fernández-
Oliver's country of origin, his age, how long he had been in China, why he had
not gone to the court in Beijing, and who had impeded him from going. Aware
of the emperor's ulterior motives, Fernández-Oliver chose his words carefully. He
said that no one had impeded him from going to Beijing and only his own deficiencies in mathematics and other skills useful to the court had prevented him
from going. The emperor asked if he were related to Father Verbiest, in part
because of the similarity in their Chinese names—Nan Huairen (Verbiest) and
Nan Huaide (Fernández-Oliver)—and Fernández-Oliver answered that they were
only of the same race. Then the emperor asked why Fernández-Oliver had not
come out together with Faglia to greet him. When Fernández-Oliver replied that
they had two churches and that Faglia had business to attend to with his Christians, the emperor laughed and said to his retainers, "Clever, clever" *(lingli, lingli)*.

At this point, Faglia approached with the two Jesuit coadjutors, Brothers

Baudino and Frapperie, who were accompanying the emperor.[47] Brother
Giuseppe Baudino (Bao Zhongyi, Zhian) (1657–1718) of Piedmont served the
emperor for many years in the court of Beijing as a physician and pharmacist.
Brother Pierre Frapperie (Fan Jixun, Shushan) (1664–1703), a Frenchman, also
served as a physician and pharmacist in Beijing; he later baptized a small son of
the Kangxi Emperor.[48] The emperor commanded that they all follow on their
horses to the governor's palace.[49] There Fernández-Oliver was interrogated by
the eminent scholar–official Tong Guowei, a maternal uncle of the emperor. (In
the following year, 1704, Tong would make an official inquiry into the widespread suffering caused by flooding in Shandong.) Other interrogators were the
scholar–official Zhang Changzhu (Chen-ki = Charki?) and a eunuch named
Zhang. Fernández-Oliver was interrogated separately and consequently missed
the meeting between the emperor and Faglia. After going to the West Church,
the scholar–official Tong accompanied Fernández-Oliver on horseback to the
East Church. Tong admired the characters on the scrolls around the altar. Fernández-Oliver presented him with some gifts from Europe and received thirty
taels of silver, for which he expressed his gratitude in Chinese style.

Fernández-Oliver and Confucian Literati

Although Fernández-Oliver appears to have been a reasonably effective leader,
there is no evidence that he attained any noteworthy degree of literacy in the
Chinese language. Although he was fluent in spoken Mandarin, it is unlikely
that he could have read more than a few characters, and certainly he could not
have composed in Chinese. His relations with Chinese literati appear to have
been characterized more by respectful distance than intimacy of the sort found
between Ricci or Aleni and literati such as Xu Guangqi of the preceding century. In fact, it is likely that the intellectual activity among the Ji'nan Christians
had declined from what it had been in 1650–1665 under the leadership of
Caballero, who composed drafts of treatises in Chinese and collaborated with
literati in refining these works. Certainly the intellectual freedom to publish
works on Christianity in Chinese had severely contracted. It is notable that the
primary achievement in Chinese letters with which Fernández-Oliver is associated was overseeing the reprinting of *The Touchstone of True Knowledge (Zhengxue
liushi)* by Caballero and Shang Huqing.

The woodblocks of this work were found when the East Church was reno-
vated in the late seventeenth century. A new edition of *The Touchstone* was prepared in which the credits page lists six Franciscans. Caballero is listed as the
author; Fernández-Oliver, Bañeza, Incarnatione, and Nieto-Diáz (Bian Shuji) are
listed as co-revisors *(tongding)* who provided the permission to publish *(nihil*

obstat), and Navarro is listed as the ecclesiastical authorizer *(zhun)* who provided the license to publish (imprimatur).[50] The woodblocks for this edition are listed as being made at the Lord of Heaven Church on Imperial Road. Shang Huqing, who had written the work with Caballero some thirty-four years before, was still alive, and Fernández-Oliver was apparently in contact with him, because Shang provided a preface dated 1698 for the new edition.[51] However, when copies of this reprinted work reached Canton, the Franciscan provincial, Manuel de S. Juan Bañeza, wrote to Fernández-Oliver on December 10, 1704, commanding that no further copies be printed or disseminated because it contained propositions that did not conform to Christian theology.[52] Although the work had previously circulated, Bañeza ordered Fernández-Oliver to lock up the woodblocks until the errors were corrected.

Fernández-Oliver spoke of the Christians uncovering woodblocks of other works that had been printed in Ji'nan. One of these was *Moxiang shengong* (The pious exercise of meditation), originally composed by Petrus de la Piñuela (Shi Duolu) in 1694 while he was in Jiangxi province. The work is a translation and adaptation of *Tratado de la oración y meditación,* a well-known work by Peter of Alcántara, O.F.M. (1499–1562). Alcántara was a mystic famous for the severity of his ascetic practices. He was also linked with the controversial Discalced reform of Spanish Franciscans. Piñuela's work was republished in Ji'nan in 1699 under the auspices of the Confraternity of the Cross at the Bu Ru Tang (Supplemented Literati Church).[53] The use of the term "Supplemented Literati" as an alternate name for the East Church indicates that the term "bu Ru" developed by Shang Huqing had received some degree of acceptance and usage in the community of Ji'nan Christians. Another work printed in Ji'nan was *Shengjiao zong du jingwen* (A general collection of prayers of the Holy Teaching), printed at the Church of the Imperial Road (East Church) in 1701–1702.[54] Most of the prayers in this work had already appeared in the *Shengjiao rike* (Daily exercises of the Holy Teaching), a collaborative Jesuit work of 1628 printed under the names of the examiners, Verbiest and F. Buglio.[55] However, the arrangement of the prayers differed. In addition, the Ji'nan prayer book contained two new prayers by Fernández-Oliver.

There are many springs in Ji'nan, and the low-lying land is subject to flooding and moisture. The old East Church suffered from this condition, and in 1698 Father Navarro wrote of the need to elevate the original pavement of the church to deal with the dampness.[56] In 1702 Fernández-Oliver oversaw the establishment of the East Church in a new building.[57] The devotion of the Ji'-nan Christians to their church was shown in the sacrifices they made to build this new church. Fernández-Oliver said it was well known that the province of Shandong was one of the poorest regions in China.[58] And yet these poor people sacrificed, to the extent of going without food, in order to raise four hundred taels, to which the clergy added thirty-three taels.[59] The new church was thirty paces (approximately ninety feet) long and fifteen paces (approximately forty-five feet) wide and contained both a baptistry and a sacristy.

A friendly non-Christian literatus, Zhu, offered to assist in decorating the new church. Zhu was a circuit intendant *(daotai)* who was not based in Ji'nan.[60] After studying books on Christianity for eight months, Zhu contributed the silver to carve a gilded inscription to hang over the altar that said, "Honor the Lord of Heaven" *(Jing Tianzhu)*. There had been some discussion between Zhu and Fernández-Oliver about the exact wording of the inscription.[61] Zhu wished to have the inscription read "Honor Heaven" *(Jing Tian)*, following the inscription written by the emperor for the Jesuit fathers in Beijing. However, Fernández-Oliver insisted that it be "Honor the Lord of Heaven," in order to distinguish between the Chinese reference to Heaven and the specific Christian reference to the Lord of Heaven (i.e., God).

In addition, a Christian baccalaureate named Kong Facundus (literally, Elegant Kong), from the family of Confucius, wrote parallel inscriptions *(dui zi)*, which were placed at the sides of the altar.[62] One of these inscriptions read: "One creator by himself is the Lord; to say that he is *Taiji* (Supreme Ultimate) or *li* (Principle) or *qi* (ether) is absolutely false." This inscription clearly distinguished the Lord of Heaven from the primary elements of Song Neo-Confucian cosmology (the Supreme Ultimate, principle, and ether). The other inscription read: "Rewards and power are given to people of excellent quality from one alone (i.e., the Lord of Heaven); requests which are made to heaven, earth, and to the idol Buddha and to Daoist immortals are ignorant offerings." Although Kong provided the parallel inscriptions along with his prestigious family name, it was apparently the eighteen taels paid by Zhu that enabled the tablets to be painted and gilded.[63]

The missionaries in Ji'nan recognized that the relationship between Christianity and Confucianism was different from Christianity's association with Buddhism, Daoism, and local deity cults. The difference in this relationship lay in the fact that Confucius was seen as a teacher rather than a deity. Fernández-Oliver joined the Jesuit Father Girolamo Franchi (Franki) (Fang Quanji) (1667–1718) of Brescia in writing a testimony to two events that reflected this difference.[64] They testified that in June 1704 the scholar–officials of Ji'nan inspected several temples in which offerings and prayers for rain had been made. However, when they found these same offerings on the bookshelves of the Confucian hall, which is referred to by Franchi as an *aula* (hall) rather than a *fanum* (temple), they had the offerings removed on the grounds that Confucius was "neither an idol or spirit, but a teacher of customs and doctrine" *(Confucio . . . neque idolum neque spiritus est, sed morum et doctrinae magister).*[65]

The other incident Franchi and Fernández-Oliver recorded brought out a more problematic element in the relationship between Christianity and Confucianism. In 1697 or 1698, a district magistrate in Shandong approached the governor in Ji'nan, who was then either Li Wei, who governed from 1697 to 1698, or Li Bing (styled Zhang Yuan) (1647–1704), who governed from 1698 to 1700.[66] This magistrate complained that a statue of Confucius had been placed together with statues of the Buddha and the Daoist Laozi in a temple when in fact Confucius differed from the others in not being a god.[67] The governor agreed with the complainant and issued a ruling *(zhi)* that this particular temple be destroyed. However, some Christians in the areas where the ruling was issued misinterpreted it to mean that the emperor wished the temples of all idols to be destroyed and began doing so. This gave rise to quarrels between the Christians and the worshippers of the deities whose temples were being assaulted. The evidence of these quarrels was apparent in the ruins still visible at the time Franchi and Fernández-Oliver made their testimony on October 12, 1705, in Ji'nan.

Anti-Jesuit Rumors

The tensions between the Jesuits and Franciscans in Shandong did not end with Valat's death in 1696. The difficulties of propagating Christianity in a province like Shandong were intensely frustrating and were felt even more keenly because of the contrast with the Jesuits at the court in Beijing. At the beginning of the eighteenth century the Jesuits in Beijing were also experiencing growing frustration in terms of making conversions but, unlike missionaries in Ji'nan, they had access to wealth and imperial power of which the Shandong Franciscans could only dream. Given this situation, the slightest pretext could ignite an accusation. One of those accusations was that the Jesuits engaged in certain money-making practices, such as usury, that were forbidden by the Catholic Church. These accusations emerged in a testimony dated October 4, 1706, at Ji'nan addressed to the papal legate, Tournon. The Tournon legation, feeling itself badly treated by the Jesuits in Beijing, offered a sympathetic ear to anti-Jesuit grievances. In evaluating these accusations, one needs to bear in mind the arrogance commonly manifested by the old Society of Jesus (prior to the dissolution of the order in 1773 and its reconstitution in 1814) as opposed to its more humble later manifestation.[68]

In his testimony, Fernández-Oliver described a discussion that he had with two non-Christians in 1702 in Ji'nan.[69] While visiting Christians, he was invited into the workshop of a man surnamed Li, where they were joined by a man named Han. Han asked why the other European priest in Ji'nan, Father Faglia, was so arrogant while Father Fernández-Oliver was so humble. Li answered that it was because Fernández-Oliver was from a poor congregation and was unable to practice commerce, whereas Faglia was from a wealthy congregation and practiced both commerce and usury. When Fernández-Oliver expressed skepticism over how Faglia could have done these things without him, a fellow European, knowing of them, Li answered that he himself had borrowed money from Faglia to the amount of several tens of taels.

Fernández-Oliver noted in his testimony that when the Portuguese Jesuit Luís de França (Zeng Leisi) (1665–1708) had returned from Beijing to Ji'nan in October or November of 1697, he had inquired of Fernández-Oliver about investing money.[70] He had asked whether it would be best to invest in land, a salt shop, or a pawnshop. The newly arrived Fernández-Oliver responded that he was ignorant of such things, but he had heard that silver invested in a pawnshop was returning a large profit.

Fernández-Oliver went on to accuse the Jesuits in Beijing of more serious offenses, including fraud. When a scholar–official surnamed Nian was sent by the emperor to Ji'nan to distribute alms, he asked Fernández-Oliver about the value of certain clocks and mathematical instruments that he had bought from the Jesuits. Fernández-Oliver responded evasively, implying that the Jesuits had overcharged Nian. Nian said that he had many such European items in his home in Beijing, having spent three thousand ounces of silver for them. He also told Fernández-Oliver that on one occasion the emperor had given the Jesuit fathers in Beijing money to distribute as alms to the hungry in Beijing. But Fernández-Oliver heard that the Jesuits had spent eight hundred taels for their own provisions, implying that the Jesuits were using money for themselves that they should have been spending on the needy.

Fernández-Oliver mentioned the case of a scholar–official surnamed Wang who had been sent by the emperor to distribute alms in Qingzhou.[71] While he was passing through Ji'nan, Wang, who liked Europeans, met with Fernández-Oliver. Wang noted that Fernández-Oliver was living in poverty, whereas the Jesuits in Beijing lived in great wealth because "they were engaging in trade and also deception" *(quia mercaturam agebant etiam decipiendo)* by selling wine and tobacco for excessive profit. Wang claimed that the Jesuits were even contracting "to rent a house to prostitutes in order to earn a larger profit" *(dare domus meretricibus, maioris utilitalis gratia).*[72] Although Fernández-Oliver noted that these were only rumors, the fact that he would include them in a written testimony to the papal legate indicates the degree of hostility felt by the Franciscans in Ji'nan toward the Jesuits in Beijing.

The hardships that the Franciscans endured in Shandong were considerable. Not only was the province poor, but it was also subject to large-scale flooding by an unpredictable river system. From April to August 1704 there was massive rainfall and flooding in which much of the province was submerged by water.[73] Many buildings collapsed, cannibalism was widespread, and bands of robbers roamed across the countryside. Because it became impractical to ride a horse under the circumstances, Fernández-Oliver went on foot with companions to deliver the annual subsidies to missions outside of Ji'nan. Coming into Qingzhou with Father Martinus Alemán (Jing Mingliang), Fernández-Oliver was robbed of his clothes by thieves. After visiting with Nieto-Díaz at Jining on the Feast of the Assumption of the Virgin Mary (August 15, 1704), he returned to Ji'nan to find that two domestic servants had died in the collapse of the mission residence.[74]

The Funeral of Father Franchi

Funeral rites were one of the most important of human activities throughout China's history. To the Chinese, the appropriate burial of one's family members and close associates was a mark of character and civilization. Because of the great importance of funerals to both the Chinese and the Christians, this was an activity that had to be reconciled through accommodation and inculturation, unlike the practice of having concubines, which was simply prohibited among Chinese Christians. From the point of view of Christianity, the act of burial was not inherently superstitious, but many features of Chinese burials were in conflict with Christianity. Some of the objections of Europeans were well founded, and others were based on misunderstandings. Consequently, both Europeans and Chinese were challenged to make difficult changes in their thinking.

These conflicts were brought to the surface in the funeral for the Jesuit Father Franchi, who was the priest at the West Church in Ji'nan from 1705 until his death in 1718. He administered nine churches and numerous oratories in Shandong in small towns outside Ji'nan, which he visited on a rotating basis while keeping his home base at the West Church.[75] According to Father Palencia, in 1709 Franchi was forbidden to practice Christianity in that area by an official who proceeded to place an idol in his church.[76] His final vows as a Jesuit had been administered by Father Romain Hinderer, S.J., on June 16, 1715.[77]

Father Hinderer conducted preliminary funeral rites for Franchi on February 13, 1718, at Ji'nan; however, the full funeral did not take place until April 10. It was presided over by Fernández-Oliver, who organized an elaborate four-day funeral at the West Church that culminated with the procession to the grave on Palm Sunday. He spent a great deal of time organizing this funeral, not merely to honor Franchi, but also to use the event to promote the fortunes of Christianity in Ji'nan.[78] The elaborate funeral procession attracted large crowds as it moved through the streets of Ji'nan to the Jesuit cemetery at Chenjialou, a site outside and to the northwest of the old inner city wall (see figure 4.1). According to one account, over fifty literati accompanied the deceased in the funeral

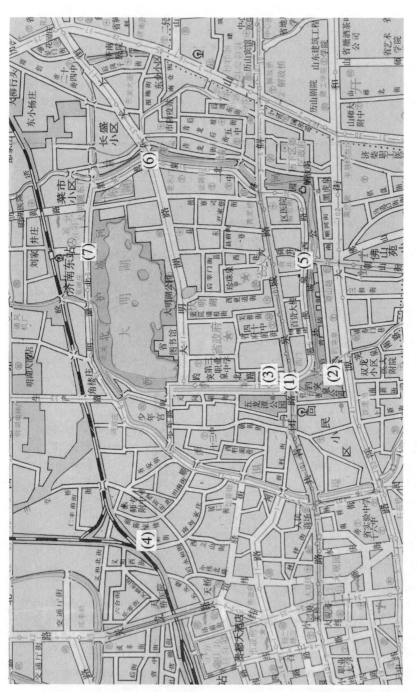

Fig. 4.1. A contemporary map of Ji'nan showing the present-day location of the West Gate (Ximen) (indicated by the numeral 1), the Fountain Springs (Baotuquan) (2), the site of the former West Church (3), the site of the former Jesuit cemetery at Chenjialou (4), and the sites of the former South Gate (5), East Gate (6), and North Gate (7). I was unable to locate the site of the former East Church.

procession while a "million" *(decies centena millia)* people—most probably intended as a figurative rather than a literal estimate—watched from the sides of the street and from the top of the city wall.[79]

When the Jesuit cemetery was founded at Chenjialou in 1637, it was located in the rural countryside beyond the city wall of Ji'nan.[80] The German Jesuit Father Bernhard Diestel (Su Na, Deye) (1623–1660) and Valat were both buried there.[81] In 1909 the Chenjialou St. Joseph Church was built on this site (see figures 4.2 and 4.3), and the remains of the Jesuits were moved to the cemetery at Hongjialou to the east of the old walled city in Ji'nan.[82]

Given the polarized atmosphere among missionaries in Shandong, it is not surprising that criticism should arise over such a prominent event as Franchi's funeral. On July 19, Bishop Della Chiesa wrote a letter from his base in Linqing to Fernández-Oliver's superior in Canton, Father J. Fernández Serrano. In this letter, Della Chiesa complained that Fernández-Oliver had violated church rulings on the Chinese rites in the funeral for Franchi and asked Serrano to investigate.[83] Consequently, on the eve of the Feast of Saint Thomas the Apostle (December 20, 1718), Fernández-Oliver returned from Beijing to find a letter from the bishop.[84] Relations between the Italian and the Spanish Franciscans appear to have been very tense, because Fernández-Oliver asked that in the future all letters from Della Chiesa and his assistant, Father Carlo di Orazio da Castorano (Kang Hezi) (1673–1755), be sent to him by way of his superior, Father Serrano. Serrano wrote to Nieto-Díaz, asking him to go to Ji'nan and pose a list of questions to Fernández-Oliver. After being delayed by illness, Nieto-Díaz finally went to Ji'nan and interrogated Fernández-Oliver on May 23, 1719, in the East Church.

One can imagine the tension at such a meeting between the two fathers. On one side was the forceful and politically attuned Fernández-Oliver who saw this as an adversarial interrogation. These were hostile questions, and Fernández-Oliver knew that they had originated with Della Chiesa. On the other hand, it is possible that he had mixed feelings toward his interrogator. Nieto-Díaz was a fellow Spanish Franciscan whereas Della Chiesa and Orazio were Italian Franciscans who served Propaganda rather than the interests of the Spanish *patronato*. And although Fernández-Oliver had criticized both Nieto-Díaz and Orazio for baptizing insincere and poorly instructed "bean curd" Christians, it is quite possible that he saw them as doing so for very different reasons. Whereas he believed that Orazio was politically ambitious and wanted to impress the authorities in Rome, Fernández-Oliver felt Nieto-Díaz was an unpolitical priest who may have been misled by his naïveté.

The first of the six questions asked why the interment was hastened so much and why it was done in the holy week before Easter with so much ostentation.[85] When Fernández-Oliver heard the question, he became angry and indignant.

Fig. 4.2. The façade (south side) of the Chenjialou Saint Joseph Church (Chenjialou Sheng Jose Tang), with the viewer facing north (address: Qian Chenjialou 63). This is the present-day site of the former Jesuit cemetery at Chenjialou (established 1637), located to the northwest of the former Ji'nan prefectural capital. The remains of the Jesuits buried in the cemetery were moved to the Hongjialou church cemetery in eastern Ji'nan when the Chenjialou Saint Joseph Church was built in 1909. The church was closed during the Cultural Revolution and reopened on December 23, 1987. Photograph: D. E. Mungello, 1997.

Franchi had died on the night of February 12/13; how could Fernández-Oliver be accused of burying him with haste when fifty-seven days had elapsed between his death and the interment on April 10?[86] Fernández-Oliver said a more logical question would have asked why the interment was so late! He had sent an announcement of Franchi's death with the servant Yin Degong to the court in

Fig. 4.3. The steeple of the Chenjialou Saint Joseph Church, with the viewer facing south. The photograph indicates how densely built up the area is. Unlike the site of the former West Church, the church has no courtyard. It is located in a maze of back alleys and is difficult to find. Photograph: D. E. Mungello, 1997.

Beijing, and he believed it was appropriate to await the messenger's return before proceeding with the funeral.

The delay was chiefly due to events caused by Della Chiesa's own assistant, Father Orazio. Orazio's poor handling of the three sectarians who appeared at the bishop's residence in Linqing on February 28, 1718, had created a public scandal that had damaged the church. (This incident is discussed in the next chapter.) Not only was Orazio responsible for publicly whipping the three sectarians and for reporting the case to the authorities, but he was also responsible for previously having baptized one of the three. (A second had been baptized by

Nieto-Díaz.) These sectarians had papers that referred to seditious activities, and by bringing their case to the authorities, Orazio was exposing Christianity to the charge of being linked with such activities. Fernández-Oliver might have delayed the funeral even longer had it not been for the governor of Shandong, Li Shude, with whom he maintained friendly relations.[87] Governor Li offered him the friendly advice that Franchi's funeral with its official honors might help counteract the bad publicity of the sectarian incident in Linqing.[88]

In response to the question of why he chose Holy Week for the funeral, Fernández-Oliver replied that he wanted to use the drama of Christ's Passion to emphasize the triumph of Christianity in a community that had been demoralized by the Linqing incident. He admitted that the pomp and ceremony of the funeral were elaborate to counter not only the effects of Orazio's poor handling of the sectarian incident but also the common Chinese criticism that Christians buried their dead with insufficient honor "as if they were dogs" (como si fueran perros).[89]

On March 13, Fernández-Oliver had met with the Christians of Ji'nan to consult with them about Franchi's funeral. It was decided that the funeral would begin on April 7 and conclude on the tenth, Palm Sunday, and that it would be open to participation by the scholar–officials.[90] Holding a funeral on Palm Sunday, the beginning of the most holy week in the Christian calendar, was a dramatic gesture. Fernández-Oliver chose this date in order to celebrate a triumph of Catholic (universal) truth and to counteract the demoralization caused by the depositions of the Linqing sectarians. Franchi's funeral was intended as a celebration of Jesus' triumphant entry into Jerusalem on Palm Sunday and the beginning of the Passion of Christ, in which evil was vanquished.

Orazio was insensitive to the subtleties of Chinese politics and unaware that it would have been far wiser to have handled the case of the three sectarians without bringing it before the authorities. When Yang Deluo was brought to the provincial capital in Ji'nan for further interrogation, Fernández-Oliver obtained a confession from him.[91] Yang's claims in the confession were dangerous for the church. He said that Della Chiesa had the authority to name emperors (zuo chaoting) and that Orazio had the authority to change customs and, in fact, was changing them in the areas where he worked. Some of Yang's followers were promising to make him emperor and because of this, he was at the church at Linqing seeking horses in order to receive the pope (jiaohua huang). Fernández-Oliver was able to have Yang Deluo's deposition suppressed and not passed along to higher official levels, where it would have caused trouble for the church. In return for the Shandong governor's compliance in this, Fernández-Oliver was all the more willing to accept the governor's advice that Franchi's funeral be expedited as a means of quieting the sectarian turbulence.

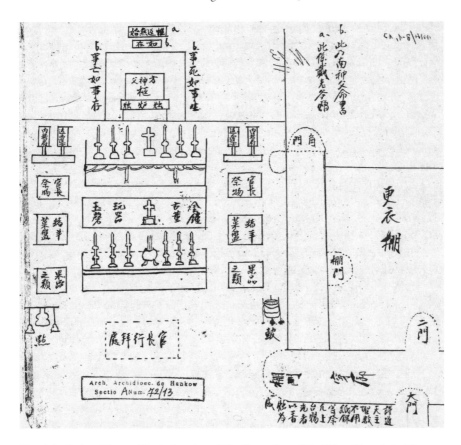

Fig. 4.4. Father Matteo Ripa's drawing of the floor plan of the West Church in Ji'nan at the time of the Jesuit Father Franchi's funeral (April 7–10, 1718). The Franciscan Father Fernández-Oliver of the East Church organized the funeral with the cooperation of the West Church parishioners. It was a major event intended to demonstrate to the Chinese public that Christians honored their dead appropriately. Note that the main entrance (lower right-hand corner) is located to the east of the church and opens into a courtyard. This same physical plan holds for the site today, although the church edifice was rebuilt in 1866 (see figures 4.5, 4.6, and 4.7). The drawing is preserved at the General Archives of the Franciscans in Rome in the Archivum Archidioecesis de Hankow, section A 72/13 (renumbered MH/8-1). Reproduced with permission of the Archivum Generale Ordinis Fratrum Minorum, Rome.

Another question that Della Chiesa raised in regard to Franchi's funeral was whether Fernández-Oliver had permitted the Chinese to offer oblations, or sacrifices, to Franchi, which would have violated the Christian prohibition on worshipping false gods. Fernández-Oliver answered that he was careful to clarify that the gifts and offerings presented by Chinese at the funeral could not be viewed as a sacrifice to the spirit of Franchi and that the only sacrifice made was in the Holy Mass offered to God.[92] He finds scriptural basis in his interpretation by citing 2 Maccabees, an apocryphal book of the Old Testament that describes the revolt of the Maccabees.[93] Apparently, Fernández-Oliver was comparing the offering of the Jew (i.e., non-Christian) Judas to the offerings of the non-Christian Chinese literati and seeing both as an anticipatory recognition of Christian resurrection. Consequently, Fernández-Oliver claimed that the Chinese were forbidden to make offerings to Franchi as a spirit; rather, the gifts were given as if Franchi were still alive.[94]

For confirmation on this and other points made by Fernández-Oliver, we can turn to a remarkable diagram of the funeral setting made by another Propaganda missionary, Father Matteo Ripa (Ma Guoxian) (1682–1746) of Naples, who was not a Franciscan (see figure 4.4).[95] Ripa, made this drawing in Beijing on December 12, 1719, based on sketches sent to him by Orazio on April 19 and May 21 of that year. Although it is possible that the Propaganda affiliation of Orazio and Ripa distorted the diagram, it is more likely that any differences would have been made in their interpretation rather than in the depiction of the church's floor plan at the time of the funeral. The West Church in Ji'nan was built, in typical Chinese style, on a north-south axis with the altar at the north end and the entrance at the south.

Ripa's diagram indicates that a statement was placed over the outer door of the entrance to the West Church (figure 4.4, lower right) that read: "The Lord of Heaven Teaching does not use paper money, ceremonial silver ingots, and other forms of sacrifice. We very much hope that those who wish to pay honor at the funeral will offer incense and candles." This was reinforced by three inscriptions from the Confucian Classics hung around the altar and prepared at the order of Fernández-Oliver (annotation in upper right-hand corner, letter "b"). Two of these inscriptions were hung to the east and west sides of Franchi's coffin, which lies just north of the upper cross. The inscriptions (letter "b" in figure 4.4) quote from the Confucian Classic *Book of Rites (Li Ji)* as follows: "Serve all the deceased in the same way that one serves the living" (east side) and "Serve all the deceased as they are served [in life]" (west side).[96]

There is also a very brief third inscription labeled with the letter "b." It is found above the coffin and reads *"ru zai"* (as if being present). This appears to be an abbreviated citation from the *Analects* 3:12, in which Confucius emphasizes the importance of the sacrificer's state of mind in making a sacrifice, hence, sacrificing "as if [the deceased] were present." Whereas previous interpretations of this passage had emphasized the importance of outward manifestations of belief in spirits, Confucius was shifting the emphasis to inner sincerity.[97] The omission of the first character—*ji* (to sacrifice)—in the *Analects* 3:12 phrase *"Ji ru zai"* (sacrifice as if [the deceased] were present) is significant. If it had been included in the inscription above Franchi's coffin, it might have been seen as implying a reference to the ritual sacrifices in Chinese ancestral worship, and such an implication would have been harshly criticized by certain missionaries. The use of these quotations from the Confucian Classics indicates some of the difficulties priests like Fernández-Oliver faced in attempting to accommodate the Confucian values of the literati with Christianity. These were delicate matters, and apparently some of his confreres were not satisfied with Fernández-Oliver's explanations.[98]

Yet another inscription found over the altar at the very top of the drawing and marked with the letter "a" states: "The nature [of the deceased, Father Franchi] returned to what is without beginning" *(Xing fan wu zhi)*. An annotation (upper right-hand corner, letter "a") indicates that this was made by a Mr. Dai *(Dai laoye)*.

The gifts presented at Franchi's funeral included money to defray funeral expenses, including the food and drink for the funeral feast.[99] Actually, Franchi's funeral in several respects followed the pattern typical of that time in northern China, including the presence of tables near the coffin for offerings to the deceased.[100] At Franchi's funeral, three pairs of tables were set out for these offerings, arranged in balanced fashion in front of the coffin, three tables to the right and three tables to the left. The pair of tables closest to the coffin was for offerings from officials. The second pair of tables was for "pork, mutton, and other edible things." The third set of tables was for fruit offerings. A feast was frequently a part of Chinese funerals, and there were catering shops that specialized in providing the equipment and preparing the meal. The food was prepared in a separate cooking area, and tables and chairs were set up for the participants. Although Fernández-Oliver indicates that such a meal was provided, no specifics are given on where or when it took place. Franchi's funeral was held in the atrium of the West Church, and preparations had already begun when the courier Yin Degong returned from delivering the news of Franchi's death to Beijing.[101]

In traditional Chinese architectural style, the entrance to a building was normally on the south side. However, Ripa's diagram of the funeral depicts the primary gate to the church on the south side, but positioned off to the east side rather than on an axis of the nave of the church (figure 4.4, lower right-hand corner), as was typical in European architecture. It is unclear whether the position of the entrance was dictated by the traditional Chinese preference for indirect rather than direct entrances into interior spaces or whether it was simply necessitated by the physical limitations of the structure of the West Church. Chinese style appears to have been followed in having an open courtyard area, only partially covered by a verandah, between the first and second entrances. After the second entrance came an area for changing from street clothes into mourning

Fig. 4.5. The site of the former West Church (address Jiangjunmiao jie 25). The façade (south side) of the Church of the Immaculate Conception (Wuyuanzui Tang) (1866) with the viewer facing north. It occupies the corner of Gao-duosi Lane (on the left side of the photograph) and Jiangjun-miao Street. The low building in front is part of the wall enclosing a courtyard that surrounds the southern and east-ern sides of the church building. The street entrance to the church is off to the right (see figure 4.6). After being closed during the Cultural Revolution, the church was reopened in December 1984. Photograph: D. E. Mungello, 1997.

clothes, another concession to Chinese funeral style. The present-day site of the church bears out much of this arrangement, although a new church edifice was built on the site in 1866 (see figures 4.5, 4.6, and 4.7).

From the courtyard and changing area one turned west into the atrium of the

Fig. 4.6. The street entrance to the Church of the Immaculate Conception (site of the former West Church) at 25
Jiangjunmiao Street. Photograph: D. E. Mungello, 1997.

church, which was placed at a right angle to the entrance and changing areas. At
the north end of the atrium Franchi's coffin lay behind a table of burning candles and incense. Above and at the sides of the coffin hung the previously
described four inscriptions. Below them was an altar with cross and candles and
below this another altar table containing, from right to left, a metal chime;
ancient utensils, such as porcelain or brass instruments; a cross; curios; and a
jade chime. Two wooden plaques were hung on each side of the altar, each of
which repeated a three-character inscription. The outside plaques read: "From
the Imperial Household Department" *(Nei Wu Fu)*. This Beijing-based department was responsible for the management of the imperial palace establishment
and consisted of approximately sixteen hundred imperial princes, imperial bond

Fig. 4.7. The main entrance and part of the southern façade of the Church of the Immaculate Conception (1866) in Ji'nan. It is located on the site of the former West Church. Photograph: D. E. Mungello, 1997.

servants, and eunuchs.[102] The inside plaques read: "To the Doctor from the Far West" *(Yuan Xi jinshi)*. The next three pairs of tables were laden with the food offerings described above. Below the last of these tables was a drum on the east side of the atrium, which was beaten to signal when a mourner arrived to make an oblation, reverence, or other act. Corresponding to the drum, on the west side of the atrium were chimes.

At the south end of the atrium, near the entrance from the courtyard, one finds a designated place where scholar–officials performed the genuflection and reverence to the deceased. Fernández-Oliver stood nearby to return the courtesy and genuflect in turn. The visitation portion of Franchi's funeral took place in the West Church on April 7, 8, and 9 (Thursday, Friday, and Saturday); the body was brought to the cemetery in a solemn procession on April 10.[103] The four grave diggers who prepared the sepulchre were Ambrosius and Joseph Wang, Franciscus Sun, and Andreas Yin.[104]

Returning to Nieto-Diaz's interrogation of Fernández-Oliver, a fifth question reflected the hostility between Orazio and Fernández-Oliver. Was it true that Fernández-Oliver had sent a malicious message to the bishop of Beijing's vicar general (Orazio) saying that he had allowed libations *(ji Tian)* or sacrifices at Franchi's interment?[105] Fernández-Oliver was indignant in responding; he felt the question was slanderous and left it to God to inflict the proper punishment for it. And yet there may have been more here than meets the eye. The message that Fernández-Oliver sent to Orazio was carried by Su Lorenzo (Laolengzuo), a former servant of Franchi's who later became a catechist under Orazio. Su was not a native of Ji'nan but had come from the village of Poligu in the Quzhou district in southern Zhili province.[106] It is likely that Su carried information about Franchi's funeral to Orazio that was, in turn, communicated to Ripa and that it was on this information that Ripa's diagram of the funeral was based.

5

Christianity and Chinese Heterodox Sects, 1701–1734

Missionary Rivalries and the Founding of Propaganda

The early development of Christianity in China has often been presented as events flowing from decisions made by the papal court in Rome or the imperial court in Beijing, but when we look at how Christianity first developed in a province such as Shandong, we see regional and local factors shaping events. Like contemporary societies, China in 1650–1785 contained a broad spectrum of religious groups ranging from lawful churches to sects engaging in secret and illegal activities. Most Christians in China at that time (both European missionaries and Chinese Christians) were trying to have their religion accepted as one of the legal and established churches. However, religious activity is often difficult to control, and it appears that Christianity in Shandong in the early eighteenth century began to be absorbed by certain illegal, native Chinese religious sects. This process was unwittingly fostered by the Italian Franciscans of the Propaganda mission.

Although all of the missionaries during these years belonged to the Roman Catholic Church, the church contained many subdivisions. Initially, there were rivalries between the various orders: Jesuits versus the mendicant orders (Franciscans, Dominicans, and Augustinians). However, even missionaries of the same order were often split by nationalistic rivalries. By rights of their monopoly (padroado), the Portuguese dominated the office of Jesuit vice-provincial of the China mission. The Portuguese authorities in Macau restricted the entry of other nationalities, particularly their greatest rivals, the Spanish, who were forced to enter China surreptitiously through the pirate-infested coast of Fujian. Certain Jesuits also saw the Portuguese monopoly as an obstacle to Christianity in China. When the Jesuit Father Verbiest requested French confreres to counter the Portuguese influence, five French Jesuits landed at Ningbo in 1687 to avoid the Portuguese at Macau. When the French requested an independent mission with their own superior, the Portuguese claimed that the padroado required them to submit to the Portuguese mission and superior.[1] The French Jesuits resisted the efforts of the Portuguese to control them and concentrated their missionary efforts in the area around Beijing and, to a lesser extent, in Jiangxi and Huguang provinces.[2]

Because such interorder and nationalistic rivalries were hindering missionary efforts not only in China but throughout the world, the papacy attempted to assert control of the situation. On January 6, 1622, Pope Gregory XV had created the Sacra Congregatio de Propaganda Fide (Sacred Congregation for the Propagation of the Faith).[3] Propaganda was headed by thirteen cardinals and charged with promoting the spread of Catholicism in overseas missions and defending the church against heretical teachings. In 1627 Pope Urban VIII founded the Collegium Urbanum in Rome as the Propaganda seminary. Although Propaganda emphasized preserving the cultures and social autonomy of non-Western lands, this theory was not put into practice in China. Moreover, because of the complexities of the Catholic Church, Propaganda initially was not able to dominate the other established missions. Consequently, in China and elsewhere, the Propaganda missionaries were added to the missionary mix as another force that competed with the other missions for power and converts. To avoid conflict with Portugal, the pope exerted control in China not through ordinary bishops but through the creation of vicars apostolic. Vicars apostolic, who were also consecrated as titular bishops, had the same episcopal powers as ordinary bishops, but they circumvented Portuguese control by ruling in the name of the pope and being controlled by Propaganda.[4] Titular bishops were assigned to an extinct see, usually in Asia Minor or northern Africa, that had lapsed owing to the rise of schismatics, heretics, or Muslims.[5]

The Missions Étrangères of Paris (M.E.P.) also played a role in Rome's grand plan for dealing with interorder and nationalistic rivalries. To implement this plan, in 1680 Propaganda sent Bishop François Pallu, M.E.P. (Fang Jige), to China as vicar apostolic and general administrator of all missions in China. Propaganda also sent five Italian Franciscans, one of whom was Monsignor Bernardino Della Chiesa (Yi Daren) (1644–1721).[6] Just prior to his departure from Venice in 1680, Della Chiesa was appointed as coadjutor (assistant) to the French vicar apostolic, François Pallu. After a very prolonged journey, Della Chiesa arrived in Canton in 1684, and after Pallu's death on October 29, 1684, he was designated vicar apostolic of the four southern provinces of China. He visited missions in Jiangxi and Fujian before being forced by illness to return to Canton in 1687. He later traveled to Hangzhou and Nanjing.

Propaganda sought to organize the Christian church in China in a hierarchy over which Rome would have direct supervision rather than merely indirect supervision by way of the Portuguese authorities. Della Chiesa became ensnared in a struggle between the Portuguese monarch, who wished to preserve the rights of the padroado, and forces in Rome centered in Propaganda, who wished to reduce the nationalistic prerogatives that were interfering with the mission of the church. Propaganda sought to expand the influence of the vicars apostolic appointed by Rome rather than the Portuguese king. However, the Portuguese king was a powerful figure and, contrary to the wishes of Propaganda, he obtained from the new pope, Alexander VIII, an agreement to divide China into three dioceses centered at Beijing, Nanjing, and Macau. In this arrangement, Della Chiesa was named bishop of Beijing.[7] However, because Della Chiesa backed Rome's prerogatives at the expense of the padroado, the Portuguese created obstacles that made it difficult for him to assume office.

In 1696, at the behest of Propaganda, the plan to divide China into three bishoprics was altered. The sizes of the bishoprics of Beijing and Nanjing were reduced, leaving nine provinces for which nine vicars apostolic were appointed.[8] The diocese of Beijing was limited to the provinces of Zhili, Shandong, and Liaodong. Della Chiesa left Nanjing in June of 1700 to assume the office of bishop in the Beijing diocese. He traveled first to Ji'nan, where he arrived on July 25. Della Chiesa and the Italian Franciscan and Propaganda missionary Father Antonio Pacecco de Frosolone (Antonius a Frusione), O.F.M. (Lao Hongen) (1669–1739), lived with the Spanish Franciscans in Ji'nan from July 1700 until September or October 1701.[9] During this time, the bishop sent Fernández-Oliver to Linqing. Later in 1701, Della Chiesa arrived at Linqing, en route to Beijing.[10] In Beijing, Della Chiesa celebrated mass in the cathedral, but while Rome had ordered that the Church of the Blessed Virgin Mary (the South Church) in Beijing be consecrated as the cathedral seat of the new bishop, the Jesuits resisted on the grounds that the church did not belong to the Portuguese padroado but had been established by their confrere Adam Schall and should rightfully remain a Jesuit church.[11] Della Chiesa came to accept their argument.

Rather than establish his episcopal residence in Beijing, where there was a strong Portuguese presence, Della Chiesa chose Linqing, which was in north-western Shandong and strategically located on the Grand Canal, the main north–south artery of China at that time (see map 1). When the papal legate, Tournon, fell ill in 1706, Della Chiesa went to Beijing for six months to minister to him. He departed with Tournon from Beijing on August 28, 1706, and accompanied the legate on his southward journey on the Grand Canal as far as Linqing.[12]

Propaganda Establishes Its Base at Linqing

When Della Chiesa established his base in Linqing, there were several competing missionary forces in the diocese of Beijing—Portuguese Jesuits, French

Jesuits, and Spanish Franciscans. The Portuguese Jesuit vice-provincial in Beijing attempted to minister to numerous Christians dispersed throughout the diocese with the aid of only two Jesuits. One of these was stationed in Zhengding prefecture and ministered to Christians in the central and southern portions of Zhili province. The other Jesuit was stationed in Ji'nan and ministered to the Christians in western Shandong and in certain towns of southern Zhili.[13] During the years when Della Chiesa was working with the Propaganda missionaries from his base in Linqing, the Jesuits at Ji'nan were, in succession, Antonio Faglia, Girolamo Franchi, and Giacomo Filippo Simonelli. There was a five-year lapse between Franchi's death in February 1718 and Simonelli's arrival in 1723, and the next year all the missionaries were expelled.[14] Spanish Franciscans were based in towns and cities in the central and western parts of Shandong.

After establishing a church at Linqing prefecture in 1701, the Italian Franciscans dedicated a church to Our Lady of Aracaeli in Dongchang prefecture in 1702 and a church at Wucheng district in 1705. All of these mission sites were in the far western part of Shandong. Because the Jesuits were unable to travel regularly to their church in Weixian in Zhili (see map 2), the Propaganda missionaries began to minister to Christians in this region as well.[15] Della Chiesa's orders to respond to the call for priests regardless of where the call originated would lead to a major confrontation with the Jesuits.

The first Italian Franciscans to make a significant contribution to the Propaganda mission in the diocese of Beijing were the above-mentioned Antonio Pacecco de Frosolone, Gabriel Antonio de San Giovanni (d. 1718), and, above all, Carlo di Orazio da Castorano.[16] San Giovanni, a member of the province of Rome, served in Shandong in the years 1702–1706 and then fell ill. He retired first to Macau and later to Manila and returned to Europe in 1715. Pacecco arrived in Shandong in 1701. In 1705 he visited Jingzhou and surrounding villages where no missionary had ever before entered and performed several baptisms, including those of the Wang family, in early 1705.[17] He also visited Weixian. Both Jingzhou and Weixian were in southern Zhili province, near the western border of Shandong. Pacecco accompanied Tournon during the papal legate's stay in Beijing and became identified with Tournon's point of view, which had been vehemently rejected by the imperial court.

The most important Italian Franciscan who served Propaganda in the diocese of Beijing was Father Orazio, who became Della Chiesa's vicar general. In 1707 Orazio made a second tour of these small Christian communities in Weixian and Jingzhou that Pacecco had visited and performed further baptisms. In 1708 Orazio visited Wucheng, which was northeast of Linqing in Shandong province, and Qinghe, which was northwest of Lingqing in Zhili province. In Chenjialou village of Qinghe district, Orazio baptized Valentin Liu and Blaise Tsai (Cai?).[18] Liu offered his house for the meetings of Christians. They continued to meet there until 1713, when their numbers became too large and François Chien (Qian?) constructed two large rooms adjoining his house to serve as a missionary residence and chapel.

After Tournon antagonized the Kangxi Emperor by promulgating the decree *Ex illa die* (1704) of Pope Clement XI , Orazio was ordered south by the emperor to retrieve copies of the promulgation and return them to the pope. After completing this task, he was left to cool his heels at the court. Out of frustration and without waiting for the emperor's permission, he left Beijing in January 1718 to return to his mission base in Linqing. The Linqing incident drew attention to Orazio's disobedience and Magistrate Wang advised him several times to return to the court, which he did in late April.

The Indefatigable Father Nieto-Díaz

Francisco Nieto-Díaz de la Concepción (Bian Shuji; (1662/63–1733), known most commonly by the surname Nieto-Díaz, from his parents Francisco Nieto and Isabel Díaz, was born in Consuegra (Toledo).[19] On February 28, 1679, at seventeen years of age, he visited the Franciscan residence in Fuensalida (Toledo); he made his vows on March 3, 1680. There is no other biographical information on Nieto-Díaz until he enrolled in the mission in 1685, at which time he was described as being of "swarthy color and with the beginnings of baldness." He would live to be seventy-six years old, serving nearly sixty years as a Franciscan and thirty-six years as a missionary in China.[20]

Nieto-Díaz arrived in Manila in 1695 and was appointed to the China mission. He and four other religious traveled on a ship to Canton, arriving on November 10. He was soon sent to Shandong where in Jining he worked with Father Bañeza and also spent some time in Ji'nan. After Bañeza's departure, Nieto-Díaz worked largely alone in Jining, except for several months when he accompanied Della Chiesa. His association with the Italian Franciscans of Propaganda was unusual among the Spanish Franciscans, and his affinity for Orazio's missionary methods would eventually evoke criticism from his Spanish confrere, Fernández-Oliver.

In February 1707 the Kangxi Emperor departed from Beijing on his sixth and final Southern Tour. He traveled south on the Grand Canal and went first to Linqing, where on March 9, 1707, Nieto-Díaz, together with six other Franciscans, gathered to be examined by the emperor to determine whether they would obtain the imperial license (*piao*) needed to remain in China.[21] Actually, Della Chiesa and Orazio had already obtained their piao. The other four were Father Incarnatione of Tai'an, Father Martinus Alemán (Jing Mingluan) of Qingzhou, Father Fernández-Oliver of Ji'nan, and Father Franciscus de San José Palencia of Dongchang.[22]

Because the emperor was occupied with other duties, the five missionaries were examined by the emperor's eldest son, Yinti, also known as Prince Zhi (1672–1734).[23] The interrogation was conducted in Manchu, with the French Jesuit Father Dominique Parrenin (1665–1741) serving as interpreter. The piao was not granted until the emperor returned from the Southern Tour. At the later interrogation on June 12 in Linqing, the five Franciscans were joined by Paccecco and two Franciscans from Shaanxi Province, Father Ioannes Baptista Maoletti a Serravalle (Ye Zongxian, Ruohan) and Father Antonio Laghi a Castrocaro (Mei Shusheng). All of them obtained the piao, except for Paccecco, who on June 16 was expelled to Macau in the company of two custodians.[24]

Around the beginning of 1709, some non-Christians filed an official accusation against Nieto-Díaz while he was passing through some villages near Dongping. As a result, he was arrested by twenty soldiers and imprisoned for fifteen days with his servants and other Christians.[25] However, five hundred people appealed to the mandarin, identifying themselves as Christians and indicating a willingness to die for Christ. Nieto-Díaz's release was secured when Father Claudio-Filippo Grimaldi (Min Mingwo) (1638–1712), a prominent Jesuit who was serving as head of the Bureau of Astronomy in Beijing, visited the governor in Ji'nan. In response to Grimaldi's emphasis on the imperial edicts allowing the European fathers and Christians to practice their faith, the governor relented and released Nieto-Díaz.

In 1714 another anti-Christian persecution broke out in Shandong and caused considerable suffering to the Christians there. The persecution was particularly acute in the region where Father Palencia served (Boxing?).[26] Palencia was imprisoned twice. In Jining he was prohibited from attending to the Christians in the churches, and in Yanshenzhen it was ordered that anyone who became a Christian would be punished.

Throughout all of this, Nieto-Díaz suffered hardships and sorrows, but he persevered. He obtained the support of some friends in Manila for his mission in Jining. He had phenomenal success in baptizing Christians in the regions of Jining and Dongping in the years 1709–1714. When he arrived in Jining, there were 1,000 Christians in the surrounding area. He baptized over 2,400 by September 19, 1709, and 1,650 more by December 31, 1709. Of these, 900 were baptized in a fifteen-day period, which would have caused quite a stir. In the villages around Dongping, Nieto-Diáz baptized 480 in two months at the end of 1711. He baptized 5,000 in 1713–1714. He ended up with a flock of more than 10,000 Christians.[27] However, he was criticized by Fernández-Oliver for being duped into baptizing members of Chinese secret societies who were seeking Christian membership as a protection against prosecution by the authorities. He was an indefatigable proselytizer, and even later, when he was banished to Canton with the other missionaries, he continued with his ministry in Shunde district, where he baptized 332 in 1729 and in 145 in 1730.

Nieto-Díaz was totally focused on his pastoral work and tried to avoid the political controversies then swirling around the mission in Shandong. He appears to have been somewhat naive politically. He did not oppose Tournon's decree of 1707, nor did he offer any resistance to the Propaganda decrees of 1704 and 1710. He took an oath to Propaganda's representative, Della Chiesa. However, Propaganda's policies provoked resistance among his flock, and when Nieto-Díaz attempted to communicate these concerns in a letter to Della Chiesa, the letter was passed on to Orazio. Because of Della Chiesa's advanced age, Orazio was in fact governing the diocese. He replied to Nieto-Díaz's letter with a harshness that the Franciscan commissioner, Father Juan Fernández Serrano, termed *"indecentísima"* (most unbecoming). In response to Serrano's order, Nieto-Díaz traveled in June 1719 to Ji'nan, where he presented Della Chiesa's list of questions to Fernández-Oliver and then transmitted the results to Serrano.

Nieto-Díaz was twice nominated to be the commissioner of the China mission—in 1715 by Diego de Santa Rosa and in 1719 by Serrano—but in both cases his nomination arrived late and became entangled with other matters.[28] In August 1721 the Franciscan provincial in Manila, Father Alonzo de la Zarza, received orders from both the minister general of the Franciscan order and Propaganda dated October 10, 1719, that the commissioner, Serrano, should depart from the mission and that he should be replaced by Fernández-Oliver. On September 3, 1721, the provincial conveyed this command to Nieto-Díaz, who received it on August 24, 1722, and forwarded it to Fernández-Oliver in Ji'nan, who accepted.

In 1720 both Fernández-Oliver and Nieto-Díaz were ill. The former was suffering from kidney stones and the latter from continual bleeding from the mouth.[29] Nieto-Díaz was still suffering from this illness when in January 1724 anti-Christian feeling reached such a point that the Yongzheng Emperor banished the missionaries to Macau. In spite of his infirmity, Nieto-Diáz was given only one day to prepare for his departure from Jining with Father Torrejón. Soldiers delivered the command with orders that if they did not depart within twenty-four hours, their furniture and luggage would be thrown into the street. The imperial command was mitigated to allow the missionaries to go instead to Canton, where Nieto-Díaz arrived at the end of October 1724.[30]

The Arrests of Christians in Jining

In 1718 almost forty men, mostly Christians, were arrested in Jining and brought to Ji'nan for a trial. They were held in the jail of the provincial surveillance commission where criminals were judged.[31] They are described by Fernández-Oliver in a letter to Orazio dated March 13, 1718.[32] They included He Jing Jacinto (Hyacinthus He Jing), also known as He Heier, a native of Wenshang.[33] At the beginning of November 1718, he was condemned to exile in Fujian.[34] However, in 1719, when it became known that he had not obeyed the exile order, he was pursued and captured in Wenshang district and sent first to Yanzhou and later to Linqing. The second jailed Christian was Li Jinglong, of whom little is known. The third was Lian N. N.[35]

At the same time, the officials in Ji'nan were questioning Yang Dele, a leader of a group of Christian sectarians in Shandong who had been sent on from the magistrate in Linqing.[36] Yang was born around 1687 of a humble family in the village Yangjiazhuang in the Chiping district. In 1718 he was thirty-one years old. Yang declared himself to be the son of God, the second person of the Holy Trinity, who would later come to sit in judgment on the living and the dead. Assuming princely authority, he distributed offices and honors. On November 11, 1718, he was led from Linqing to the official tribunal in Ji'nan and was sentenced at the beginning of November to exile in Fujian province. However, in early 1719 when the sectarians were allowed to return to their villages, it was discovered that Yang had not gone into exile, and a search for him was conducted. What was of greater concern to the missionaries is that Yang Dele in his deposition to the officials in Ji'nan had made certain damaging claims about Bishop Della Chiesa in Linqing. Yang's claims that Della Chiesa and his companions had received authority from the pope in Rome to change the customs of China and to create emperors amounted to accusing Della Chiesa of sedition.[37]

Fernández-Oliver believed that the authorities would soon detain Paulus Zhang, from the village of Yaotou, in Dong'e district. Zhang had been baptized by Nieto-Díaz and appointed by Orazio as a lay leader of several parishes (*zong huizhang* [praefectus generalis christianitatum]).[38] Around 1717 Father Franchi made an accusation about Zhang to the viceroy, but the verbal accusation was rejected.[39] Fernández-Oliver did not trust Zhang and wrote that "he is as knavish as the rest; and so Your Fathership [Orazio] should be careful of him."[40] Although the mandarins gave orders to seize and punish Christians in many areas, Fernández-Oliver noted that in Ji'nan the nonbelievers were not bothering the Christians, particularly those who had been Christians for a long time.[41]

Secret meetings by Christians, such as the Confraternity of the Passion, were dangerous and yet necessary. They were dangerous because they reinforced the tendency of literati to associate Christianity with heretical and subversive teachings, such as the White Lotus Teaching. But they were necessary because for groups accused of heretical teachings, meeting in secret was one way to avoid the official prohibitions on their teachings.[42] The very strong sense of Confucian orthodoxy that developed among literati in seventeenth- and eighteenth-century China caused them to associate being different, false, and subversive with the category of *xiejiao* (heterodox teaching). Traditionally, quasi-religious secret societies, such as the Red Turbans, Yellow Turbans, and White Lotus Teaching, were all associated with protest and rebellion by lower-class members of society. The association of Christianity with heterodox teachings in China was based upon more than Chinese xenophobia toward a foreign teaching. Like the secret societies, Christianity was often accused by the literati of prohibiting ancestor worship, meeting in small groups, using magical techniques to control followers, and deceiving the people.[43] These accusations were reinforced by the fact—more and more true after the lapse of the conversion of eminent figures after 1611—that Christianity found its greatest following among the same lower social classes who joined the secret societies.

Not only did Christianity and the White Lotus Teaching draw many of their members from the same lower classes, but some individuals were, or were suspected by officials of being, members of both groups simultaneously. In September 1719 the provincial governor of Shandong complained to Fernández-Oliver that a certain Meng Erya, a literati-degree holder and catechist who had been supported by Orazio, was in fact a member of the White Lotus secret society.[44] The White Lotus Society (Bailian She) was not a highly integrated organization but rather a label for a number of different peasant movements which were quasi-Buddhist and subversive.[45]

Fernández-Oliver believed that the confusion between Christianity and the White Lotus Teaching was intentionally cultivated, because some White Lotus adherents in Shandong around 1703 called their teaching *Tianzhujiao* (Lord of Heaven Teaching), the name used by Christianity.[46] Fernández-Oliver claimed that the White Lotus Teaching used the name Tianzhujiao in an attempt to confuse the authorities and circumvent the prohibition on the White Lotus sect. The district of Zhangqiu, part of Ji'nan prefecture, was one of the more prosperous districts in Shandong, and Fernández-Oliver wished to purchase a building there to establish a church. What particularly motivated his wish to establish a church in Zhangqiu was the presence there of the secular Lord of Heaven teaching.[47] The teaching's adherents were said to be followers of the prohibited White Lotus Teaching who were using the name of Christianity to circumvent the prohibition. Whenever the people of Zhangqiu heard Fernández-Oliver speak of the "Lord of Heaven Teaching," they were terrified and opposed it because of its association in their minds with the banned White Lotus Teaching. Fernández-Oliver wanted to establish a church in Zhangqiu in order to distinguish Christianity from these false associations.

Fernández-Oliver Protests the Baptism
of Secret Society Members

On May 2, 1718, Fernández-Oliver wrote a long letter to Father Kilian Stumpf (Ji Li'an, Yunfeng) (1655–1720) of Würzburg, a prominent Jesuit in Beijing who had served as president of the Chinese Bureau of Astronomy since 1711 and also as Jesuit visitor of China and Japan during the years 1714–1718. The letter was about how a Chinese secret society had caused great difficulty for the Christian church in Shandong. This sect had various names but was known most commonly as the Natural Teaching or Natural Sect (Xinglijiao).[48] Fernández-Oliver claimed that the sect originated from an ancient secret society called the White Lotus Society (Bailian She), which had existed in the time of the Ming dynasty and which the mandarins had attempted to suppress, punishing thousands of men and women with death. (Actually, the White Lotus Society can be traced back to Mao Ziyuan [ca. 1086/88–1166] of the Southern Song dynasty.)[49] Fernández-Oliver wrote that in the first year of the Kangxi Emperor's reign (1662), some remnants of this society organized around the leadership of Liu Mingde, also known as the Great Lord Liu.[50] Liu was a soldier active in the province of Henan, though he was a native of Wenshang district in Shandong. As Liu's reputation grew in Shandong, Henan, and elsewhere, the mandarins began to persecute Liu and his followers. The members of this society were able to ransom themselves with silver, and they changed the name of the sect and continued with their rites. In addition to the principal name, Natural Sect, the group was known as the White Lotus Sect, Emptiness Sect (Kongzi Jiao), Principle Sect (Li Jiao), Abstaining from Food with One's Name (Benming zhai), Sect of the Goblins (Pihouzi jiao), and other names.[51]

Fernández-Oliver claimed that this Natural Sect was divided into two groups, one associated with civil officers (*wen*) and the other with military officers (*wu*).[52] The civil officers consisted of headmen of different regions who possessed the seal necessary to authenticate documents in their regions. The mandarins bribed them with silver, which these civil officers distributed to needy members. Great emphasis was placed on secrecy, and all members were required to recite an oath or chant to preserve this secrecy. This oath consisted of an "eight-character mantra" *(bazi zhengyan)*: "Eternal Parents in our original home in the world of true emptiness" *(Zhenkong jiaxiang wusheng fumu).*[53] This chant they recited on bended knees three times during the night, each time for almost three-quarters of an hour, first placing incense in a censer that they set outside their windows.[54] During the day they also prayed three times, although they did not kneel during the day. They worshiped the sun, which they called "Lord" *(laoye)*; at night they worshiped the moon, which they called "Mother Goddess" *(nainai)*. Fernández-Oliver claimed that men and women met together at night in secret to recite their chants as well as to preach and to plan acts of rebellion. Their failure to observe customary distinctions of age and sex made them radical in the eyes of contemporary Chinese society. They recognized other members by signs, whether certain expressions of the eyes or certain movements of the hands, and the like. If a guest arrived at their homes, they fed him; they did not oblige him to give them silver, nor a calling card, nor a *diezi* (saucer or plate) as a gift, because they believed that that person might someday become king.

Fernández-Oliver wrote that the military officers of the Natural Teaching secret society were divided into eight classes, named after the famous Eight Trigrams *(Ba gua)* of the *Book of Changes (Yijing)*.[55] Each trigram *(gua)* contained a hierarchy of officers, including a provincial military commander *(tidu)* and a regional commander *(zongbing)*.[56] In regard to the prayers and customs, they were like the civil officers *(wen),* except that did not pay much attention to their women and they did not care much about what happened to their sect, because when a rebellion began, they cut themselves loose and formed other associations. Fernández-Oliver stated that they managed the soldiery and stole ancient iron swords, which they were accustomed to place on the roofs of their houses for decoration. In Jining they even stole in the night the cross that the blacksmith had placed on the door of Nieto-Díaz's women's chapel *(Shengmu Tang)*. Fernández-Oliver claimed that they all employed various superstitions and diabolical enchantments, as well as diabolical medicines to excite lechery.[57]

He was particularly critical of both Orazio, based in Dongchang, and Nieto-Díaz, based in Jining, for baptizing insincere Christians who were members of secret societies.[58] In his letter of 1718 to the Jesuit vice-provincial, Father Stumpf, Fernández-Oliver wrote that a number of sectarians decided to be baptized so that they might be protected by Christianity against charges of membership in an illegal secret society. Whereas both Fernández-Oliver and Franchi had refused to baptize them, they were able to go to Jining and deceive Nieto-Diaz into baptizing "thousands" of them. They sought rosaries, crosses *(shenghao),* and calendars of festival days *(zhanli dan)* to place on the doors of their houses. They did this to identify themselves as Christians and receive the protections of Christianity, but their understanding of the religion was so meagre that they often hung the symbols incorrectly.

Fernández-Oliver claimed that the numbers of these secret society members who sought baptism were so great that Nieto-Díaz divided the task of baptizing them with Orazio, who was seeking to make his reputation in Rome by baptizing large numbers of Chinese. Orazio baptized so many Christians that he assigned the catechist Paulus Zhang to assist him.[59] Around 1717 Franchi had complained to the viceroy about Zhang, but the verbal accusation was rejected. However, these Christians baptized by Nieto-Díaz and Orazio were so poorly instructed that they were referred to as "bean-curd *(doufu)* Christians," a name that was said to be commonly used in the house of Bishop Della Chiesa in Linqing.

Embarrassing Incidents

An embarrassing incident in 1718 linked baptized Chinese Christians with popular religious sects. On February 28 at 2 p.m. in Linqing, three men came to the church where Della Chiesa was residing. They created a scene and were confronted by Orazio.[60] The three men were Li Yeshi, Zhan Chengjie, and Niu San Jiaohuazi (Niu the Third Brother).[61] Although all three were said to be Christians, only two had been baptized, one by Orazio and the other by Nieto-Díaz.[62] Although the motivation of the three is unclear, they clearly were troublemakers whose appearance lent support to Fernández-Oliver's criticism that Orazio and Nieto-Díaz had been duped into baptizing people who were using Christianity to shield them from arrest.[63]

One of these three men carried two bundles wrapped in yellow cloth *(baofu)* on his shoulders. In a haughty, arrogant manner, they claimed that they were sent by the Great Lord *(Dazhu)* and that they carried a mandate *(jiezhi)* to Della Chiesa from this Great Lord. They demanded that they be permitted to present their mandate directly to the bishop. In the commotion, they forced their way into the residence, reaching the main dining room *(yaofang)* near the entryway to the house and next to the kitchen. At this point the servants blocked their advance and stripped them of one of the yellow bundles. They brought it inside to Orazio, who opened it to find red papers painted with meaningless strokes. In the meanwhile, the menservants pressed the three intruders to turn over the other bundle, which they claimed carried a note *(danzi)* from their Great Lord, but they refused to give it up, saying very haughtily that it was of a sacred nature and should not be touched without burning incense *(xiangzhu)*.

Orazio called them into his presence, whereupon they arrived making signs and bowing three times in the direction where they pretended a holy image to be. Orazio asked them where they had come from, and they answered that they had been sent from Macau by the Great Lord. However, they were unable to give the true location of Macau. Rather than placing it in the far south of China, they said it was not very far to the east, that is, near Dongchang prefecture and Chiping district, which is in Shandong province, just west of Ji'nan. This revealed not only that their claims as Christians were suspect but also a gross ignorance and lack of education. They identified their Great Lord as Yang Dele.[64] They said he was—and here the blending of Christianity with Chinese secret societies becomes evident—an uneducated man *(baiding)* who was a Great Lord, and even the second person of the Christian Trinity (that is, equivalent to the Son, or Jesus), and that he would judge the living and the dead. However, they said that their Great Lord was not a Christian. When asked why they had come to Linqing, they said to deliver this note.

The second yellow bundle contained red and yellow paper with Chinese writings about Liu Mingde, also known as the Great Lord Liu, who was said by Fernández-Oliver to be a leader of the White Lotus offshoot, the Natural Sect.[65] The Chinese writings in these bundles were poorly composed and made reference to sedition. Orazio had these men publicly whipped and bound. After consulting with Della Chiesa, he presented the case to the magistrate of Linqing, Wang Jingting.[66] The danger of this situation for Christians was compounded by the delicate position of Orazio, who in 1716 had antagonized the Kangxi Emperor by assisting Tournon in promulgating the decree *Ex illa die* (1704) of Pope Clement XI in China and who had been ordered to retrieve copies of the document. The Linqing incident drew attention to Orazio's disobedience, and Magistrate Wang advised him several times to return to the court, which he did in late April of 1718.[67]

On August 30, 1719, Fernández-Oliver wrote to Orazio to thank him for the books that Orazio's servant, Pedro Sun, had brought and to inform him of the judicial proceedings against two Christians.[68] The first of these, Thomas Wang Ermu from the village Mengjialou, was accused of killing his wife of seventeen years. The couple had had a serious argument, and the following day Madame Wang was found dead and Wang himself half crazed. The wife's family (surnamed Lian) lodged a complaint with the tribunal at Yanggu district, which referred the case to the next level at Yanzhou prefecture. The district magistrate *(zhixian)* at Yanggu, referred to as Venerable Wang, is praised by Fernández-Oliver for handling the case expeditiously, and the accused Wang was given twenty to thirty blows and then released.

The second case involved Julian Meng Erya, also of the village of Mengjialou. Meng had entered the literati ranks at the lowest level by attaining the status of a *shengyuan* (a candidate who passed the qualifying examination), also known as a *xiucai* (licentiate). The attainment of such a status would not have entitled Meng to appointment to official office, but it would have bestowed a certain amount of social prestige along with exemption from corporal punishment and the labor tax. Such men were often threats to the regime, particularly if they were talented, because they often failed to advance to higher-ranking literati status. Their personal frustration combined with their social prestige to make them dangerous leaders of the poor against the state. The governor claimed that Meng Erya was an evildoer and should not be supported by Christians. He was brought before the Yanggu district tribunal on the charge of murder. He and his son-in-law were accused by a group of non-Christians of murdering his daughter because she no longer wished to be a Christian.

The case against Meng Erya was complicated by Orazio's association with him. On September 25 Fernández-Oliver again wrote to Orazio, informing him that an official proclamation *(gaoshi)* had been placed on the West and South Gates of Ji'nan by the magistrate *(weili or weizhengtang)* of Ji'nan, surnamed Zhu. When Fernández-Oliver learned of these proclamations on September 14, he went to the governor of Shandong (Li Shude?) in Ji'nan. The governor-general said that he was amenable to removing one phrase from the proclamation that referred to the Lord of Heaven Church and Orazio. The deleted phrase spoke of "a report containing particular circumstances on the cause regarding Meng Erya and others who are working in the Lord of Heaven church and in the administration of it by that one with the surname Kang (Orazio)."[69] However, the governor-general said that Meng Erya and his associates had been part of a perverse sect called the Principle Sect, which was part of the White Lotus Teaching.[70] The governor-general claimed that this Meng was a "wicked man" *(xing wu de ren)* who should not be admitted to the Lord of Heaven church. He further said that Orazio had grievously erred in befriending Meng and his companions.

In March 1719, Orazio went for the first time to Sanlizhuang, a village one mile from the town of Jingzhou, and baptized thirty-four persons. In nearby Qingcaohe, a devout Christian named Ignatius Fei established a chapel in his house and also built rooms for the residence of the priest and his associates.[71] Orazio took into his service Lorenzo Su, the former servant of Father Franchi, who carried a report on Franchi's funeral to Orazio. Su had been baptized in Beijing.[72] He had originally been the only Christian in his entire region, but under the influence of Orazio, Su's whole family was converted, and their village, Poligu, became the third small residence of the Italian Franciscans in that region. Su was the author of a pamphlet mentioned by Ripa in a letter of May 20, 1718.[73] After the Jesuits abandoned their mission in Zhengding prefecture in southern Zhili, Orazio assumed the ministry of it in 1721.[74]

Bishop Della Chiesa died at seventy-eight years of age on December 20, 1721. In deference to Chinese culture, many European missionaries who died in China were buried with elaborate funerals. Della Chiesa's funeral took place on April 7, 1722. It was celebrated by Orazio and Nieto-Díaz and was attended by over four hundred Christians. His remains were buried in a cemetery four and a half miles south of Linqing.[75] Over the grave, Orazio erected a tombstone with Della Chiesa's name and family coat of arms as well as a chapel. However, over time and because of anti-Christian animosity, the grave was desecrated and the identifying tombstone broken and scattered.[76] In 1920 Pope Benedict XV, a distant relative of Della Chiesa, instigated an investigation to locate the grave.[77] A Chinese priest, Father John Yuan, discovered a fragment of Della Chiesa's tombstone in a Chinese pagoda called Tianningsi near Linqing. This fragment contained a Latin inscription and the Della Chiesa coat of arms.[78] Della Chiesa's remains and the tombstone fragment were located and transferred to the new mission cemetery of Hongjialou in the eastern part of Ji'nan. A reinterment ceremony took place in the cathedral there on December 2, 1920.[79]

Propaganda Missionaries Establish an Underground Mission

On January 11, 1724, the Yongzheng Emperor issued an edict that expelled to Macau all the missionaries except those engaged in the work of the imperial court.[80] The missionaries were given several months to prepare for their departure, and during this interval the Jesuits at the court obtained permission for the missionaries to reside at Canton rather than at Macau. However, this permission was withdrawn in 1732 and the missionaries were expelled to Macau. As part of this edict, the churches in the provinces were confiscated and the practice of Christianity was declared illegal. Rather than confining themselves to Canton, Macau, and Beijing and abandoning the Christians in the provinces, the missionaries went underground. The Propaganda missionaries were instrumental in founding an underground church in western Shandong and southern Zhili. This secret apostleship had been initiated in 1706 when Father Johannes Müllener returned to his flock after having been expelled for not obtaining the imperial patent (piao). He was later followed by Italian Franciscans, Spanish Dominicans, Spanish Augustinians, and priests of the Missions Étrangères of Paris.[81] When the expulsions of 1724 began, the Italian Franciscans were the first to revive these tactics of an underground church. They were followed by other missionary groups, including the Jesuits.

Orazio was able to avoid receiving formal notification of the Yongzheng Emperor's expulsion edict until March 28, when the authorities in Dongchang prefecture conveyed the official word and gave him six months to depart. He used this time to visit his Christians and to admit numerous catechumens to baptism.[82] However, Orazio was able to obtain permission to travel to Beijing instead of departing for the south. He went first to Haidian, a village northwest of Beijing where Propaganda had a house, and arrived at the residence of the Propaganda missionaries in Beijing on November 29.

For the next two years, Orazio lived at Haidian and Beijing.[83] While some of the Propaganda missionaries returned illegally from Canton to minister secretly to their flocks, Orazio felt that because he was the official vicar-general of the diocese of Beijing, misbehavior on his part might bring harm to the Christians in southern Zhili and western Shandong. Consequently, he waited until he was able under the pretext of convalescence or visiting friends to make one visit each year to these Christians. He made the first of these visits in April 1727. In addition, he attempted to establish a refuge by having his catechist, Joseph Lo, purchase a house in Dezhou in northwestern Shandong; however, he was unable to find a good Christian family that would occupy the house.[84]

Although Orazio felt that his official position prevented him from ministering to an underground church in the area of the Propaganda missions, he had no compunction about other Propaganda missionaries taking on this clandestine service. Propaganda had sent two Italian Franciscans to be used in the China mission.[85] One, Tiburce Airoldi, had died at Canton on July 24, 1726, but the other, Simpliciano Sormano, was waiting in Canton. Sormano was born at Canegrate (near Milan), became a member of the religious province of Milan, and was promoted to the college of San Bartolomeo all'Isola at Rome (see figure 6.1). He arrived in Canton in 1725, and after Orazio's many entreaties, the Propaganda procurator at Canton, Father Dominic Perroni, C.R.M., allowed Sormano to depart at the end of 1727. Sormano arrived on January 11, 1728, in the Christian community of Sanlizhuang in Jingzhou. After spending two months in Haidian studying the Chinese language and learning about the mission, Sormano visited almost all of the Propaganda mission communities in southern Zhili and western Shandong and baptized over two hundred neophytes. He spent the summer in Chenjialou in the small oratory prepared by Orazio.

When Orazio made his annual visit to Jingzhou in January 1729, he learned that Sormano had fallen gravely ill in the Pingyin district in Shandong. Orazio nursed him for a short time but then was forced by the terms of his residence in China to return to Beijing. Sormano appears to have been an extremely devout priest whose severe fasts and other mortifications of the flesh weakened him and brought on a return of his illness. Orazio was forced to return to Haidian, and he decided that Sormano's condition required that he be sent to Canton. Consequently, Sormano left Haidian on August 3, 1729, and never returned.[86] In his visit to "Tsu-chieh" (near Jingzhou in southern Zhili) and former Jesuit Christian communities in Weixian in 1731, Orazio performed 227 baptisms. However, Orazio continued to seek a full-time priest for these missions. This priest was found in Giovanni-Antonio Buocher, O.F.M., who proved to be far more effective than Sormano and, in fact, was an outstanding organizer of the underground church in southern Zhili and northwestern Shandong.

Orazio had been the sole Franciscan active in the Propaganda mission of China during the years 1707–1728. However, by the early 1730s, his work as a Propaganda missionary in China was nearing an end. When Monsignor François M. Garetto, assistant of the vicar apostolic of the provinces of Shanxi and Shaanxi, suggested that Orazio return to Rome to defend the cause of the Propaganda mission to China, Orazio, with Buocher in place, was easily convinced.[87] In October 1733 Orazio passed through the Propaganda missions, making farewell visits. At Qingcaohe (a subdivision of Jingzhou) he met with the leaders of the different Christian communities in the house of his old and faith-ful associate, Ignatius Fei. Orazio continued on to Dezhou, accompanied by Fei and his longtime servant and catechist, Giovanni Zhou. Delegations from the Shandong districts of En and Dong'e met him along the way and, in traditional Chinese style, accompanied him for several miles. Orazio arrived at Canton on December 12 and embarked for Europe on January 26, 1734, leaving China after thirty years of service.[88]

6

Shepherds, Wolves, and Martyrs in the Underground Church

The Spirit and the Flesh in the Mission Field

Great contrasts appear to be part of human nature, and the conflict between the spirit and the flesh has never been resolved. Whereas the spiritual realm is difficult to achieve, the sensual passions are difficult to tame. Moreover, it is by no means clear that sensual impulses are completely antithetical to supersensual impulses, and in certain areas, such as Italian Renaissance works of art, the sensual treatment of religious figures such as David, the Madonna, and Jesus greatly enhance the spirituality of these works. But in other cases, sensual feelings have interfered with spiritual aims, particularly for priests dedicated to a life of the spirit. Such was the scandal and tragedy of two Propaganda missionaries, Fathers Bevilacqua and Randanini, who served in western Shandong and southern Zhili in the years 1736–1741.

The scandal of these two missionaries was brought into sharper contrast by the near heroic qualities of other Franciscan missionaries in Shandong, including Father Caballero and even the superior of these two Propaganda missionaries, Father Buocher. Giovanni Antonio Buocher, O.F.M. (1701–1763), was born in Portoferraio on the island of Elba. He entered the Observant Franciscan order in 1719 in the religious province of Tuscany. After studying for one year (1729–1730) in the missionary college of S. Bartolomeo all'Isola in Rome, he was appointed to the China mission and arrived in Canton on August 5, 1731.[1] Buocher reached the residence at Haidian on March 17, 1732, and he continued to work as a Propaganda missionary in the diocese of Beijing until 1753. During that time he became the main organizer of the underground church in the provinces of Shandong and Zhili.[2] He was superior of the Propaganda mission from 1736 until 1753.

During the first few months after Buocher's arrival, Orazio taught him rudimentary Chinese phrases and other basics of the mission before sending him on

June 20 to Qingcaohe (in Jingzhou). During these few months that Buocher and Orazio were together before the latter's departure from Haidian on October 21, the two men formed a bond. This bond continued in later years when Buocher shared in private correspondence with Orazio the most confidential details of problems he was facing with Bevilacqua and Randanini. Orazio and Buocher shared a missionizing intensity for making converts rather than a pastoral sensitivity toward the flaws and subtleties in human nature. Both were outstanding priests for the Propaganda mission where the people tended to be poor, provincial, and theologically unsophisticated. Buocher's success was indicated in the rising number of baptisms.

Buocher assumed the ministry of more than 3,000 Christians, almost all of whom had been baptized by Orazio. Because the situation in Shandong was so dangerous for missionaries, Buocher turned his attention first to Zhili. His residence alternated between Qingcaohe and Jianjialou, but he was also often at "Tsu-chieh" and in the village subdivisions of Weixian. These villages were so obscure that they are very difficult to locate today. Later in Shandong he extended his ministry to Linqing, Dongchang prefecture, and Wucheng. By the end of 1735, he had revived all of the previous missions. Soon after his arrival in 1732, Buocher reported baptizing 140 people, half of them adults, but by the end of 1735 the number of those baptized had increased to 800, of whom 500 were adults.[3] He achieved all of this in spite of the fact that he was forced to operate as an underground priest.

Because of the harsh persecutions of Christians, especially in Shandong, Buocher took care to have several hiding places where he could take refuge outside of the district where the persecution was occurring. These included a small residence at Zhenjialou and several rooms in Poligu in Quzhou district in Zhili, in the house of Su Lorenzo. Buocher worked as a Propaganda missionary in southern Zhili and western Shandong for twenty years (1732–1753). His abilities were recognized with his appointment as titular bishop of Rosalie and coadjutor to the vicar apostolic of Shanxi and Shaanxi provinces. He was sent to Shanxi, where he was consecrated on December 16, 1753. He was arrested in Shanxi at the end of 1755 and expelled to Macau, where he arrived on October 4, 1756.[4]

The Scandal of Father Bernardino Bevilacqua

Bernardino Maria Bevilacqua was born in Scala in Calabria, a remote region in the southwestern tip of the Italian peninsula. He entered the Observant branch of the Franciscans in the province of Cosenza. He was sent by Propaganda to the China mission, arriving in Macau in 1734.[5] Bevilacqua joined the Propaganda missionaries in Shandong and Zhili provinces in the spring of 1736 and was placed at Qingcaohe. The records tell us very little about his origins, but he was ill suited to the heavy demands placed upon the Propaganda missionaries. Caballero in the 1650s had complained about being isolated in the residence in Ji'nan for days on end when he lacked knowledge of the Chinese language and contacts with people. And yet he was able to endure this adversity because of his stable personality and spiritual resources. As Caballero and other Spanish Franciscans in Shandong developed greater contacts with the Chinese there, this isolation was reduced. The situation with the Propaganda missionaries was different. After 1732, when the missionaries were expelled to Macau, the Italian Franciscans serving Propaganda traveled secretly to their mission sites in Shandong and Zhili. They served in these remote towns and villages as part of an underground church, in constant fear of being discovered. For some of these missionaries, this isolation was simply a burden to bear, but for others, it unleashed passions that were harmful to the mission.

Bevilacqua remained in the mission field for only two years, from the spring of 1736 until the spring of 1738, when Buocher expended precious mission funds to hustle him out of Shandong-Zhili as a scandal was breaking. Buocher wrote that Bevilacqua was "a debauched Calabrian, lover of priapism, and that a harem was composed from the Chinese Christians" *(calabrese scostumato, affetto da priapismo, e che s'era fra le cristiane cinesi costituito un harem)*.[6] Bevilacqua used his priestly authority to seduce Chinese Christian acquaintances and penitents, both married women and unmarried girls.[7] In the small towns and villages where he worked, Bevilacqua attempted to convince these women, and especially the young girls, that they were not sinning but rather making an act of charity toward a needy person. Bevilacqua's sexual partners may also have included males.[8]

Some of the details of Bevilacqua's behavior are described in Buocher's letter of September 20, 1738, to Orazio.[9] In the body of the letter, Buocher spoke in general terms of Bevilacqua being "mad" or "insane" *(amattito)* or suffering from "madness" *(mattia)*.[10] But clearly these were not clinical terms for Buocher, because he also described this madness as "filthiness" *(sozzetto)* that involved "diabolical things" *(cose diaboliche)*. The madness was not immediately evident because Bevilacqua appeared outwardly to be healthy. However, stressful situations brought his malady to the surface.

Missionaries to China were very guarded in communicating information in written form for fear that it might be used against them by their enemies. The Jesuit missionaries in China sometimes wrote to their superiors in Rome using a coded language. However, the Italian Franciscans used other means. Buocher sought to guard the confidentiality of his letter, first, by including the details in a secret appendix, which is five times the length of the original two-page letter.

In addition, he described the most delicate topics using a phonetic Chinese, a romanization of the Chinese characters that would have been comprehensible only to someone, such as Orazio, who was fluent in Mandarin *(guanhua)*, a dialect of northern China used by Chinese officials.

In the secret appendix, Buocher wrote that Bevilacqua's madness first manifested itself in 1737, approximately one year after his arrival.[11] It took various forms, including extravagant spending of mission funds for frivolous projects and ill-tempered treatment of Chinese workers. His temper caused him to dismiss three or four menservants, and his behavior led to the removal of the catechist, Li Giovanni, from the mission.

It is difficult to glean a sense of individual personalities of Chinese Christians mentioned in missionary correspondence because the letters sought mainly to give details of mission activities, such as baptisms and finances. However, occasionally enough is revealed to begin to draw a picture of certain individuals. Li Giovanni had a long association with Propaganda missionaries. He appears to have begun working under Orazio as a servant and, over time, evolved into a catechist. However, Li's flaws led him eventually to be dismissed from the mission, and his association with Bevilacqua was the immediate cause of his dismissal. Buocher claimed that Li was lazy and noted that even Orazio had found him slothful. Buocher, with his scathing and colorful language, referred to Li as "arrogant pus" *(marcia superbia)* and described Li's relationship with Bevilacqua in contradictory terms.[12] On one hand, Li was said to cater to Bevilacqua's bad behavior, and, on the other hand, Li was said to have carried a knife with the intention of killing Bevilacqua and another servant. Buocher did not take the threat of murder seriously because "they are all scarecrows" *(sieno tutti suoi spauracchi)*.[13] Buocher dismissed Li, but Li nursed a grudge and continued to speak ill of Buocher and other Europeans. By contrast, Buocher said that his own servant, Lo Giuseppe, was well behaved.[14]

Buocher wrote that Bevilacqua engaged in inappropriate frivolity and flirtation with Chinese girls and young women. He observed that Bevilacqua was healthy and cheerful so long as things went well, but whenever they had a disagreement, Bevilacqua fell ill. He told people that in order to heal his illness, he needed to be around the more amorous and loving people of his homeland. Buocher, who was more French than Italian and who wrote Italian as a second language, regarded this as a very strange comment.[15] He repeatedly referred to Bevilacqua as "the Calabrian" *(il Calabrese)*, as if it were a pejorative term.

Although Buocher was reluctant to leave Bevilacqua by himself, the persecution of Christians forced him to do so. The new missionaries, Randanini and Nadasi, had arrived at Jingzhou in January 1738 to join the Propaganda mission.[16] The persecution forced Buocher to leave Randanini in the company of Bevilacqua in Qingcaohe for three months while he took Nadasi with him to

Jianjialou.[17] Around the feast day of Saint Joseph (March 19) 1738, an official edict against Christianity was issued, and Buocher withdrew with Nadasi to Weixian. He also wrote to the Christian catechist and elder Fei Ignatius, saying that if the situation became dangerous, he should lead Bevilacqua and Randanini to Haidian. Soon afterwards, a letter arrived from Fei containing news so shocking that Buocher was forced to go immediately to Qingcaohe.

Buocher described the scandalous features of this "filthy tragedy" using Chinese phrases. When he arrived at Qingcaohe, there was a dramatic scene in which Bevilacqua handed Buocher a knife, ostensibly to take revenge for Bevilacqua's misdeeds, but the move was, in fact—as Buocher noted—a ploy for sympathy. Buocher, who did not yet know the extent of Bevilacqua's misdeeds, felt some sympathy, but this changed when the details were revealed. A train of mothers, brothers, and uncles, as well as Fei Ignatius, came with their complaints over Bevilacqua's behavior. In describing the explosive details, Buocher wrote in Chinese that that "devil cheated a lot of girls and also some young married women" by sexually defiling them.[18]

In one notable instance, a fourteen-year-old girl came to Bevilacqua in the course of religious activities with an irregular menstrual cycle *("iue king po tiao," i.e., yue jing potiao)*. He offered to regularize her cycle (!) and, in the process, violated the girl sexually.[19] The girl, completely distraught, did not make a scene in front of a number of women nearby nor in front of her future bridegroom, but went home and tried to hang herself. Her parents discovered her attempt and, after making a physical examination and becoming infuriated, rushed to Bevilacqua's house to confront him. The scandal was made even worse by the fact that the family had been newly converted to the faith.

Another Christian woman, named Lorenza, told Buocher that Bevilacqua had "violated the sixth commandment" by committing adultery with the wife of her nephew, the same woman who only a few months before had been baptized by Bevilacqua with the water of holy baptism. Other young girls, weeping, came forward to reveal to Buocher that Bevilacqua had also violated them. These included two young girls of only twelve or fourteen years of age, though the scandal to Chinese eyes lay more in Bevilacqua's violation of the girls' virginity than an act of pedophilia. For eighteenth-century Chinese, twelve years was considered the onset of marriageable age for females.

Buocher wrote to Orazio that he was so upset by the situation that he considered killing himself or running away. Somehow, though, we might doubt these words, because Buocher was, above all, a problem solver and his skills in that area soon became apparent. Chinese society of that time was preoccupied with the sexual purity of women. This preoccupation was reflected in the strict separation of the sexes in religious gatherings. A Chinese formulation of church regulations from around 1690 entitled *Shengjiao guicheng* states: "In the village when the women hear mass in the chapel, it is absolutely forbidden for men to enter into the interior and even to look in from the outside."[20] Buocher dealt with the uproar quickly and efficiently. While one young woman was threatening to hang herself, another turned to her non-Christian parents for help, and yet another turned to a magistrate. Buocher quickly told Fei Ignatius and his household—Christian converts were often members of the same extended family—that he would give everyone satisfaction. He did so, first, by sending Bevilacqua away. Second, he paid silver to a number of the aggrieved families. And third, he was persuasive in explaining that the entire affair had been created by Satan in order to destroy the work of God.

Buocher needed not only to appease the aggrieved parties but also to prevent news of this scandal from coming to the attention of the enemies of the Propaganda missionaries. He did so by obtaining a vow of silence from all parties involved and imposing on them, as a matter of conscience, a prohibition on further discussion of the affair, even among members of the same family. With priestly modesty, Buocher claimed that he succeeded in dealing with the affair, not through his own efforts, but through the assistance of Saint Joseph, the husband of the Virgin Mary, who had become the patron saint of the missions to China.[21]

Buocher's comments reveal a mixture of embarrassment and disgust. Bevilacqua claimed that he was not a scoundrel but was compelled by a nature that could not be changed.[22] Buocher compared Bevilacqua's explanation to that of a thief who claims that he is compelled to steal by dire need. He mocked Bevilacqua's claim that he was led by an irresistible force to commit these acts by saying that the force was probably a satyr itself. Buocher was able to explain Bevilacqua's behavior to the Chinese Christians as a "temporary case of madness" and demonic possession. He emphasized that this was very unusual conduct for a European. But Bevilacqua's behavior was not the first case of mental instability in the Propaganda mission in western Shandong. Father Simpliciano Sormano, who had served the Propaganda mission from January 1728 until August 1729, increased his fasting and mortifications to such an extent that his health was injured.[23] Buocher believed that both Sormano and Bevilacqua suffered from mental derangement, but whereas Sormano's illness tended toward spiritual matters, Bevilacqua's inclined toward diabolical things.[24]

On September 20, 1738, Buocher wrote a report from Jingzhou to Arcangelo Miralta, C.R.M., who was the Propaganda procurator in Macau during the years 1732–1750.[25] In this letter, Buocher complained bitterly about "the craziness in that Father Bernadino" (La matti in di questo Padre Bernardino) that had exposed the mission to great danger.[26] Buocher justified the additional expenditures for special assistance to remove Bevilacqua from the mission field on the grounds that, although he was unworthy, it was worth the expense to remove him before he exposed the mission to further danger. Buocher referred to Bevilaqua's sin as "filthyish" *(sozzetto)* and said that it "tends toward a diabolical ending" *(tende verso fini diabolici),* adding that perhaps the "Hateful Demon" *(il Demonio Maledetto)* already commanded a large part of Bevilaqua's perverse intentions.

Bevilacqua arrived in Macau on June 3 and was met by Father Miralta, who escorted him to a Franciscan convent, probably the Convent of Holy Mary of the Angels (Santa Maria Angelorum). He was placed under the care of Antonio de la Concepción (An Duoni), O.F.M. (1665/1667–1749).[27] Father Concepción was a revered figure who labored in the China mission for fifty-two years, having first landed in Fujian province in 1697. He was based mainly at Canton until 1633 and then, after the missionaries' expulsion, at Macau until his death in 1749. Most of his work was devoted to caring for the sick as a physician, surgeon, and pharmacist, but he also served in an administrative capacity in managing the household and as procurator. Concepción was a benign figure who ministered to need, whether in Christians or non-Christians. When Bevilacqua encountered him in 1738, Concepción was a septuagenarian who was more inclined to minister to his suffering than to condemn his behavior in the manner of Buocher.

Bevilacqua appears to have suffered a mental and physical collapse. The loving care by Brother Antonio, as Bevilacqua referred to him, restored Bevilacqua's mental health in about one month. But it was judged that Bevilacqua was not yet physically healthy enough to undertake the long sea journey back to Europe, and he was later moved to a Dominican convent. Bevilacqua claimed that he would be willing, while biding his time, to use his knowledge of Mandarin in the service of the church.

Two years later, Bevilacqua was still in Macau and still not physically able to make the return voyage. During this time, he became a pathetic figure, waiting to depart and writing letters to clerics in Rome who might be able to help him. He complained in a letter of December 8, 1740, that in the previous October he had suffered from such a malign fever and vehement indigestion that he could not get out of bed for fifteen to twenty days.[28] He was finally restored to health by Concepción, who gave him an emetic. One might consider these symptoms to be the exaggerations of a hypochrondiac, but they are supported by an independent observer. On October 14, 1740, Bevilacqua was examined by a physician, Juan Vizente Peisieo, and judged physically incapable of making the sea voyage.[29] He was found to be suffering from a nearly continuous discharge of urine (due to a venereal infection?), lack of appetite, weakness of the stomach and the whole body, indigestion, and hypochrondia.

This illness could have been aggravated by his unhappy life in Macau. He lived in isolation, with little human contact. He had no income and was completely dependent upon Miralta and other clerics for his sustenance. He rarely left the convent and suffered from a melancholy sadness.[30] Bevilacqua's letters from Macau at this time reveal a humility that is hard to reconcile with the acts of an aggressive sexual predator. Possibly he had been persuasive in a gentle way in his seductions. In any case, he appears to have been crushed and humiliated by his behavior and blames no one in particular for his actions, but only a state of ill health. In his letters from Macau, he is obsessed with his health; while, on one hand, he appears to have been a hypochondriac, on the other hand, his obsession with health could also be explained by its being the key to his returning home and escaping his humiliating condition in Macau. He finally departed from Macau in 1742 and traveled to Mylapur in India, where he worked in the service of the bishop of Saint Thomas before eventually returning to Italy.

Of Bevilacqua's family we know only that he had a brother. On December 8, 1740, he wrote to Father Prone Colmo and other priests at the Convent of Stefano del Cacco in Rome.[31] In this letter he asked if his brother, Signore Alessandro Bevilacqua, had replied to the Reverend Father Abbot Lucarelli.[32] Had his family abandoned him over his disgrace? Bevilacqua's last years, like his origins, remain obscure.

The Scandal of Father Alessio Randanini

Alessio Randanini was born in Rome in 1693. He entered the order of the Observant Franciscans in the province of Rome and was associated with the church of San Pietro in Montorio, which is located on Janiculum Hill (Gianicolo).[33] This steep ridge is located on the west side of the Tiber River, beginning near Saint Peter's Piazza on the north and extending to the south. Randanini was an instructor at the nearby missionary college of San Bartholomeo all'Isola in Rome, and perhaps he and Bevilacqua met there before the latter's departure for China. This college took its name from the church of San Bartolomeo all'Isola, which is located on Tiber Island (Isola Tiberina) in the Tiber River, one mile west of the Roman Forum.[34] The church was rebuilt in 1624 by the Roman architect Orazio Torriani, who designed the façade that stands today (see figure 6.1).[35]

Together with Father Hermenegildo Nadasi (d. January 14, 1755) of Brescia, Randanini left Rome in 1736 and arrived at Jingzhou in southern Zhili in January 1738. He spent three months alone with Bevilacqua in Qingcaohe from January until March.[36] This contact occurred just prior to Bevilacqua's removal to Macau and exposed Randanini to Bevilacqua's turmoil. In his report of October 10, 1738, Miralta noted that Randanini and two other Italian Franciscans (Buocher and Nadasi) as well as two Spanish Franciscans were hidden in the provinces of Shandong and Zhili.[37]

Fig. 6.1. The Church of San Bartolomeo all'Isola, Rome. This was the site of a Franciscan missionary college where Fathers Boucher, Bevilacqua, Randanini, and Nadasi studied before departing for China to participate in the Propaganda mission in western Shandong and southern Zhili provinces. Alinari/Art Resource, New York.

Randanini arrived at "Sce hu scian" in Dongping on November 18, 1738.[38] Because of the anti-Christian persecutions in Shandong, the Propaganda missionaries had not established a residence in this region. Randanini spent twenty-five pesos in constructing a missionary dwelling. However, the village site was inconvenient because it was remote, far from the markets where provisions were purchased, plagued by thieves as well as hostile gentiles, and far away from the Christians. Acting on the advice of older missionaries, Randanini built two small rooms in "Leu kuang hoang" of Chiping district. The timber for the house was obtained through the assistance of a Christian named Gao Marcus.[39] However, problems in Shandong forced Randanini to flee across the western border of Shandong into Zhili. He arrived at the village of Poligu, part of Quzhou, on January 5, 1740.[40] He spent seventy pesos in constructing a three-room building in Poligu that included a residence and a chapel dedicated to Our Lady of Grace (Beatis Maria Virginis Gratia).[41] This became the third small residence of the Propaganda missionaries in the diocese of Beijing. However, the site was not advantageous for missionary work. Later a chapel was built in "Mamingtang" in Linqing, which Buocher blessed with a Roman rite on October 12, 1741.[42]

In the period from November 20, 1738, to September 11, 1741, Randanini recorded baptisms of 105 people. Even granting that the restrictions imposed by his illegal residency limited his effectiveness, the number of his baptisms is unimpressive, particularly when compared with the number of baptisms recorded by Buocher. This is one of several indications that Randanini's talents were not a good match for being an underground priest in a remote region of eighteenth-century China. Randanini had been raised in the sophisticated environment of Rome, and his work as a professor at the College of San Bartolomeo all'Isola indicates an intellectual mentality. He appears to have taught theology there.[43] In China he was forced to live in secrecy in an extremely provincial and unintellectual environment.

Randanini has left several lists that include the baptisms he performed while serving in the Propaganda mission as well as a list of his journeys of ministry, including the distance that he traveled in Chinese miles (li) on each trip.[44] The list records under each entry the baptismal name and age, the date and place of the baptism, the names of the Christian parents (the non-Christian parents' names are omitted), and the name and residence of the godmother or godfather.[45] Nearly all of the names represent baptismal names of Latinized form and European origin. The list of baptized individuals contains fifty-six females and forty-nine males; two-thirds of those baptized were less than three years old. Randanini had some success in increasing the numbers of baptisms: four in 1738, ten in 1739, twenty-three in 1740, and sixty-eight in 1741. While the parents were Christians in fifty-seven cases, in thirty-six cases they were gentiles. In seven cases the father was Christian and the mother gentile, while in only two cases was the reverse true. In one case the father was a Christian and the mother an apostate Christian; in another case the mother was an apostate and the father was a gentile. In one case the parents are listed as "idolatrous," a vague reference that might refer to the worship of Buddhist, Daoist, or local deities.

Only one godparent was listed at each baptism. In most cases, the sex of the godparent matched the sex of the baptized person. In a few cases, a godfather was listed with a baptized female; however, in no case was a godmother listed with a baptized male. A few names of godfathers appear repeatedly: Su Laurentius

(Lorenzo) of Poligu in Quzhou (nine times), Fortunatus of Weixian (six times), Iu (Ie) Iuniponis of "Ta ciai" (Dazhao? Tachai?) (five times), and Kao the Headman of "Ciai scan" in Pingyin (three times). Godmothers whose names recur are Agata of "Cian hu scai" in Weixian (five times), Maria of "Zi bi" in Weixian (five times), Marta of Weixian (four times), and Lucia of "Sce Ho Scian" in Dongping (three times).

The isolation of some of these towns was remarkable. On December 18, 1740, Randanini, accompanied by Su Lorenzo, braved the bitter cold and the danger of highwaymen to travel to the village "Lu scia cioang," near the prefectural city of Guangping.[46] There he heard the confession of an eighty-eight-year-old woman who, because of the absence of priests, had not made her confession for thirty-two years.[47] No missionaries had visited the village since an anti-Christian persecution twenty-two years earlier (1718). In addition, he baptized seven people: Thomas (eight years of age), Joseph (four years), Jacobus (four years, two months), Agatha (nine years, three months), Petrus (thirty-four years, three months), Lucia (fifty-nine years), and Agnes (fifty-six years).[48] Whereas all the children had Christian fathers and gentile mothers, the parents of the adults were listed as gentiles. Su Lorenzo served as godfather for Petrus and Lucia.

The baptismal list indicates that in 1738 and 1739, Randanini's activity was focused in Dongping, Pingyin, Dong'a, and Chiping, which are all in Shandong. However, beginning early in 1740, his activity moved westward out of Shandong province and just across the border into Zhili, where he divided his time between Weixian and Quzhou, with occasional visits to Guangping and to Linqing, which was barely within Shandong (see map 2). Was the intensity of persecution the only reason for this shift in mission territory, or could there have been another reason?

In a letter of September 19, 1740, to Cardinal Vincenzo Petra, prefect of Propaganda in Rome, Randanini asked permission because of his weakness to serve in another mission or even to return to Rome. Randanini spoke of a complaint against him and of his being "disobedient in an Adam-like way" (d'obbedire adamusim).[49] He claims that he had been waiting for a reply to "this matter" for two years. Two years before would have been late 1738. What was "this matter"? It appears to have involved his sexual activity.

Randanini seems to have been a more stable personality than Bevilacqua; however, they both were accused of sexual improprieties with Chinese women. In his letter to Orazio of August 22, 1740, Buocher described an incident in which Randanini, on a trip to the market accompanied by a boy servant, attempted to buy the sexual services of a Chinese gentile woman.[50] The woman was scandalized, and a group of gentiles carried a complaint to the house of the parish head and elder, Su Lorenzo, who silenced the complainant with money. This incident gives some indication of the lay leadership roles that Chinese played in the church. Su had been converted by Orazio around 1718 and had been a Christian for over twenty years. He was viewed as an important mediating figure between the Chinese people and the European priests, with some degree of authority. Su's presence in Poligu probably was one of the reasons why Randanini chose to build a residency and chapel there.[51] Su is listed as godfather at baptisms in the chapel of Our Lady of Grace in Poligu by Randanini on January 13, 1740; July 24, 1740; December 18, 1740; April 2, 1741; April 29, 1741; and November 11, 1741.[52]

Father Nadasi became so upset by the events surrounding Randanini's seduction attempt that he fled "in a most shameless manner," according to Buocher, to Jianjialou.[53] Nadasi wrote to Randanini, suggesting that he flee to Macau or elsewhere. He also wrote to Buocher, seeking to remedy the situation. However, Buocher did not give much credence to his comments, including his criticism that the manservant Lo Giuseppe was a false Christian.

Randanini and Bevilacqua were bound together by some link, though the exact nature of the bond is difficult to define. The distance between Bevilacqua's home in a remote area of the Italian peninsula in Calabria and Randanini's home in Rome meant that they probably did not meet until they prepared for missionary work in Rome. Buocher believed that the three months they spent together in Qingcaohe from January through March of 1738 caused Randanini to become infected with Bevilacqua's sickness and that this exposure led Randanini eventually to engage in a similar sort of sexual abuse of Chinese Christians. The extent to which Randanini may have been influenced by Bevilacqua may be debated. It is clear that in attempting to have sexual relations with Chinese women, both were guilty of breaking their priestly vows of chastity. Moreover, they endangered the entire Propaganda mission by doing so in a society that was very protective of women's chastity and in a country that had banned foreign priests from the provinces. Yet, Randanini's behavior was less flagrant than Bevilacqua's. While Bevilacqua exploited his authority as a priest in attempting, and succeeding in, the seduction of young girls and newly married women, Randanini was accused of attempting to solicit the sexual services of a non-Christian woman as a prostitute. Buocher implied that there were other instances of sexual transgressions on Randanini's part, but it is not clear what they were.

Bevilacqua and Randanini reacted in different ways to the exposure of their secret sexual activities. Whereas Bevilacqua suffered a physical and mental collapse, Randanini appears to have had a more resilient nature. He appealed to Father Miralta, the Propaganda procurator based in Macau, for material assistance to aid in amending his behavior.[54] But Buocher was skeptical of Randanini's desire to "live the life of a saint" and regarded it as mere talk. Although Randanini spoke of wanting to change himself and make himself saintly, a companion noted that he acted amorously and disgracefully. While Randanini apparently convinced the Augustinians in Macau of his sincerity, Buocher believed that they had been duped and stated that the behavior of Bevilacqua and Randanini had so scandalized the Chinese Christians and been so destructive of the church in China that both of them had to be removed from the area.

When in September 1739 Buocher discovered Randanini's sexual seduction of Chinese Christians, he wrote about it to Orazio using a biblical metaphor: "In the past year I discovered that not the wolf but a shepherd acting as a wolf was devouring the sheep."[55] Buocher claimed that Randanini reacted very aggressively to Buocher's attempts to help him. He called upon the patron saint and "principal protector" of the Christian missionaries to China, Saint Joseph, in his struggle with Randanini and wrote that it was "easier to save the sheep from the wolf than from the shepherd." And yet, one wonders how objective Buocher's portrayal of the situation was. From Randanini's arrival in the Shandong–Zhili mission field, Buocher had complained about his attitude. While the evidence is strong that Randanini did follow Bevilacqua in sexually seducing Chinese, it also appears that Bevilacqua and Randanini were very different personalities and that Buocher lacked the subtlety to distinguish between them. By contrast, Buocher wrote that Father Nadasi "behaves well" and would very likely last as a missionary.

The Tenuous State of the Propaganda Missionaries, 1736–1785

Hermenegildo Nadasi, O.F.M., was born in 1703. He was a Franciscan in the religious province of Brescia and studied at the college of San Bartolomeo all'Isola in Rome, where Randanini taught. Propaganda sent him to western Shandong, where he arrived in early 1738 with Randanini. Whereas the service of Bevilacqua and Randanini in China was short-lived, Nadasi continued to serve in the Propaganda mission of southern Zhili and western Shandong for seventeen years. He suffered from chronic inflammation of the legs and died on January 14, 1755, at Zhaojiazhuang, a village subdivision of Weixian.[56] He was buried at Linqing near the gravesite of Bishop Della Chiesa.[57]

At the time of Nadasi's arrival, the Christians in Shandong endured more official harassment than Christians in Zhili, but anti-Christian edicts were also issued in Zhili, and Buocher, the senior Propaganda missionary, had difficulty finding Christians who would risk giving lodging to a European priest. He assisted Nadasi in finding refuge at Zhaojiazhuang in Weixian with the family of Thomas Ren, a pious and wealthy parish leader (*huizhang*).[58] Buocher also permitted Nadasi to use the residence at Jianjialou. Buocher assigned Nadasi to these two districts and to the nearby district in Shandong. He kept Jingzhou and several missions in western Shandong for himself, although this region had recently witnessed a severe case of persecution in the incident involving the Spanish Franciscan, Father Almadén.

Antonio de la Madre de Dios de Almadén (An Duoni), O.F.M., was born in 1697 at Almadén and entered the Franciscan order in the province of San José on February 20, 1713. He arrived in the Philippines in 1724 and came to Canton in 1725. In April 1729 he reached Shandong, where he undertook an underground ministry. He was arrested by the governor of Shandong in 1737 and sent to Beijing. Later he was returned to his mission in Shandong, where he was imprisoned with eight of his Christians in "Shininchow" and eventually expelled from Shandong in 1739.[59] His forced march in chains through Shandong and Zhili was very demoralizing to the Christians there.

By 1740, after thirty-five years of effort, the Italian Franciscans of the Propaganda mission in western Shandong and southern Zhili ministered to a total of twelve hundred practicing Christians. When one considers that Caballero had himself baptized five thousand people in the nearby area around Ji'nan in 1650–1664, one sees that in the century between 1650 and 1750, it became more difficult to make Christian converts in Shandong.

In addition to the churches that they had founded, the Propaganda missionaries also began to minister to older Christian communities that had been founded by the Jesuits but then neglected because of lack of personnel and other reasons.[60] The lack of priests had made it impossible for the Jesuits to minister to southern Zhili and western Shandong during the period of the persecution from 1724 to 1736. During the years 1720–1734, the Jesuits had only three Chinese priests in their ranks: Fan Shouyi, Lihe (Louis Fan), S.J. (1682–1753); Gong Shangshi, Guanruo (Thomas da Cruz), S.J. (1666–1746); and He Tianzhang, Qiwen (François-Xavier Rosario He), S.J. (1667–1736) of Macau.[61] For a period of eighteen years (1716–1734), no Jesuit missionaries visited the former Jesuit churches in southern Zhili. During the winter of 1740–1741, Thomas Ren of the village of Zhaojiazhuang built a small residence and small public oratory and offered it to Propaganda as a gift. Ren gave the deed to Father Nadasi, who forwarded it to Father Miralta, the Propaganda procurator at Macau. Miralta anticipated the favorable reaction of Rome by accepting the gift and ordering the Propaganda missionaries to offer gifts in return, including a picture of the Virgin Mary. He then passed the deed on to Propaganda headquarters in Rome.

When Juan Bañeza de Lucera, O.F.M., of Saint Agnes in Apulia arrived on February 10, 1741, Buocher sent him to stay for several months in the residence at Zhaojiazhuang.[62] This was intended as a way of preventing a young missionary without experience or knowledge of the Chinese language from bringing attention to the mission.[63] Unfortunately, his arrival in Zhaojiazhuang came to the attention of the Jesuit vice-provincial in Beijing, Domingos Pinheiro (Pinheyro) (Chen Shance, Jingzhi), S.J. (1688–1748).[64] Pinheiro viewed this as an appropriation of a Jesuit area and in a letter dated March 29, 1743, to Buocher ordered the Propaganda missionaries out of Zhaojiazhuang.[65] Pinheiro had the letter delivered by the Chinese Jesuit Louis Fan Shouyi.[66]

This was an unfortunate jurisdictional dispute in which the interests of the Christians in Zhaojiazhuang were disregarded. Although the Christians at Zhaojiazhuang were attached to Father Lucera and resisted his removal, Buocher ordered Lucera to avoid the house of Thomas Ren as much as possible, unless he was summoned because of illness. The matter was referred to the Propaganda headquarters and to the Jesuit father general, François Retz (1730–50), for a decision.[67] Rome insisted on a compromise. Early in 1744 the Jesuit vice-provincial in Beijing sent Father Joseph Shen Dongxing, or Saraiva (Sarayva), S.J. (1709–1766), to Weixian to prepare a text of agreement for a division and sharing of missions. After much wrangling, this document was signed by the Chinese priest and the Italian Franciscans on June 11, 1744, and ratified by the bishop of Beijing on November 10.[68] The text of the agreement was forwarded to Rome and approved by Propaganda on September 26, 1746.

Lucera worked in the Propaganda mission of southern Zhili and western Shandong for many years. After Nadasi's death in January 1755, Lucera toiled on alone until the arrival of Father Pius Liu Biyue the Elder in December 1757. By the time Mariano Zaralli (Mei), O.F.M., arrived in March 1763, Lucera had become frail and blind, and it was difficult for him to minister to twenty-three hundred Christians. He turned his major duties over to Zarelli and withdrew to a small refuge at Pingyin district in Shandong, where his ministerial responsibilities were reduced to caring for five hundred Christians.[69] Yielding to Zaralli's entreaties, Lucera delayed his departure to Macau, but finally, after thirty-four years of service, he departed for Macau on July 19, 1775. He died at a convent in Macau on March 4, 1779.

Meanwhile, Zaralli brought a tremendous enthusiasm to the Propaganda mission in Zhili and Shandong. He was born at Norma, Italy, in 1726 and became an Observant Franciscan of the Roman province. He was guided to Shandong by Luke Li Song of Gujiafen, a Christian layman and pillar of the church in Shandong.[70] Upon his arrival on March 2, 1763, Zaralli established his mission base at Zhaojiazhuang and eventually became the superior of the Propaganda mission in Zhili and Shandong.[71] He founded a chapter of the Society of Piety (Renci Hui) and revived the Franciscan Christian community at Guangping in Zhili, where he noted the profound faith of a parishoner named Lucio Li.[72] After the consecration in 1780 of Damascène Sallusti as the new bishop of the diocese of Beijing, Zaralli was named the vicar of all Christians in the interior of the provinces of Zhili and Shandong. All Christians in southern Zhili were placed under the jurisdiction of the Italian Franciscans, and Zaralli was given the power to confer the sacrament of confirmation. While most Christians in Shandong accepted this situation, several catechists and Chinese priests, including Father-Adrian Zhu Xingyi, supported the Portuguese in their opposition to Sallusti.[73]

Zaralli was joined in Shandong shortly after Easter 1774 by Antonio Maria Sacconi (Kang Andang), O.F.M. (1741–1785), of Osimo. From 1774 to 1780 Sacconi worked out of Zhaojiazhuang and Weixian.[74] He became so fluent in spoken and written Chinese that he would later be called upon to serve as interpreter during the Great Persecution interrogations in Beijing in 1785.[75] After being named titular bishop of Domitiopolis and vicar apostolic of Shanxi and Shaanxi provinces, Sacconi departed the Zhili–Shandong mission in October 1780.

Father Pius Liu Biyue the Elder (1718–1786)—who is distinguished from his contemporary, Father Pius Liu Biyue the Younger, also known as Pius Liu Zizhen (1718–1785)—was born in Sichuan province and sent to Naples to study in the Collegio Cinesi founded by Father Matteo Ripa.[76] Liu was ordained in Naples in 1747 and returned to China in 1758 as a Propaganda missionary in Zhili–Shandong. He was first assigned to Jingzhou and Dezhou, where he ministered to Christians who had been without a shepherd since the death of the Chinese priest, Giovanni Battista Gu Ruohan (1701–1763) of Beijing, an earlier graduate of the Collegio Cinesi in Naples who had been ordained there in 1734.[77] Because Liu's presence in Jingzhou was aggravating the situation of Christians and leading to persecution, he was sent in 1778 to Manchuria and eventually to Beijing. In the aftermath of the Great Persecution of 1784–1785 when circumstances made it impossible to send a European to minister to the Christians in Shandong-Zhili, Liu was chosen to go instead. However, because of weakness caused by his advanced age, he died in the Christian community of Qingzhou in central Shandong on October 18, 1786.[78]

The End of the Spanish Franciscan Mission in Shandong

While the Italian Franciscans under the auspices of Propaganda served Christians in southern Zhili and western Shandong, the Spanish Franciscans continued to serve Christians in western and central Shandong. However, they labored under increasingly difficult conditions. Five Spanish Franciscans who served in Shandong between the middle of the eighteenth century and the Great Persecution of 1784–1785 were all initially buried in the Li family cemetery in the village of Gujiafen, east of Ji'nan. (Their remains were moved to the church at Hongjialou in Ji'nan in 1904, where they may be found today.) Luke Li Song had been the son of a Christian father, and apparently the entire family also converted and, owing to the kinship of such villages, most of Gujiafen became Catholic.

Little is known of the first two of these five Spanish Franciscans to be buried at Gujiafen. The first was Juan de Villena (Wei), O.F.M. (1697–1744), of Villena (Alicante), who entered the Franciscan order in the religious province of Saint Joseph in Spain in 1713.[79] After traveling to the Philippines in 1721 and Canton in 1722, he was sent to Shandong, where he is said to have been a virtuous and zealous missionary. In 1727 when he and the Italian Franciscan Orazio were on the verge of being captured at their hiding place in Shandong, they fled to Beijing and asked to be hidden there.[80] Villena died in Zhangqiu district on December 27, 1744. The second of these missionaries to be buried at Gujiafen was Manuel de San Juan Capistrano, also known as Manuel de Mieses, O.F.M. (1702–ca. 1754). A provincial's report stated that in spite of poor health, Capistrano accomplished in ten years what it took most other missionaries twenty years to achieve.[81] However, Capistrano's red hair made him stand out among the Chinese and brought him undesired attention, which, in an underground apostolate, meant danger.

More is known of the other Spanish Franciscans buried at Gujiafen. José de la Encarnación, O.F.M. (1737–1777), was born in Madrid and took the Franciscan habit in December 1753 in Avila. He arrived in Manila in July 1765 and chose to go to Shandong as a companion to Father Matías Garcia Ferrara. Traveling first to Macau and then to Beijing, they arrived in Ji'nan on May 30, 1766.[82] Encarnación excelled in the study of spoken and written Chinese. It is difficult to distinguish his individual accomplishments because his lists of people receiving the sacraments, except for the years 1766 and 1769, were usually combined with those of his coworker, Garcia Ferrara.

Matías Garcia Ferrara de Santa Teresa y Alcazar (Guo), O.F.M. (1717–1790), was born in the village of Alcazar de San Juan, Spain, and entered the Franciscan order in 1735. He was ordained in 1742 and volunteered for missions in East Asia. He entered the East Asian Franciscan province of Greater San Gregorio and arrived in Manila in 1747. After an abortive attempt as a missionary in Cochin China, he arrived in Shandong in 1756. Between November 1756 and the middle of 1757, Ferrara visited thirty mission stations, heard 1,188 confessions, administered 1,087 communions, and baptized 169 people, mostly children.[83] The situation in the provincial capital of Ji'nan had deteriorated to the point that there were only 114 Christians. The earlier Portico (Portiúncula) Church, also known as the East Church, had been confiscated by Chinese officials, forcing the Franciscans to teach and administer the sacraments out of their residence.[84] Ferrara's ill health prevented him from fully exercising his ministry.[85] In 1769 he suffered from chronic bleeding of the mouth, but he survived.[86] During the Great Persecution of 1784–1785, agents of the Chinese government sought to arrest him, but he was able to elude them, in part because the Chinese were seeking him under the false name of Lixing'a.[87] He died in 1790, after serving as a missionary in Shandong for thirty-four years.

The last missionary to be buried at Gujiafen was Buenaventura de Astorga del

Sagrado Corazón de Jesús (Li), O.F.M. (1721–ca. 1801).[88] He was born in Astorga (Léon), Spain, and took the habit in the Discalced Franciscan province of San Pablo, where he made his profession of faith in 1745. He arrived in Manila in 1759 and went to Shandong by way of Macau in 1762. He worked in Shandong for two years, but his red hair and ruddy complexion caused him to stand out, and his overly candid personality made for difficulties with the Chinese, who refused to hide him.[89] He returned to Macau and Manila and spent 1667–1669 in Cochin China, specifically Cambodia, but because of a disagreement with his superiors, he returned to Shandong. The exact date of his return there is unknown, but he is recorded as being in Shandong in 1778. He worked primarily in Linqu district. He was the fifth Spanish Franciscan to be buried in the Li family cemetery in Gujiafen, where the Chinese date on his stele gives the year of his death as 1801. Astorga was the last Spanish Franciscan to serve in Shandong. The Spanish government was losing interest in the China mission and discontinued its financial support shortly thereafter.[90]

Conclusion

The Great Persecution of 1784–1785 was a dramatic ending to the Propaganda mission in southern Zhili and western Shandong and to the Spanish Franciscan mission in western and central Shandong. However, the conditions that led to this persecution had been developing for decades. Given that the missionaries had been working illegally in these regions since the Yongzheng Emperor's expulsion edict of 1724 and because the Qianlong Emperor had not reversed this expulsion, it was only a matter of time before the government cracked down in a campaign of arrests. The Qianlong Emperor was particularly prone to exaggerate subversive threats to Manchu rule in China. In May 1784 when four Italian Franciscans sent by Propaganda were discovered to be surreptitiously traveling from Canton to Shanxi province, suspicions of their subversive intent were compounded by a Muslim rebellion then under way in the northwest of China.[91] This led to extensive governmental searches for the hidden missionaries, most of whom were found and sent to Beijing for interrogation. Several of them died in the process, creating Christian martyrs.

Seen within the larger perspective of the history of Sino-Western relations, the Great Persecution marked the end of a era. The long reign of the Qianlong Emperor (r. 1736–1796/99) was the last in which China would exert a clear dominance over foreigners from the Far West. After 1799, Western imperialism began with ever greater force to impinge upon a China in decline, and this caused a slight shift in the Chinese view of Christianity. We have seen in Shandong how Christianity began to be absorbed at the popular level into the indigenous tradition of sectarian heterodoxies. The absorption of Christianity into this tradition was done not by European missionaries but in spite of them. It was a spontaneous movement led by Chinese common people and stimulated by Chinese economic, religious, and social forces. In their preoccupation with expanding their lists of baptisms, some of the European missionaries, such as Orazio and Nieto-Díaz, appear to have been oblivious to the fact that Christianity was being absorbed by these sectarian traditions. Other missionaries, such as Fernández-Oliver, saw the problem but were unable to resolve it. This was an early sign of Christianity's assimilation into Chinese culture and of the powerlessness of missionaries to control these forces of assimilation.

When Chinese history is viewed from the perspective of great political forces (whether based in Europe or at the court of Beijing), the Macartney Embassy of 1792–1793 is often seen as a watershed event, symbolizing a reversal in the relative positions of strength between China and the West. The dominance of China was giving way to the dominance of the West. However, from the point of view of the history of Christianity and the assimilation of Christianity into Chinese culture, this shift had the negative effect of arresting the indigenizing process by strengthening foreign forces in China. Not only was the power of foreign diplomats and generals increased, but the power of foreign missionaries to control the development of Christianity was also strengthened. This had the effect of weakening the forces of assimilation. Whereas during the sixteenth and seventeenth centuries Christianity had been becoming more Chinese in ways that the missionaries could not control and often opposed, after 1799 the missionaries were in a position to stop those indigenizing forces that they did not support. This had the effect of making Christianity more foreign.

And yet, the view from the capitals of great nations is not the whole picture. When one looks at the regional history of Christianity in western Shandong and southern Zhili in the years 1650–1785, we see that conversions were made that, fostered by the indigenous Chinese values of filial piety, were passed down from generation to generation and survived into modern times. Many villages converted by missionaries long ago remain Christian today.[92] These developments appear to have had a history somewhat separate from those focused on in the capital. This may explain why, after it looked as though Christianity had been exterminated in China during the Cultural Revolution of 1966–1976, it reemerged from the ashes. This phenomenon appears to have been fostered by the development of underground churches of the sort that flourished in western Shandong and southern Zhili after the missionaries were officially banned by the Yongzheng Emperor in 1724. The thirst for spirituality caused human ingenuity to find a way to compensate for the absence of a formal freedom of religion in China. It appears that the underground church in China played (and continues to play) this essential role in Chinese culture.

Postlude: Requiescat in Pace

On September 1, 1703, eighteen years after being recruited in Spain for the China mission, Father Fernández-Oliver wrote to the priest who recruited him and who over the years had served as a spiritual counselor. In this letter to Father Michael Sánchez, he said:

> Regarding the foreign roads along which the Lord, who is the sole protector of this mission, calls his children, I might fill many pages with what I have seen and heard. I will merely say that I express gratitude to Your Paternity for having brought me from Europe and America—a wise man does not need a long explanation—in order to come to where I see the mercy of God in abundance. In the past year, coming down a road that I must have traveled on more than sixty times, without knowing how, I went astray and came to find what the Lord wanted me to look for, which was an abandoned boy who shortly after being baptized, died. And I found my way back to the road, doubtless in payment for having placed that soul in his Father's kingdom. And where I hope, through the great mercy of the Lord, I also prepare to go, in spite of experiencing so many detours in my life, to where that little angel has already gone.[1]

Notes

Introduction

1. For a description of seven different bases of anti-Christian feeling in China, see D. E. Mungello, *The Great Encounter of China and the West, 1500–1800* (Lanham, Md.: Rowman & Littlefield, 1999), 37–42.

Prelude

1. *Sinica Franciscana,* vol. 2, *Relationes et epistolas Fratrum Minorum saeculi 16 et 17,* ed. P. Anastasius van den Wyngaert, O.F.M. (Quaracchi-Florence: Collegium S. Bonaventurae, 1933), 461, 519. (Hereafter cited as S.F. 2.)

2. S.F. 2: 461.

3. S.F. 2: 520.

4. *Sinica Franciscana,* vol. 3, *Relationes et epistolas Fratrum Minorum saeculi 17,* ed. P. Anastasius van den Wyngaert, O.F.M. (Quaracchi-Florence: Collegium S. Bonaventurae, 1936), 405. (Hereafter cited as S.F. 3.)

5. *Sinica Franciscana,* vol. 8, *Relationes et epistolas Fratrum Minorum Hispanorum in Sinis qui a. 1684–92 missionem ingressi sunt,* ed. P. Fortunatus Margiotti, O.F.M. 2 parts (Rome: Segreteria delle Missioni, 1975), 969. (Hereafter cited as S.F. 8.)

6. A duplicate copy of the drawing of the cross found its way to Father Philippo Bonanni, head of the Athanasius Kircher Museum in Rome (Musaei Kircheriani Romae). The Franciscan commissioner, Father J. Fernández Serrano, also received a copy of the sketch, which he forwarded to the provincial in Manila. This apparition was only one of several sighted in China. Father R. Hinderer, S.J., sent copies of the same images to Rome in 1722 and noted that two apparitions had appeared in Shandong and two others in Zheijiang province, the second of which caused terror in Hangzhou.

7. S.F. 2: 464.

8. S.F. 2: 465.

9. S.F. 3: 523.

10. S.F. 3: 531.

Chapter 1

1. *Sinica Franciscana,* vol. 2, *Relationes et epistolas Fratrum Minorum saeculi 16 et 17,* ed. P. Anastasius van den Wyngaert, O.F.M. (Quaracchi-Florence: Collegium S. Bonaventurae, 1933), 317. (Hereafter cited as S.F. 2.) See also article on Caballero by Antonio Sisto Rosso, O.F.M., "Caballero, Antonio de (Santa Maria)," in *Dictionary of Ming Biography,* ed. L. Carrington Goodrich and Chaoying Fang (New York: Columbia University Press, 1976), 24.

2. Georges Mensaert, O.F.M., "Les Franciscains au service de la Propagande dans la Province de Pékin, 1705–1785," *Archivum Franciscanum Historicum* 51 (1958): 311 n., lists Father M. Alcazar (d. 1790) as the last Spanish Franciscan in Shandong, but Father B. de Astorga served in Shandong until his death in 1801.

3. Rosso, "Caballero," 24.

4. The Chinese name Li Yufan for Father Morales is identified by Paul Pelliot in Henri Cordier, *Bibliotheca Sinica* (Paris: Librairie Orientaliste Paul Geuthner, 1922–24), vol. 5, col. 3910. Morales is the author of the work *Shengjiao xiaojing jie* (Filial piety explained in terms of Christianity), a Chinese text with Spanish translation. This work forms part of the entry Borgia Cinese 503 in the Vatican Library. See Paul Pelliot, *Inventaire sommaire des manuscrits et imprimés chinois de la Bibliothèque Vaticaine,*rev. and ed. Takata Tokio (Kyoto: Instituto Italiano di Cultura Scuola di Studi sull'Asia Orientale, 1995), 54.

5. Antonio Sisto Rosso, O.F.M., *Apostolic Legations to China of the Eighteenth Century* (South Pasadena, Calif.: P. D. & Ione Perkins, 1948), 107.

6. S.F. 2: 363 n. 5.

7. Rosso, "Caballero," 25.

8. Rosso, "Caballero," 26. .

9. S.F. 2: 453.

10. S.F. 2: 391.

11. S.F. 2: 454.

12. S.F. 2: 455.

13. S.F. 2: 410.

14. S.F. 2: 457.

15. S.F. 2: 410.

16. S.F. 2: 457–58.

17. S.F. 2: 410–11.

18. S.F. 2: 411.

19. S.F. 2: 459.

20. S.F. 2: 431, 442–43.

21. S.F. 2: 459.

22. S.F. 2: 460.

23. S.F. 2: 460–61.

24. S.F. 2: 413.

25. S.F. 2: 419.

26. S.F. 2: 415–16.

27. S.F. 2: 419.

28. S.F. 2: 416; Joseph Dehergne,*Répertoire des Jésuites de Chine de 1552 à 1800* (Rome: Institutum Historicum S. I., 1973), 71.

29. S.F. 2: 417.

30. S.F. 2: 418.

31. S.F. 2: 421.

32. S.F. 2: 422.

33. S.F. 2: 423–24.

34. See D. E. Mungello, *The Forgotten Christians of Hangzhou* (Honolulu: University of Hawaii Press, 1994), 134–36.

35. S.F. 2: 425–26.

36. S.F. 2: 426.

37. S.F. 2: 428.

38. S.F. 2: 412.

39. Father Juan Pastor, O.F.M., was a Spaniard who had arrived in the Philippines in 1628–1629. He served as minister provincial for the three-year term 1652–1655 and died in 1666. Communication between the Philippines and Ji'nan was so slow that Caballero was unaware of Pastor's election as the new Franciscan provincial until over a year after the event.

40. S.F. 2: 430.

41. S.F. 2: 430.

42. S.F. 2: 432.

43. S.F. 2: 430–31.

44. S.F. 2: 442.

45. S.F. 2: 433, 442.

46. S.F. 2: 433–34. At the time, there were four Jesuits residing at the Hangzhou church, including the newly elected Jesuit vice-provincial, Father Simão da Cunha, S.J. (1589–1660), and the former vice-provincial, Father Manuel Dias, S.J., the Younger.

47. S.F. 2: 434.

48. S.F. 2: 424.

49. S.F. 2: 435.

50. S.F. 2: 436, 441.

51. S.F. 2: 441.

52. S.F. 2: 437.

53. S.F. 2: 438–39, 448–49.

54. S.F. 2: 443. Father Alonso de San Francisco served as provincial from his election on January 21, 1655, until his death on May 1, 1656.

55. S.F. 2: 445.

56. S.F. 2: 446.

57. S.F. 2: 446–47.

58. S.F. 2: 447.

59. S.F. 2: 437–38.

60. S.F. 2: 468–70.

61. S.F. 2: xliv, 459.

62. S.F. 2: 469.

63. S.F. 2: 489.

64. S.F. 2: 451.

65. Dehergne, *Répertoire*, 71. De Ferrariis would serve as procurator at Macau in 1657–1659.

66. S.F. 2: 473.

67. S.F. 2: 467.

68. S.F. 2: 474.

69. S.F. 2: 471.

70. S.F. 2: 475, 484. Francisco de San Diego, O.F.M., was trained in the the Franciscan province of San Gabriel in Spain, arrived in the Philippines in 1616, and after occupying various offices, was made the commissioner visitor in 1648. In 1656–1658 he served as provincial. He died in 1659 and so was deceased when Caballero wrote his letter of thanks for the aid.

71. Victorio Riccio (Li), O.P., was born in Florence, joined the Dominican order in 1635, came to the Philippines in 1648, and arrived in China in 1659. He died in Manila in 1685. S.F. 2: 475 n. 3.

72. Francisco Varo (Wan Jiguo, styled Daojin), O.P., was born in Hispali, Spain, on October 4, 1627. He was ordained as a Dominican in 1642 and arrived in the Philippines in 1648. He came to China in 1649 and died in Canton on January 31, 1687. S.F. 2: 397 n. 4.

73. S.F. 2: 476, 484.

74. S.F. 2: 484.

75. S.F. 2: 477.

76. Johannus a Capistrano, O.F.M., was born in Leon and was a member of the Franciscan province of San Paulo. He arrived in the Philippines and, after holding various offices, served as provincial in 1658–1660. He died in Manila in March 1662. S.F. 2: 478 n. 1.

77. Sebastian Rodriguez, O.F.M., was born in 1619. A graduate of the Franciscan province of Saint John the Baptist, he arrived in the Philippines in 1644 and, after holding various officies, died in Manila on July 11, 1679. S.F. 2: 398 n. 1.

78. S.F. 2: 479.

79. S.F. 2: 483.

80. S.F. 2: 489.

81. S.F. 2: 490.

82. S.F. 2: 490–91.

83. S.F. 2: 449–50.

84. S.F. 2: 450.

85. S.F. 2: 465.

86. S.F. 2: 491–92.

87. S.F. 2: 493.

88. S.F. 2: 496.

89. S.F. 2: 472.

90. S.F. 2: 480.

91. S.F. 2: 481, 483.

92. S.F. 2: 477.

93. S.F. 2: 484.

94. S.F. 2: 487.

95. S.F. 2: 487–88.

96. S.F. 2: 488.

97. S.F. 2: 414

98. S.F. 2: 484.

99. S.F. 2: 486.

100. S.F. 2: 499.

101. Antonio de San Gregorio (Antonius a sancto Gregorio), O.F.M., was a native of Salices, or San Felices de los Gallegos. He made his profession of faith on March 10, 1611, in the Franciscan province of San Paulo and arrived in the Philippines in 1621, where after filling various offices he was elected minister provincial in 1632. After a visit in 1635 to Mexico, he returned to Manila and was elected vice-provincial on September 17, 1639, and minister provincial in 1649. S.F. 2: 361 n. 1. He died in 1662 in a convent of his order.

102. S.F. 2: 361–64.

103. S.F. 2: 498.

104. S.F. 2: 499.

105. S.F. 2: 500.

106. S.F. 2: 520.

107. S.F. 2: 503.

108. S.F. 2: 545.

109. S.F. 2: 547.

110. S.F. 2: 547–48.

111. S.F. 2: 549–50.

112. S.F. 2: 551.

113. S.F. 2: 552.

114. Matthew 10:16: "Look, I send you out like sheep among wolves; be wary as serpents, innocent as doves" (New English Bible); Luke 10:3: "And look, I am sending you like lambs among wolves" (NEB).

115. S.F. 2: 328.

116. S.F. 2: 329. In his biographical article on Caballero, Rosso wrote that the epitaph on Caballero's grave was composed by his first convert and the first Chinese bishop, Luo Wenzao (Gregory Lopez), O.P. (d. 1691), who had the epitaph engraved in stone (Rosso, "Caballero," 30). The inscription was later seen and reproduced in the nineteenth century by Elijah C. Bridgman in the *Chinese Repository* 8 (1839): 389–90; and by William C. Hunter in *Bits of Old China* (London: Kegan Paul, Trench, 1885), 68–70.

Chapter 2

1. In discussing the contents of this second work in Chinese, Caballero drew from the commentary on chap. 14 of the apocryphal Book of Wisdom by the French theologian Nicolas of Lyra, O.F.M. (ca. 1270– ca. 1349), entitled *Biblia Sacra,* vol. 3, col. 1960.

2. *Sinica Franciscana*, vol. 2, *Relationes et epistolas Fratrum Minorum saeculi 16 et 17,* ed. P. Anastasius van den Wyngaert, O.F.M. (Quaracchi-Florence: Collegium S. Bonaventurae, 1933), 427. (Hereafter cited as S.F. 2.) In a letter of December 15, 1653,

to a new Franciscan provincial, Caballero wrote that he had "made and composed in their letters and Chinese language three books in their style" (S.F. 2: 430).

3. S.F. 2: 428.

4. Fang Hao, *Zhongguo Tianzhujiao shi renwu chuan* (Biographies of historical personages in the Chinese Catholic Church), 3 vols. (Hong Kong: Gongjiao Renlixue Hui, 1970–1973), 2: 112; and Fang Hao, *Fang Hao liushi zidinggao* (The collected works of Marius Fang Hao, revised and edited by the author on his sixtieth birthday) (Taipei: Taiwan Xuesheng Shuju, 1969), 234.

5. In the introduction to *Bu Ru wengao*, Shang states that he was baptized by Jinliang Bi xiansheng shenfu, that is, Bi Fangji, *zi* Jinliang, or the Jesuit Father Francesco Sambiasi (1582–1649). This baptism would appear to have taken place while Sambiasi was living in the region of Shandong and Nanjing in 1631–1643, before being designated by the southern Ming court as ambassador to Macau in March 1645.

6. *Shandong tongzhi* (Gazetteer of Shandong province) (1934–1935) 2: 2197; and *Wei xianzhi*, comp. Wang Songfen, 2 vols., facsimile of 1760 ed. (Taipei, 1976), 353.

7. Fang, *Zhongguo, ,* 2: 112.

8. Shang Huqing, *Tian Ru yin* (Ji'nan, 1664), Shang preface, p. 2a.

9. Shang, *Tian Ru yin*, Shang's preface, p. 2a.

10. Shang, *Tian Ru yin,* Shang preface, p. 2a–b.

11. Shang Huqing, in collaboration with Antonio Caballero a Santa Maria (Li Andang) *Tian Ru yin*, with a preface by Wei Xuequ of Jiashan (Ji'nan, 1664). Published at the West Church.

1. Copy in Biblioteca Apostolica Vaticana (BAV), Borgia Cinese 334.9° (reprinted) and 349.8° (cf. Courant 7148, Bibliothèque nationale de France [BNF]). 3 + 2 + 25 folios. The main text consists of pages with eight vertical lines across and 20 characters per line. Allowing for blank areas between sections and at the beginning and end, one estimates the main text to consist of approximately 7,500 characters (48 pages x 160 characters per page = 7,680 characters).

2. Copy in Beitang Library identical, except for the inclusion of a title page missing from BAV copy. See H. Verhaeren, C. M., "Boite aux renseignements nova et vetera: Notes bibliographiques," *Bulletin catholique de Pékin* 30 (1943): 183–90.

3. Copy in BNF, Courant 7148 (appears to be identical to BAV copy).

4. Copy in Zikawei Library (Shanghai). Transcribed copy with each full page having eight lines and 24 characters per line; missing prefaces by Wei and Shang, contains a 3-page preface by Run Wangbi, Shang's son, undated.

12. This *Tian Ru yin* was mentioned by Father José Navarro, O.F.M., the Franciscan commissioner of the China mission, who visited Ji'nan in 1698, in a letter dated February 8, 1698, to Father Jean Basset, the "provicarius" of Maigrot (*Sinica Franciscana*, vol. 8, *Relationes et epistolas Fratrum Minorum Hispanorum in Sinis qui a. 1684–92 missionem ingressi sunt*, ed. P. Fortunatus Margiotti, O.F.M.[Rome: Segreteria delle Missioni, 1975], 292-93. [Hereafter cited as S.F. 8.]). In claiming that *Tian Ru yin* draws from the *Da xue* (Great Learning) and *Si shu* (Four Books), Navarro revealed his unfamiliarity with Chinese texts, since the *Da xue* is one of the Four Books. But Navarro's brief description of the contents was based upon an informed source because he stated that the work explains the Four Books in terms of a "*litteraliter sensu catholico*" (literal Catholic sense). In this manner Caballero was said to prove not only fundamental teachings of natural religion

(first cause, rewards and punishment, immortality of the soul) but also some mysteries of grace. Caballero reconciled the Christian and Literati teachings through the use of metaphors of baptism and penitence. Navarro claimed that he had a copy of the *Tian Ru yin* in his possession.

13. See James Legge, trans., *The Chinese Classics,* vol. 3, *The Shoo King or the Book of Historical Documents,* (Oxford: Oxford University Press, 1893), IV.iii.2.2; and Shang, *Tian Ru yin,* 1b. The notion of imprints is captured in Romans 1: 20: "His invisible attributes, that is to say, his everlasting power and deity, have been visible, ever since the world began, to the eye of reason, in the things he has made" (New English Bible). "Ever since the creation of the world, his invisible nature, namely, his eternal power and deity, has been clearly perceived in the things that have been made" (Revised Standard Version).

14. I am grateful to Professor Derk Bodde for his assistance in translating this passage. Private letter of Bodde to the author, January 29, 1996.

15. *Li ji* (Book of rites), chap. 48. See *Shisan jing zhu shu* (Notes and commentary on the Thirteen Classics), a photolithographic edition based on *Shisan jing zhu shu jiaokan-ji,* compiled by Ruan Yuan and originally printed in 1806, 2 vols. (Beijing: Zhonghua Shuji Chuban, 1980), 2: 1600 bottom.

16. Shang, *Tian Ru yin,* 2b.

17. This version of *Tian Ru yin* has the slightly variant title of *Tian Ru yin zheng* and is preserved in the Zikawei Library (Shanghai). Xu Zongze's work *Ming-Qing jian Yesuhui shi yizhu tiyao* (A summary of Jesuit translations made in the late Ming and early Qing periods) (Taipei: Zhonghua Shuju Gufen Youxian Gongxi, 1958), 130–31, reproduces the preface but omits the closing names.

18. Shang Huqing, *Tian Ru yin zheng,* Run Wangbi preface, 2.

19. Shang, *Tian Ru yin zheng,* Run Wangbi preface, 1.

20. Shang, *Tian Ru yin zheng,* Run Minbi preface, 1–2.

21. *Lun Yu* 14:37, as translated in Wing-tsit Chan, *A Source Book in Chinese Philosophy* (Princeton, N.J.: Princeton University Press, 1963), 43. Cf. Legge, *Chinese Classics,* 1: 289.

22. Shang, *Tian Ru yin,* Run Wangbi preface, 2. On Zhang Xingyao, see D. E. Mungello, *The Forgotten Christians of Hangzhou* (Honolulu: University of Hawaii Press, 1994), 149.

23. Fang Hao, *Zhongguo* 2: 110.

24. Fang Yi et al., *Zhongguo renmin da cidian* (Comprehensive dictionary of Chinese biographies) (Shanghai: Commercial Press, 1921; reprint, Taipei: Commercial Press, 1979), 1743; and Verhaeren, "Notes bibliographiques," 188.

25. Huang Yilong, "Zhongxiao beifang yu shizijia: Mingmo Tianzhu-jiao-tu Wei Xuelian qiren," *Xinxue* 8, no. 3 (1997): 77. See also Frederic Wakeman Jr., *The Great Enterprise* (Berkeley and Los Angeles: University of California Press, 1985), 1: 274 n.

26. Arthur Hummel, ed., *Eminent Chinese of the Ch'ing Period* (Washington, D.C.: United States Government Printing Office, 1943), 671, 893; and L. Carrington Goodrich and Chaoying Fang, eds., *Dictionary of Ming Biography* (New York: Columbia University Press, 1976), 275, 708, 1306.

27. Shang, *Tian Ru yin,* Wei Xuequ preface, p. 1a, 2a–b.

28. Shang, *Tian Ru yin,* Wei Xueqin preface, p. 1b.

29. Shang, *Tian Ru yin,* Wei Xuequ preface, p. 2b.

30. *Zhengxue liushi* exists in the following forms: (1) Two copies in BAV: Borgia Cinese 369.11° (Pelliot-Takata, p. 39); Raccolta Generale Oriente 247. 3° (Pelliot-Takata, p. 84). The Vatican copy of the *Zhengxue liushi* was reprinted in the collection *Tianzhujiao dongchuan wenxian sanbian* (Third collection of documents on the spread of Catholicism to the East), ed. Wu Xiangxiang, 6 vols. (Taipei: Taiwan Xuesheng Shuju, 1972) 1: 89–266. (2) Three copies in BNF, Courant 7154 (appears to be identical to BAV copy), 7155, 7156 (without prefaces). (3) The Zikawei Library of Shanghai has a partial handwritten copy missing the last one-third of the work. Otherwise, the Zikawei copy is identical to the BAV printed copy.

31. Shang, *Tian Ru yin* (BAV copy), preface, p. 2a.

32. Shang, *Tian Ru yin zheng*, Run Wangbi preface, 3.

33. Shang Huqing, *Zhengxue liushi* (BAV copy), 1a.

34. S.F. 8: 113–14.

35. Shang, preface to *Zhengxue liushi*, p. 4a.

36. Shang, preface to *Zhengxue liushi*, p. 2b.

37. Shang, preface to *Zhengxue liushi*, p. 3a. Cf. *Zhongyong* (Doctrine of the mean), chap. 1.

38. Shang, preface to *Zhengxue liushi*, p. 3b.

39. The introduction is dated the fifteenth day of the eighth lunar month in the third year of the Kangxi reign (October 4, 1664). Shang Huqing, *Bu Ru wengao*, introduction, 11.

40. Run Wangbi in his preface to *Tian Ru yin zheng* (p. 3) wrote that the work consisted of four parts.

41. Unable to obtain access to the original copy of the *Bu Ru wengao* in the Zikawei Library (Shanghai) or even a microfilm or photocopy thereof, I was forced to rely upon a copy that had been transcribed by hand about 1979 owned by the Sinologisch Instituut in Leiden. This copy divides the work into four parts, each with separate pagination as follows: pt. 1, 1–105 (the table of contents of the entire work is found on 1: 2–3 and the introduction on 1: 4–11); pt. 2, 1–70; pt. 3, 1–87; and pt. 4, 1–112. All endnote references that follow are to the transcribed copy.

42. Shang, *Bu Ru wengao*, introduction, 1: 10.

43. Lisha was located in the Licheng district, which was an earlier name for the provincial capital of Ji'nan. *Zhongguo gujin diming dacidian* (Comprehensive dictionary of ancient and modern Chinese place names), ed. Zang Lihe (Shanghai: Commercial Press, 1931; reprint Hong Kong: Commercial Press, 1982), 1220–21.

44. Shang, *Bu Ru wengao*, 1: 12, 3: 1.

45. Bernhard Karlgren, *The Book of Odes: Chinese Text, Transcription, and Translation* (Stockholm: Museum of Far Eastern Antiquities, 1950), 229; and Arthur Waley, *The Book of Songs* (London: George Allen & Unwin, 1937; reprint, New York: Grove, 1960), 142.

46. Legge, *Chinese Classics*, 5: 288, 290.

47. *Bu* is found in the following: *Mencius* Ib.4 (two occurrences), IIIa.1, IIIb.4, VIb.7, VIIa.13.

48. Xu Wending, *Taixi shuifa* (Western hydraulics) in *Tianxue chuhan* (The first collection of writings on the Heavenly Learning, ed. Li Zhizao, 52 *juan* (1628; reprint, Taipei: Taiwan Suesheng Shuju, 1965) 3: 1506. *Taixi shuifa* was later included in Xu's

Nongzheng quanshu (An encyclopedia on agriculture), 60 *juan* (1625–1628) and eventually copied in this form into the *Siku quanshu* (Complete library in four branches of literature). See Hummel, *Eminent Chinese,* 317–18.

49. *Zhongguo renmin dacidian,* 1610–11; and Goodrich and Fang, *Dictionary of Ming Biography,* 237–39.

50. Meng Ruwang (José Monteiro, S.J.), *Tianxue lueyi* (A summary of the Heavenly Teaching), 26a, in *Tianzhujiao dongchuan wenxian xubian* (A continuation of a collection of writings from the Eastern mission of the Catholic Church), ed. Wu Xiangxiang, (Taipei: Taiwan Xuesheng Shuju, 1966), 2: 899.

51. Prime Minister Qian Saian (i.e., Qian Shisheng) of Wutang is quoted as stating: "By replacing what our *ru* have lost, Christianity is unique, and conserves and reforms the other sects." This quotation is found in the prefatory material to chap. 2 in Lionel M. Jensen, *Manufacturing Confucianism* (Durham, N.C.: Duke University Press, 1997), 78. The passage is attributed to Father Joao Monteiro with no other identification of the source.

52. Shang, *Bu Ru wengao,* introduction, 1: 4.

53. Shang, *Bu Ru wengao,* introduction, 1: 4.

54. Zhu Xi, *Sishu zhangju jizhu,* 1a. Cf. Legge, *Chinese Classics,* 1: 382; Chan, *Source Book,* 97.

55. Shang, *Bu Ru wengao,* 1: 12.

56. Arthur Waley, trans., *The Analects of Confucius* (London: George Allen & Unwin, 1938), 90. Cf. the translation by Wing-tsit Chan: "A man who reviews the old so as to find out the new is qualified to teach others" (*Source Book,* 23).

57. Shang, *Bu Ru wengao,* introduction, 1: 5.

58. Chan, *Source Book,* 36.

59. Shang, *Bu Ru wengao,* 2: 29–30.

60. Shang, *Bu Ru wengao,* introduction, 1: 6.

61. Shang, *Bu Ru wengao,* introduction, 1: 6.

62. The transcribed copy of the *Bu Ru wengao* at my disposal refers to Father Sambiasi as "Jinliang Bi xiansheng shenfu" (the Reverend Father Master Jinliang Bi). Sambiasi's Chinese name is normally presented as Bi Jinliang (Fangji). He was born in Cosenza, which was in the southern Kingdom of Naples. He entered into the Jesuit novitiate in 1602 at twenty years of age and departed for the Indies in 1609.

63. After Sambiasi was forced to leave Beijing, instead of returning to Macau, he was assisted by the literatus Ignatius Sun Yuanhua (d. 1632) in going to Jiading, just northwest of Shanghai. There he was hospitably provided with lodgings and a chapel in a school. This incident is mentioned in A. Semedo, *Histoire universelle de la Chine* (Paris, 1645), 336 f., cited in Louis Pfister, S.J., *Notices biographiques et bibliographiques sur les Jésuites de l'ancienne mission de Chine, 1552 à 1773.* Variétés Sinologiques 59 and 60 (Shanghai: Imprimerie de la mission catholique, 1932–34; reprint [2 vols. in 1], Taipei: Chinese Materials Center, 1976), 137. Sun was a native of Jiading who had attained the juren degree in 1612 (Hummel, *Eminent Chinese,* 686). He studied mathematics and weaponry under Xu Guangqi. In 1630 he was appointed governor of Dengzhou and Laizhou in the Shandong peninsula, but he fell into disgrace and was executed by the Ming authorities in 1632, over the protests of his mentor, Xu Guangqi.

64. Daniello Bartoli, *Dell'historia della Compagnia de Giesu: La Cina* (Rome, 1663), 1109 f., cited in Pfister, *Notices biographiques,* 139.

65. Joseph Dehergne, *Répertoire des Jésuites de Chine de 1552 à 1800* (Rome: Institutum Historicum S.I., 1973), 238; Pfister, *Notices biographiques,* 138.

66. Shang, *Bu Ru wen gao,* introduction, 1: 6–7.

67. Western dates were not part of Shang's presentation, but I have added them for historical clarification.

68. Shang, *Bu Ru wengao,* introduction, 1: 7.

69. Shang, *Bu Ru wengao,* introduction, 1: 9.

70. Shang, *Bu Ru wengao,* introduction, 1: 7.

71. Shang, *Bu Ru wengao,* introduction, 1: 7–8.

72. Shang, *Bu Ru wengao,* introduction, 1: 8.

73. Shang, *Bu Ru wengao,* introduction, 1: 9.

74. Shang, *Bu Ru wengao,* 1: 12.

75. Shang, *Bu Ru wengao,* 1: 32.

76. Shang, *Bu Ru wengao,* 1: 32–33.

77. Shang, *Bu Ru wengao,* 1: 33.

78. Shang, *Bu Ru wengao,* 2: 4.

79. Shang, *Bu Ru wengao,* 2: 15.

80. Zhang Xingyao, *Tianjiao mingbian zixu,* reprinted in Xu Zongze, *Ming-Qing jian,* 122. The original source of this phrase was the Neo-Confucian philosopher Lu Xiangshan (Jiuyuan) in *Lu Xiangshan quanji,* 36 juan (1521; reprint, Hong Kong, n.d.), *juan* 36, p. 317.

81. Shang, *Bu Ru wengao* 1: 42. The term *gongshi* (engineer) was probably borrowed by Shang from Father Giulio Aleni's *Sanshan lunxue ji,* 1 juan (Hangzhou, ca. 1627), in *Tianzhujiao dongchuan wenxian xubian,* ed. Wu Xiangxiang, 1: 444 (f. 5b).

82. Shang, *Bu Ru wengao* 1: 43.

83. Shang, *Bu Ru wengao,* 2: 7.

84. Shang, *Bu Ru wengao,* 2: 8.

85. Anne Birrell, *Chinese Mythology: An Introduction* (Baltimore: Johns Hopkins University Press, 1993), 24.

86. Shang, *Bu Ru wengao,* 1: 34.

87. Shang, *Bu Ru wengao,* 1: 34-35.

88. Shang, *Bu Ru wengao,* 1: 35.

89. Derk Bodde, "Myths of Ancient China," in *Essays on Chinese Civilization,* ed. Charles Le Blanc and Dorothy Borei (Princeton, N.J.: Princeton University Press, 1981), 62–65.

90. Cao Xueqin, *The Story of the Stone,* trans. David Hawkes. (Harmondsworth, England: Penguin, 1993) 1: 47.

91. Bodde, "Myths of Ancient China," 62. See illustration in Yuan Ke, *Dragons and Dynasties: An Introduction to Chinese Mythology,* trans. Kim Echlin and Nie Zhixiong. (London: Penguin, and Beijing: Foreign Language Press, 1991), 6.

92. The term *Daotong* (Transmission of the Way) was first developed in the Song, and the earliest occurrence has been traced to 1136 by James T. C. Liu. (See John Winthrop Haeger, "The Intellectual Context of Neo-Confucian Syncretism," *Journal of Asian Stud-*

ies 31 [1972]: 504.) Although new to the twelfth century, the term was an elaboration of a continuous literati tradition and the mark of the tradition's creative vitality.

93. Shang, *Bu Ru wengao*, 1: 35.

94. Shang, *Bu Ru wengao*, 1: 31. Ode 235, translated in Chan, *Source Book*, 113. Cf. *Odes* I.i.I.7 (Legge, *Chinese Classics*, 1: 431), cited in *Doctrine of the Mean* 33:6 (Legge, *Chinese Classics*, 1: 433).

95. Legge, *Chinese Classics*, 1: 385, 454; and Chan, *Source Book*, 98

96. The copy of the *Wanwu benmo yueyan* cited here is preserved in the BNF, Chinois 6971; 2, 23 folios. 156; 2,640 characters (eight lines per page and 15 characters per line). This is a copy of the reprint made ca. 1680 at the Gospel Church (Fuyin Tang) located in the eastern part of Yangren Alley in the western suburbs of Canton, also known as Zhujiang. The church was located at the Small South Gate (Xiaonanmen) on Huata Street. See Joseph Dehergne, S.I., "La Chine du Sud-Ouest: Guangxi (Kwangsi) et Guangdong (Kwangtung), Étude de géographie missionnaire," *Archivum Historicum Societatis Iesu* 45 (1976): 18, 22–24. Also see Antonio Sisto Rosso, O.F.M., "Pedro de la Pañuela, O.F.M.," *Franciscan Studies* 8 (1948): 273–74.

97. Antonio de Santa Maria Caballero, preface to *Wanwu benmo yueyan*, preface, 1a.

98. Caballero, *Wanwu benmo yueyan*, 1b.

99. Caballero, *Wanwu benmo yueyan*, 1a, 23a.

100. Caballero, *Wanwu benmo yueyan*, 9a.

101. Caballero, *Wanwu benmo yueyan*, 9b.

102. S.F. 2: 427.

103. S.F. 2: 428.

104. Goodrich and Fang, *Dictionary of Ming Biography*, 30.

105. Father Antonio Sisto Rosso estimated that *Wanwu benmo yueyan* was reprinted at Zhujiang "about 1680," but he gives no documentation for that date. Goodrich and Fang, *Dictionary of Ming Biography*, 30.

Chapter 3

1. *Sinica Franciscana*, vol. 3, *Relationes et epistolas Fratrum Minorum saeculi 17*, ed. P. Anastasius van den Wyngaert, O.F.M. (Quaracchi-Florence: Collegium S. Bonaventurae, 1936), 333. (Hereafter cited as S.F. 3.)

2. *Sinica Franciscana*, vol. 7, *: Relationes et epistolas Fratrum Minorum Hispanorum in Sinis qui a. 1672–81 missionem ingressi sunt*, ed. Georgius Mensaert, O.F.M., in collaboration with Fortunato Margiotti and Sixto Rosso, O.F.M. (Rome: Segretaria delle Missioni, 1965), 123. (Hereafter cited as S.F. 7).

3. S.F. 7: 123–24..

4. S.F. 7: 125.

5. S.F. 7: 126.

6. S.F. 3: 463, 466–67.

7. S.F. 3: 464.

8. S.F. 3: 467.

9. S.F. 3: 465.

10. S.F. 3: 468.

11. S.F. 3: 468–69.

12. Charles O. Hucker, *A Dictionary of Official Titles in Imperial China* (Stanford, Calif.: Stanford University Press, 1985), 89.

13. S.F. 3: 470.

14. S.F. 3: 470.

15. In one letter, Paschale mentioned 350 pesos and in another letter, 400 pesos. S.F. 3: 472, 478.

16. S.F. 3: 472.

17. S.F. 3: 478.

18. S.F. 3: 474–75.

19. S.F. 3: 490–91.

20. S.F. 3: 476.

21. S.F. 3: 477.

22. S.F. 3: 477.

23. S.F. 3: 490.

24. S.F. 3: 510–11.

25. S.F. 3: 493.

26. S.F. 3: 509.

27. S.F. 3: 509–10.

28. S.F. 3: 482–83.

29. S.F. 3: 220–22, 495.

30. S.F. 3: 496.

31. S.F. 3: 498.

32. S.F. 3: 497.

33. S.F. 3: 216–17.

34. S.F. 3: 218–19.

35. S.F. 3: 512.

36. S.F. 3: 513.

37. S.F. 3: 220.

38. S.F. 3: 506–7.

39. S.F. 3: 498–99.

40. S.F. 3: 223.

41. S.F. 3: 225.

42. S.F. 3: 226.

43. S.F. 3: 531.

44. S.F. 7: 1217.

45. S.F. 7: 1218.

46. S.F. 7: 1219.

47. See S.F. 7: 1227; and Joseph Dehergne, "Les missions du nord de la Chine vers 1700," *Archivum Historicum Societatis Iesu* 24 (1955): 265.

48. S.F. 7: 1221.

49. S.F. 7: 1221; and S.F. 8: 825–26.

50. S.F. 7: 1222.

51. *Sinica Franciscana,* vol. 8, *Relationes et epistolas Fratrum Minorum hispanorum in*

Sinis qui a. 1684–92 missionem ingressi sunt, ed. Fortunatus Margiotti, O.F.M. 2 parts (Rome: Segreteria delle Missioni, 1975), 145. (Hereafter cited as S.F. 8.)

52. S.F. 8: 146.

53. S.F. 8: 155.

54. Lin Fujun and Shi Song, eds., *Qing shi biannian* (Annals of Qing history), 3 vols. (Beijing: Zhongguo Renmin Daxue Chubanshe, 1988), vol. 2, pt. 1, 490; and letter of Father J. Valat to Noyelle de Car, May 1685, Jap.-Sin. 163, sheet 275r–275v.

55. Maxwell K. Hearn, "Document and Portrait: The Southern Tour of Paintings of Kangxi and Qianlong." In *Chinese Painting under the Qianlong Emperor: The Symposium Papers in Two Volumes,* ed. Ju-hsi Chou and Claudia Brown. *Phoebus* 6, no. 1 (1988): 92–93.

56. Jonathan D. Spence, *Ts'ao Yin and the K'ang-hsi Emperor, Bondservant and Master.* (New Haven: Yale University Press, 1996), 126.

57. Hearn, "Document and Portrait," 111.

58. Hearn, "Document and Portrait," 112.

59. Hearn, "Document and Portrait," 113, 116.

60. S.F. 8: 155.

61. S.F. 8: 157.

62. S.F. 3: 743.

63. S.F. 3: 743 & S. F., viii, 159.

64. S.F. 3: 743; S.F. 8: 157; Lin and Shi, *Qing shi biannian,* vol. 2, pt. 1, 490.

65. S.F. 8: 158.

66. S.F. 3: 743 & S.F. 8: 159.

67. S.F. 8: 159.

68. S.F. 3: 744; and D. E. Mungello, *The Forgotten Christians of Hangzhou* (Honolulu: University of Hawaii, 1994), 60–61.

69. S.F. 8: 57.

70. S.F. 8: 58.

71. S.F. 8: 59.

72. S.F. 8: 69.

73. S.F. 8: 70–71.

74. S.F. 8: 72.

75. *Sinica Franciscana,* vol. 9, *Relationes et epistolas Fratrum Minorum Hispanorum in Sinis qui annis 1697–98 missionem ingressi sunt,* comp. and annotated by Father Fortunatus Margiotti, O.F.M.; prepared for publication and corrected by Fathers Gaspar Han (Han Chengliang) and Antolin Abad, O.F.M. (Madrid: Segreteria delle Missioni, 1995), 574. (Hereafter cited as S.F. 9.)

76. Lorenzo Perez, "La venerable orden tercera y la Archicofradia del Cordón en el Extremo Oriente," *Archivo Ibero-Americana* 33 (1930): 64.

77. S.F. 9: 574.

78. S.F. 9: 575.

79. S.F. 9: 576.

80. S.F. 9: 577.

81. S.F. 9: 578.

82. S.F. 9: 581.

83. Palencia cared for Christians in the small towns of the Linqu, Qingzhou (now

Yidu), Shouguang, Xincheng, Putai, Gaoyuan, Boxing, Mengyin, Xintai, Weixian, Laizhou (Yixian), Dengzhou (now Penglai), and Yizhou districts. S.F. 9: 582.

84. S.F. 9: 582.
85. S.F. 9: 583.
86. S.F. 9: 583–84.
87. S.F. 9: 585.
88. S.F. 9: 588.

Chapter 4

1. *Sinica Franciscana, vol. 8, Relationes et epistolas Fratrum Minorum Hispanorum in Sinis qui a. 1684–92 missionem ingressi sunt,* ed. Fortunatus Margiotti, O.F.M. (Rome: Segreteria delle Missioni, 1975), 819. [Hereafter cited as S.F. 8.]

2. S.F. 8: 853 n.
3. S.F. 8: 820.
4. S.F. 8: 842, 846, 847.
5. S.F. 8: 841.
6. S.F. 8: 842.

7. S.F. 8: 843. Jean Charbonnier, M.E.P., translates *huizhang* as "local community leader" in his article "The Interpretation of Christian History," in *Historiography of the Chinese Catholic Church, Nineteenth and Twentieth Centuries,* ed. Jeroom Heyndrickx, C.I.C.M. (Leuven: Ferdinand Verbiest Foundation, 1994), 41.

8. 1 Timothy 5: 17–18 states: "Elders who do well as leaders should be reckoned worthy of a double stipend, in particular those who labor at preaching and teaching. For Scripture says, 'You shall not muzzle a threshing ox' ; and besides, 'the worker earns his pay'" (New English Bible).

9. S.F. 8: 844.
10. S.F. 8: 845.

11. A book in Chinese printed in 1683 entitled *Rule of the Holy Rope (Shengsu Guitiao)* explained the rules of receiving the scapular and the sacred rope of SaintFrancis. S.F. 8: 845.

12. S.F. 8: 846.
13. S.F. 8: 847.

14. Christopher F. Black, *Italian Confraternities in the Sixteenth Century* (Cambridge: Cambridge University Press, 1989), ix, 1.

15. Black, *Italian Confraternities,* 7–8.

16. Louis Pfister, S.J., *Notices biographiques et bibliographiques sur les Jésuites de l'ancienne mission de Chine, 1552 à 1773,* Variétés Sinologiques no. 59 and 60. (Shanghai: Imprimerie de la Mission Catholique, 1932–34; reprint [2 vols in 1] Taipei: Chinese Materials Center, 1976), 226–27.

17. See Gail King, "Christian Charity in Seventeenth-Century China," *Sino-Western Cultural Relations Journal* 22 (2000): 13–30; and Joanna F. Handlin Smith, "Benevolent Societies: The Reshaping of Charity during the Late Ming and Early Ch'ing," *Journal of Asian Studies* 46, no. 2 (1987): 309–35.

18. H. Verhaeren, C.M., "Ordonnances de la Sainte Eglise" (*Shengjiao guicheng*), *Monumenta Serica* (Peiping) 4 (1939–40): art. 23, p. 465; art. 33, p. 472.

Shortly before 1940, Father Verhaeren, the librarian of the Beitang Library in Beijing, discovered in that old collection a Chinese text of church regulations. The text was undated and signed only with the characters *Li bei*. Verhaeren interpreted the signature as a traditional literati form in which the author out of modesty (and to create a witty puzzle) signs a work with the second and last character of his two-character given name (*ming*), in this case, "Li." "Bei" referred to his collaborators. Verhaeren traced the origin of the work to a meeting of missionaries held during their expulsion to Canton during the years 1665–1671. The abbreviated signature is said to be that of Father Feliciano Pacheco (Cheng Jili, 1622–1687), who as Jesuit vice provincial during the years 1669–1669 and 1672–1673, would have had the authority to sign such a document during that time. (Verhaeren, "Ordonnances de la Sainte Eglise," 451–53).

19. Fernández-Oliver to Bañeza, 1703, S.F. 8: 854–55.

20. *New Catholic Encyclopedia* 5: 954–55, s.v. "Flagellation."

21. *New Catholic Encyclopedia* 4: 895, s.v. "The Discipline."

22. Yang Liansheng, "Daojiao zhi zibo yu Fojiao zhi zipu" (The self-pummeling of Daoism and the self-beating of Buddhism), in *Tsukamoto Hakushi Shoju Kinen Bukkyoshi Gakuronshu* (Essays on the history of Buddhism presented to Professor Zenryu Tsukamoto on his retirement) (Kyoto: Research Institute for Humanistic Studies of Kyoto University, 1961), 962–69.

23. Yang, "Daojiao zhi zibo," 968.

24. Jonathan Chaves, "Moral Action in the Poetry of Wu Chia-chi (1618–84)," *Harvard Journal of Asiatic Studies* 46 (1986): 4222.

25. "Third Orders," *New Catholic Encyclopedia* 14: 93–97; 4: 154.

26. P. Lorenzo Perez, "La venerable orden tercera y la Archicofradia del Cordón en el Extremo Oriente," *Archivo Ibero-Americano* 33 (1930): 63; and A. Caballero, letter of November 20, 1649, in *Sinica Franciscana,* vol. 2, *Relationes et epistolas Fratrum Minorum saeculi 16 et 17,* ed. Anastasius van den Wyngaert, O.F.M. (Quaracchi-Florence: Collegium S. Bonaventurae, 1933), 394. (Hereafter cited as S.F. 2.)

27. Perez, "La venerable orden tercera," 64.

28. Perez, "La venerable orden tercera," 63.

29. Perez, "La venerable orden tercera," 64.

30. S.F. 8: 821.

31. *Sinica Franciscana,* vol. 7, *Relationes et epistolas Fratrum Minorum Hispanorum in Sinis qui a. 1672–81 missionem ingressi sunt,* ed. Georgius Mensaert, O.F.M., in collaboration with Fortunato Margiotti and Sixto Rosso, O.F.M. (Rome: Segretaria delle Missioni, 1965), 46 (hereafter cited as S.F. 7); and S.F. 8: 854.

32. S.F. 8: 854.

33. S.F. 7: 46.

34. S.F. 8: 877.

35. S.F. 8: 824.

36. S.F. 8: 877 n.

37. S.F. 8: 878 n. The title is "Ku ji Sheng Fangjige Sanhui Gui." The first folio is reproduced in S.F. 8, table 10 (between pages 878 and 879). The entire text is preserved in Castorano (Orazio), *De rebus sinensibus,* doc. 1.

38. S.F. 8: 849.

39. S.F. 8: 850.

40. S.F. 8: 850–51.

41. S.F. 8: 851.

42. Maxwell K. Hearn, "Document and Portrait: The Southern Tour of Paintings of Kangxi and Qianlong," in *Chinese Painting under the Qianlong Emperor; The Symposium Papers in Two Volumes*, ed. Ju-hsi Chou and Claudia Brown, *Phoebus* 6, no. 1 (1988): 92.

43. Lin Fujun and Shi Song, eds., *Qing shi biannian* (Annals of Qing history) (Beijing: Zhongguo Renmin Daxue Chubanshe, 1988.), 2: 2, 214.

44. Fernández-Oliver to Bañeza, 1703, in S.F. 8: 858.

45. Testimony by Fernández-Oliver presented to papal legate M. de Tournon, October 4, 1706, in S.F. 8: 869.

46. Fernández-Oliver writes that the emperor encounted Faglia "fifteen leagues" (about forty-five miles) outside the city, but the distance is unlikely to have been that great. Fernández-Oliver to Bañeza, 1703, in S.F. 8: 859.

47. S.F. 8: 852 n. 2; and Joseph Dehergne, S.I., *Répertoire des Jésuites de Chine de 1552 à 1800* (Rome: Institutum Historicum S. I., 1973), 27. After the Kangxi Emperor's tour passed through Ji'nan, Fernández-Oliver wrote a short letter dated March 25, 1703, to the Belgian Jesuit Father Antoine Thomas in Beijing, thanking him for the assistance of the Beijing fathers in the emperor's tour and commenting favorably on the behavior of the Jesuit Brothers Baudino and Frappieri, who accompanied the emperor (S.F. 8: 852).

48. S.F. 8: 822; and Dehergne, *Répertoire*, 27, 101.

49. Fernández-Oliver to Tournon, 1706, in S.F. 8: 870.

50. Shang Huqing and Li Andang [Antonio Caballero, O.F.M.], *Zhengxue liushi* (The touchstone of True Knowledge), p. 1a, reprinted in *Tianzhujiao dongchuan wenxian sanbian* (Third collection of documents on the spread of Catholicism to the East), ed. Wu Xiangxiang (Taipei: Taiwan Xuesheng Shuju, 1972), 1: 93.

51. Shang and Li, *Zhengxue liushi* (The touchstone of True Knowledge), pp. 2a–4b; reprint ed., 1: 95–100.

52. S.F. 8: 114. Permission to print the work had been given by the Franciscan commissioner Father José Navarro. This permission had probably been secured during Navarro's brief visit to Ji'nan in 1698. He departed from Canton on April 6 and arrived on June 13, the day of Saint Anthony of Padua (1195–1231), in Shandong province at Jining, where Nieto-Díaz was the priest. He moved on to Taian and then to Ji'nan. Finally, the title page noted that the work had been printed with woodblocks at the Tianqu Tianzhu Tang (the Lord of Heaven Hall located on the Imperial Way), which was another name for the East Church. S.F. 8: 878 and table 10.

53. The first page of *Moxiang shengong* indicates that the work was written by Father Shi Duolu, Zhenduo (Petrus de la Piñuela, O.F.M.), and revised jointly by Father En Maoxiu (José Navarro, O.F.M.), Father Li Anding, Weizhi (Augustinus a Sancti Paschale, O.F.M.), and Father Mai Ningxue, Zhiwen (Bernardino de las Llagas Mercado, O.F.M.). For more information on Piñuela, see Antonio Sisto Rosso, "Pedro de la Piñuela, O.F.M., Mexican Missionary to China and Author," *Franciscan Studies* 8 (1948): 250–74.

54. Fernández-Oliver to Bañeza, 1703, S.F. 8: 856; Paul Pelliot, *Inventaire sommaire des manuscrits et imprimés chinois de la Bibliothèque Vaticaine*, rev. and ed. Takata Tokio

(Kyoto: Instituto Italiano di Cultura Scuola di Studi sull'Asia Orientale, 1955), . 85, 92. As of July 1996, *Shengjiao zongdu jingwen* was still missing from the Vatican Library. A description of the contents of this Franciscan prayer book printed in 1701–2 in Ji'nan is found in Paul Brunner, S.J., *L'euchologe de la mission de Chine, editio princeps 1628 et développements jusqu'à nos jours*. (Münster: Aschendorffsche, 1964), 99–108.

55. Brunner, "L'euchologe de la mission de Chine," 84–85.

56. S.F. 8: 821.

57. There is some uncertainty about whether a new East Church was built or whether the old East Church was simply extensively reconstructed. In spite of the contradictory references, I interpret it to have been a radical reconstruction of the original church.

58. S.F. 8: 855.

59. S.F. 8: 821, 855.

60. S.F. 8: 821, 855–56, 868.

61. S.F. 8: 868.

62. S.F. 8: 869. Cf. S.F. 8: 856.

63. S.F. 8: 855–56.

64. S.F. 8: 862–64.

65. S.F. 8: 864.

66. Arthur Hummel, ed., *Eminent Chinese of the Ch'ing Period* (Washington, D.C.: United States Government Printing Office, 1943), 451.

67. S.F. 8: 862-863.

68. See J. S. Cummins, *A Question of Rites: Friar Domingo Navarrete and the Jesuits in China* (Aldershot, England: Scolar, 1993), 8, 22–32 et passim.

69. S.F. 8: 866.

70. S.F. 8: 866–67. Dehergne, *Répertoire*, 100, places França in Ji'nan on October 13 or November 13, 1696.

71. S.F. 8: 867–68.

72. A French translation of this passage reads: "de louver leurs Maisons a le prostituées publiques pour a tirer un plus grand profit." See "Déclaration faite à Monsieur le Cardinal de Tournon par le Reverend Père Michel Fernandez," in *Anecdotes sur l'état de la religion dans la China* (Paris, 1739), 2: 314.

73. S.F. 8: 822.

74. S.F. 8: 822–23.

75. Pfister, *Notices biographiques*, 566.

76. S.F. 9: 581.

77. Dehergne, *Répertoire*, 100.

78. Fernández-Oliver indicated that the funeral negotiations were complex and vexing. See his letter to Orazio, March 13, 1718, in S.F. 8: 952.

79. K. Stumpf, S.J., "Regestum generale funerum patris Franchi," in Castorano (Orazio), *De rebus sinensibus*, doc. 23, cited in S.F. 8: 973–74.

80. S.F. 8: 973 n.

81. In 1847 Father Benjamin Brueyre, S.J. (Li Xiufang Yaming), visited the Chenjialou cemetery and found gravestone epitaphs for Diestel and Valat, but not for Franchi. Brueyre, letter of September 30, 1847, in *Lettres des Nouvelles Missions*(1846–1852), 2: 135–40 (82nd letter). Also see Brueyre's letter dated September 30 at Ji'nan, in *Annales de la propagation de la foi* (Lyon, 1849), 21: 309.

82. When I visited the site in March 1997, I found a dedication stone with parallel inscriptions in Chinese (left) and Latin (right) over the entrance to the Chenjialou Saint-Joseph Church. The year of dedication given in the Latin inscription is MDCCCCIX (1909). After being closed during the Cultural Revolution, the church was reopened on December 23, 1987. See Jean Charbonnier, M.E.P., ed., *Guide to the Catholic Church in China/Zhongguo Tianzhujiao zhinan* (Singapore: China Catholic Communications, 1989), 284.

83. *Sinica Franciscana, vol. 6, Relationes et epistolas primorum Fratrum Minorum Italorum in Sinia (saeculis 17 et 18),* ed. Georgius Mensaert, O.F.M., in collaboration with Fortunato Margiotti, O.F.M., and [Antonio] Sixto Rosso, O.F.M. (Rome: Segreteria delle Missioni, 1961), 745–46.

84. S.F. 8: 970.

85. S.F. 8: 971.

86. S.F. 8: 972.

87. R. G. Tiedemann, "Christianity and Chinese 'Heterodox Sects': Mass Conversion and Syncretism in Shandong Province in the Early Eighteenth Century," *Monumenta Serica* 44 (1996): 376.

88. S.F. 8: 973.

89. S.F. 8: 974.

90. Letter of Bishop Della Chiesa to Fr. F. Serrano, O.F.M., May 10, 1720, in *Sinica Franciscana,* vol. 5, *Relationes et epistolas Illmi D. Fr. Bernardini della Chiesa O.F.M.,* ed. Anastasius van den Wyngaert, O.F.J., and Georgius Mensaert, O.F.M. (Rome: Collegium s. Antonii, 1954), 757. (Hereafter referred to as S.F. 5.)

91. S.F. 9: 286–87.

92. S.F. 8: 975.

93. S.F. 8: 975. The heroic Jewish leader Judas Maccabeus led a successful revolt against the tyrannical Syrian ruler Antiochus IV. In freeing Judah, Maccabeus reoccupied Jerusalem and rededicated the Temple (165 B.C.), an event celebrated by the feast of Hanukkah. In the passage 2 Maccabees 12:43, which Fernández-Oliver cites, a number of Jews had fallen in battle because they carried under their tunics amulets sacred to the idols of Jamnia, which violated the Mosaic First Commandment. Judas offered an atoning sacrifice to free the dead from their sin by levying a contribution from each man, which yielded two thousand silver drachmas. This amount he sent to Jerusalem as a sin offering. According to the passage in 2 Maccabees, in doing so, Judas was anticipating the resurrection because it would have been foolish to pray for the dead if he had not expected them to rise again.

94. S.F. 8: 976.

95. A second version of Ripa's drawing of the West Church floor plan exists. It differs only slightly from the first version and appears to be a later version because identifying letters and numbers have been added to the drawing. This second version is reproduced in S.F. 8: table 12 (between pages 976 and 977). It first appeared in Matthaeus Ripa, *Giornale de' viaggi fatti da me D. Matteo Ripa diviso in tre parti,* October 3, 1717 (Archivum Generale Ordinis Fratrum Minorum, Romae). However, a letter dated October 10, 2000, from Father Ponciano Macabalo, O.F.M., the current secretary general of the Franciscan Mission in Rome, informed me that the original of this second version of Ripa's drawing was, at the moment, lost.

96. The phrases "*Shi si ru shi sheng*" and "*Shi wang ru shi cun*" are from *Li ji*, chapter *Zheng Yi*, in *Shisan jing zhu shu* (notes and commentary on the Thirteen Classics), a photolithographic edition based on *Shisan jing zhu shu jiaokanji*, compiled by Ruan Yuan and originally printed in 1806, 2 vols. (Beijing: Zhonghua Shuju Chuban, 1980), 1639 top.

97. E. Bruce Brooks and A. Taeko Brooks, trans., *The Original Analects: Sayings of Confucius and His Successors* (New York: Columbia University Press, 1998), 82. Cf. James Legge, trans., *The Chinese Classics* (Oxford: Oxford University Press, 1893), 1: 159; and Arthur Waley, trans., *The Analects of Confucius* (London: George Allen & Unwin, 1938), 97.

98. S.F. 8: 975 n. 29.

99. S.F. 8: 976.

100. See Susan Naquin, "Funerals in North China: Uniformity and Variation," in *Death Ritual in Late Imperial and Modern China*, ed. James L. Watson and Evelyn S. Rawski (Berkeley and Los Angeles: University of California, 1988), 41.

101. S.F. 8: 976 n. 31.

102. Charles O. Hucker, *A Dictionary of Official Titles in Imperial China* (Stanford, Calif.: Stanford University Press, 1985), 84.

103. S.F. 8: 952 n. 20.

104. Castorano (Orazio), *De rebus sinensibus*, doc. 23.

105. S.F. 8: 971 & S.F., ix, 288.

106. S.F. 5: 746.

Chapter 5

1. Antonio Sisto Rosso, O.F.M., *Apostolic Legations to China of the Eighteenth Century* (South Pasadena, Calif.: P. D. & Ione Perkins, 1948), 127; and Virgile Pinot, *La Chine et la formation de l'esprit philosophique en France (1640–1740)* (Paris, 1932), 86.

2. Georges Mensaert, O.F.M., "Les Franciscains au service de la Propagande dans la province de Pékin, 1705–1785," *Archivum Franciscanum Historicum* 51 (1958): 163.

3. *New Catholic Encyclopedia*, 11: 840–41, s.v. "Propagation of the Faith, Congregation for the"; and Henri Daniel-Rops, *The Church in the Eighteenth Century*, trans. John Warrington (Garden City, N.J.: Image Books, 1966), 103. The official title of Propaganda was changed in 1967 to Congregatio pro Gentium Evangelizatione de Propaganda Fide (Congregazione per l'Evangelizzazione dei Popoli o "de Propaganda Fide").

4. Kenneth Scott Latourette, *A History of Christian Missions in China,* (London: Society for Promoting Christian Knowledge, 1929), 113.

5. *New Catholic Encyclopedia* 14: 176–77, s.v. "Titular Bishop."

6. Rosso, *Apostolic Legations,* 126. Della Chiesa was born in Venice. He entered the Franciscan order at the age of nineteen and was ordained in 1663 and given the name of Bernardus. He belonged to the Franciscan province of Assisi. *Sinica Franciscana*, vol. 5, *Relationes et epistolas Illmi D. Fr. Bernardini della Chiesa O.F.M.,* ed. Anastasius van den Wyngaert, O.F.J., and Georgius Mensaert, O.F.M. (Rome: Collegium s. Antonii, 1954), 3. (Hereafter cited as S.F. 5.)

7. Anastase Van den Wyngaert, O.F.M., "Le patronat portugais et Mgr. Bernardin della Chiesa," *Archivum Franciscanum Historicum* 35 (1942): 8.

8. Wyngaert, "La patronat portugais," 22.

9. *Sinica Franciscana,* vol. 8, *Relationes et epistolas Fratrum Minorum Hispanorum in Sinis qui a. 1684–92 missionem ingressi sunt,* ed. Fortunatus Margiotti, O.F.M. 2 parts (Rome: Segreteria delle Missioni, 1975), 821. (Hereafter cited as S.F. 8). Cf. S.F. 5: 7; and J. J. Heeren, "Bishop Della Chiesa and the Story of His Lost Grave," *Journal of the North-China Branch of the Royal Asiatic Society* 54 (1923): 187.

10. S.F. 5: 7.

11. Wyngaert, "Le patronat portugais," 26–27.

12. S.F. 5: 7–8 ; and Rosso, *Apostolic Legations,* 170.

13. Georges Mensaert, O.F.M., "Les Franciscains au service de la Propagande dans la Province de Pékin, 1705–1785," *Archivum Franciscanum Historicum* 51 (1958): 163–64.

14. Mensaert, "Les Franciscains," 170 n.

15. Mensaert, "Les Franciscains," 164–65.

16. There were other Franciscans who served the Propaganda mission in the diocese of Beijing for only a short time in the early 1700s, as described in Mensaert, "Les Franciscains," 167 n. The Polish missionary Father Placidus Albrecht de Valcio, O.F.M. (1662–1728) remained only a few months before illness forced him to return to Canton. Cf. *Sinica Franciscana,* vol. 9, *Relationes et epistolas Fratrum Minorum Hispanorum in Sinis qui annis 1697–98 missionem ingressi sunt,* comp. and annotated by Fortunatus Margiotti, O.F.M.; prepared for publication and corrected by Gaspar Han (Han Chengliang) and Antolin Abad, O.F.M. 2 parts (Madrid: Segreteria delle Missioni, 1995), 931–33. (Hereafter cited as S.F. 9.) José Francisco de Langasco, O.F.M. remained one year but was forced by officials to leave China. In 1704 Brother Vicente de Roiate, O.F.M., was sent to Cochin China, and Juan Bañeza Bonassisa de Illiceto, O.F.M. went to Mexico.

17. Mensaert, "Les Franciscains," 166.

18. Mensaert, "Les Franciscains," 167–68.

19. *Sinica Franciscana,* vol. 10, : *Relationes et epistolas s Fratrum Minorum Hispanorum in Sinis qui annis 1696–98 missionem ingressi sunt,* comp. and ed. Antonius S. Rosso, O.F.M.; prepared for publication and corrected by Fathers Gaspar Han (Han Chengliang) and Antolin Abad, O.F.M. (Madrid: Segretaria delle Missioni, 1997), 373. (Hereafter referred to as S.F. 10.)

20. S.F. 10: 381.

21. S.F. 10: 388–89.

22. S.F. 10: 390.

23. In the following year, 1708, Yinti was entrusted with the care of the degraded heir, Yinreng, but Yinti was disgraced in that same year. Arthur Hummel, ed., *Eminent Chinese of the Ch'ing Period* (Washington, D.C.: United States Government Printing Office, 1943), 929–30.

24. S.F. 10: 143 n. 4.

25. S.F. 10: 375; and S.F. 9: 580–81.

26. S.F. 10: 376.

27. S.F. 10: 376–77.

28. S.F. 10: 378.

29. S.F. 10: 380.

30. In the infirmary in Canton, Nieto-Díaz regained his health within less than a year. He was then assigned to minister in Shunde district, one day's journey south of Canton, and there he remained until August of 1732, when all the missionaries were expelled to Macau. From Macau he traveled to Manila with Fathers Diego de Santa Rosa, Francisco de Palencia, and Silvestre Marco. Although elderly and ill, he was sent to Laguna to assist the rector, Father Blas de los Yélamos. When his condition became aggravated, he went to the infirmary of Santa Cruz de Bay, where he died on October 11, 1739.

31. *Anchasi*, a provincial judge of accused criminals. Charles O. Hucker, *A Dictionary of Official Titles in Imperial China* (Stanford, Calif.: Stanford University Press, 1985), 103–4, no. 13, explains that this is an abbreviation for *Tixing Ancha Shisi* (Provincial Surveillance Commission) (495–96, no. 6446), an office during the Ming and Qing dynasties in charge of judicial matters and investigations. Each province had such an office, of which there were a total of eighteen in the Qing period.

32. S.F. 8: 951.

33. S.F. 5: 762, no. 10.

34. S.F. 5: 767, no. 18.

35. Other imprisoned Christians were Francis (Francesco) Lu Jiulin and his son. Lu originated in Jining, where he was baptized by Nieto-Díaz, and was a leader of the sectarians. Also included were Thomas Gao Zhongmei, who was also a leader of the sectarians; Lu's neophyte, Wang Xihao, of whom nothing is known; Mu Taizhong, of whom nothing is known, and his son; Julius Su Tianzhang, a leader of the sectarians, originally from Jining, but baptized by Fernández-Oliver in Ji'nan; Li Jiahai, of whom nothing is known; Thomas Shang, a sectarian of Dongping subprefecture in Taian prefecture; Ignatius Zhang Yinjin of the Feicheng district in Taian prefecture; and Peter Hai Sejing, of whom nothing is known.

36. S.F. 8: 953; S.F. 9: 286.

37. S.F. 8: 953–54.

38. May 2, 1718, no. 5; and S.F. 5: 608–15. See R. G. Tiedemann, "Christianity and Chinese 'Heterodox Sects': Mass Conversion and Syncretism in Shandong Province in the Early Eighteenth Century," *Monumenta Serica* 44 (1996): 353.

39. S.F. 5: 764, no. 13; see also S.F. 5: 611–14, 766.

40. S.F. 8: 951.

41. S.F. 8: 952.

42. B. J. Ter Haar, *The White Lotus Teachings in Chinese Religious History* (Leiden: Brill, 1992), 220.

43. Ter Haar, *White Lotus Teachings*, 220–224.

44. S.F. 8: 985–88.

45. Ter Haar, *White Lotus Teachings*, 1–15 and passim.

46. S.F. 8: 929. Ter Haar, *White Lotus Teachings*, 252–53, refers to *Tianzhujiao* being used as an alternate name for the White Lotus Teaching in the late eighteenth century, but he finds it puzzling and offers no clear explanation.

47. S.F. 8: 857–58.

48. S.F. 8: 955.

49. Ter Haar, *White Lotus Teachings*, 65.

50. S.F. 5: 606, 759, 764.

51. S.F. 8: 955–56.

52. S.F. 8: 956.

53. Susan Naquin, *Millenarian Rebellion in China: The Eight Trigrams Uprising of 1813* (New Haven: Yale University Press, 1976), 24–31.

54. S.F. 8: 956–57.

55. S.F. 8: 957.

56. *Tidu*, supreme commander of a province. Cf. Hucker, *Official Titles*, 498 (no. 6482): provincial military commander, rank 1B, leader in the Green Standards (*luying*).

57. S.F. 8: 957–58.

58. S.F. 8: 959.

59. S.F. 8: 951–52, 959.

60. A brief biography of Orazio appears in S.F. 5: 438 n. . 3. The visit of the three Chinese to Bishop Della Chiesa's residence in Linqing is described in the letter of Fernández-Oliver to K. Stumpf, S.J., May 2, 1718, in S.F. 8: 961–65.

61. Castorano (Orazio), *De rebus sinensibus*, doc. 73.

62. S.F. 8: 961–65.

63. The incident is summarized in Tiedemann, "Christianity and 'Heterodox Sects,'" 341.

64. S.F. 8: 962.

65. S.F. 8: 955.

66. *Xiu Linqing zhouzhi* (Revised Linqing Department Gazetteer) (1785), cited in Tiedemann, "Christianity and 'Heterodox Sects,'"341 n. 3.

67. S.F. 8: 963–64.

68. S.F. 8: 985–86.

69. S.F. 8: 987.

70. S.F. 8: 988.

71. Mensaert, "Les Franciscains," 169.

72. S.F. 5: 770.

73. Matthaeus Ripa, "Diario, 1718." Manuscript in Archivum Archidioecesis de Hankow in Sinis, section A. Archivum General Ordinis Fratrum Minorum, Rome, cited in S.F. 5: 707 n.

74. Mensaert, "Les Franciscains," 171.

75. Heeren, "Lost Grave," 192.

76. Actually, Della Chiesa was not the only cleric buried at this site. In 1755, another member of the Propaganda mission, Father Hermenegildo Nadasi, O.F.M., was also buried there.

77. S.F. 5: 9; and Heeren, "Lost Grave," 193–94.

78. Four photographs of the tombstone are reproduced in Heeren, "Lost Grave," opposite page 194.

79. The Hongjialu Sacred Heart Church is located east of the former walled city of Ji'nan and near present-day Shandong University. It is also the site of the Holy Spirit Seminary (Shengshen Beixiu Yuan) founded in December 1988.

80. Mensaert, "Les Franciscains," 171–72.

81. Mensaert, "Les Franciscains," 173 n.

82. Mensaert, "Les Franciscains," 173.

83. Mensaert, "Les Franciscains," 173–74.

84. Mensaert, "Les Franciscains," 174.

85. Mensaert, "Les Franciscains," 174–75.

86. After recovering, Sormano was sent to the Propaganda mission in Cambodia. He died at Thonol (?) on July 21, 1752. Mensaert, "Les Franciscains," 176.

87. Mensaert, "Les Franciscains," 178.

88. Mensaert, "Les Franciscains," 178.

Chapter 6

1. Bernward H. Willeke, O.F.M., "Studia Preliminari pro 'Sinica Franciscana,'" April 6, 1996.

2. Georges Mensaert, O.F.M., "Les Franciscains au service de la Propagande dans la province de Pékin, 1705–1785," *Archivum Franciscanum Historicum* 51 (1958): 177.

3. Mensaert, "Les Franciscains," 178–79.

4. On the order of Propaganda, Buocher made an apostolic visit to Tongking in 1762. He died in Macau on December 5, 1765. Daniel Van Damme, O.F.M., *Necrologium Fratrum Minorum in Sinis,* 3d ed.(Hong Kong: Tang King Po School, Kowloon, 1978), 166–67. First edition compiled by Joannes Ricci, O.F.M. (1934); second edition compiled by Kilian Menz, O.F.M. (1944).

5. Van Damme, *Necrologium,* 27.

6. Letter of Buocher to Orazio, July 20, 1738,published in Gherardo De Vincentiis, *Documenti e titoli sul privato fondatore dell'attuale R. Istituto (antico "Collegio dei Cinesi" in Napoli) Matteo Ripa sulle Missioni in China nel secolo 17 e sulla constituzione e consistenza patrimoniale della antica fondazione.* (Naples: Melfi & Joele, 1904), 437.

7. De Vincentiis, *Documenti e titoli,* 439.

8. De Vincentiis, in summarizing the contents of the secret appendix to Buocher's letter of September 20, 1732, to Orazio, wrote that Bevilacqua's activity "does not appear to have excluded sexual relations of the brother even with the stronger sex" *(Nè sembra escluso il commercio del frate anche col sesso forte).* De Vincentiis, *Documenti e titoli,* 439.

9. Buocher to Orazio, Qingcaohe, September 20, 1738. Biblioteca Nazionale Napoli (hereafter abbreviated BNN), MS. XI-B-70, f. 590–95.

10. BNN, MS. XI-B-70, f. 590v.

11. BNN, MS. XI-B-70, f. 591r.

12. Buocher to Orazio, October 16, 1737, BNN, MS. XI-B-70, f. 583-84, cited in De Vincentiis, *Documenti e titoli,* 437.

13. Buocher to Orazio (?),July 20, 1738, f. 59r, cited in De Vincentiis, *Documenti e titoli,* 440.

14. Buocher to Orazio, July 26, 1739, BNN, MS. XI-B-70, f. 599–600, cited in De Vincentiis, *Documenti e titoli,* 441.

15. BNN, MS. XI-B-70, f. 591v.

16. BNN, MS. XI-B-70, f. 590r.

17. BNN, MS. XI-B-70, f. 592r.

18. BNN, MS. XI-B-70, f. 592r.

19. BNN, MS. XI-B-70, f. 592v.

20. H. Verhaeren, C.M., "Ordonnances de la Sainte Eglise (*Shengjiao guicheng*)," *Monumenta Serica* (Peiping) 4 (1939–40): 463, 475 (article 33).

21. Saint Joseph's status as patron saint of the China missions dated from the expulsion of missionaries from the Chinese mainland, when twenty-three missionaries signed a petition on January 26, 1668, requesting that Saint Joseph be designated the patron saint of China. The petition was signed by nineteen Jesuits, three Dominicans, and one Franciscan, Antonio Caballero. Father Intorcetta carried their request to Rome, where it was approved by the Holy See in 1660. Joseph Dehergne, S.J., "Les Jésuites de Chine et la dévotion à saint Joseph," *Cahiers de joséphologie* (Montreal) 15 (1967): 1–2. See also *Butler's Lives of Patron Saints*, ed. Michael Walsh (Wellwood, England: Burns & Oates, 1987), 263–66.

22. BNN, MS. XI-B-70, f. 592v.

23. Mensaert, "Les Franciscains," 175–76; and *Sinica Franciscana*, vol. 9, *Relationes et epistolas Fratrum Minorum Hispanorum in Sinis qui annis 1697–98 missionem ingressi sunt,* comp. and annotated by Fortunatus Margiotti, O.F.M.; prepared for publication and corrected by Gaspar Han (Han Chengliang) and Antolin Abad, O.F.M. 2 parts (Madrid: Segreteria delle Missioni, 1995), lxxxiii, xcviii. (Hereafter cited as S.F. 9.)

24. BNN, MS. XI-B-70, f. 590v. Also see the letter of Buocher to Castorano, dated July 20, 1738, published in De Vincentiis, *Documenti e titoli,* 438.

25. G. Buocher, O.F.M., "Relatio: Stato delle missioni de PP. Osservanti Italiani di S. Francesco in fondate in Cina," Archivo Storico della Sacra Congregazione per l'Evangelizzazione dei Populi o 'de Propaganda Fide,' Vatican (hereafter cited as APF). Scritture Originali della Congregazione Particolare nell'Indie e Cina (hereafter cited as SOCP), v. 42 (1739), f. 159–164v. Father Miralta (Min Mingwo; 1682–1751) of Piamonte joined the Clérigos Regulares de la Madre Dios on February 11, 1700, and went to China with the papal legate Carlo Antonio Ambrosio Mezzabarba in 1719. He was in Tonking in 1722 and then was a missionary in Jiangxi, Zhejiang, and Jiangsu provinces until 1724, when the persecution forced him to go to Canton. He made a trip to Manila in 1726 and then was expelled in 1732 to Macau, where he remained as mission procurator of Propaganda until 1750, when he accompanied Bishop Hilario de Santa Rosa to Rome. He died the following year in Marino on December 21. He was knowledgeable in Chinese and compiled an Italian–Chinese dictionary. *Sinica Franciscana*, vol. 10, *Relationes et epistolas Fratrum Minorum Hispanorum in Sinis qui annis 1696–98 missionem ingressi sunt,* comp. and ed. Antonius S. Rosso, O.F.M.; prepared for publication and corrected by Gaspar Han (Han Chengliang) and Antolin Abad, O.F.M. 2 parts (Madrid: Segreteria delle Missioni, 1997), 774 n. (Hereafter cited as S.F. 10).

26. Buocher, "Relatio," f. 160r.

27. Letter from Brother Bernadino Maria di Scala, at Macau to unnamed person in Rome, November 30, 1738, APF, SOCP, v. 1739, f. 253r. A biography of Antonio de la Concepción, O.F.M., is found in S.F. 9: 617–30.

28. Letter from Bevilacqua at Macau to Father Prone Colmo in Rome, December 8, 1740, APF, SOCP v. 1742–45, f. 191r .

29. Certificate of health by Juan Vizente Peisieo, surgeon and anatomist, dated October 14, 1740, and sent with letter for Bevilacqua dated December 8, 1740, at Macau to Rome, APF, SOCP, v. 1742, f. 189r.

30. Bevilacqua to Colmo, f. 191r, 191v.

31. The names on the envelope to which Bevilacqua addressed this letter are the Most Very Reverend Father Mr. Prone Colmo, Father Don Giuseppi Marziali Monaco Silvestrino, and, in his absence, to the Most Reverend Father Abbot Lucarelli and, in his absence, to the Most Reverend Father Abbot Josi. Bevilacqua letter dated December 8, 1740, at Macau, f. 190r.

32. Bevilacqua to Colmo, f. 192r.

33. Buocher in his letter to Orazio of September 26, 1739, refers to Randanini as "*quel P. di San Pietro Montoris,*" BNN, MS. XI-B-70, f. 600r.

34. The church San Bartolomeo all'Isola was first constructed by the German emperor Otto III (980–1002) over the ruins of the Roman temple of Aesculapius (Christopher Hibbert, *Rome: the Biography of a City* [London: Viking, 1985], 340). It was restored in 1113 and again in 1180, when it was rededicated to Saint Bartholomew. A flood in 1557 demolished the church, although the twelfth-century Romanesque campanile survives.

35. Leonard von Matt and Franco Barelli, *Rom: Kunst und Kultur der "Ewigen Stadt" in mehr als 1000 Bildern* (Cologne: Verlag M. DuMont Schaubert, 1975), 273.

36. BNN, MS. XI-B-70, f. 592r & f. 599v.

37. APF, SOCP 42 (1739), f. 19v.

38. A. Randinini, *Beneficia facta,* APF, Scritture riferite nei Congressi, v. 22, f. 394r. Hereafter cited as SRC.

39. Randinini, *Beneficia facta,* 394v.

40. A. Randanini, "Loca Missionis provinciarum Xantung et Peking," APF, SOCP v. 22 (1740–1741), f. 388r.

41. Mensaert, "Les Franciscains," 180–81.

42. Randinini, *Beneficia facta,* f. 394v–395r.

43. Buocher in his letter of August 22, 1740, to Orazio refers to Randanini as a "Teologo" (theologian), but in sarcasm. Gherardo de Vincentiis, *Documenti e titoli sul privato fondatore dell'attuale R. Istituto (antico "Collegio dei Cinesi" in Napoli) Matteo Ripa sulle Missioni in China nel secolo XVIIIe sulla constituzione e consistenza patrimoniale della antica fondazione* (Naples: Melfi & Joele, 1904), . 463.

44. Randanini's lists are preserved in the Propaganda Archives in Rome, APF, SOCP, v. 22 (1740–1741), f. 375–395r.

45. A. Randanini, "Liber baptizatorum in diocese Xangtung et Pekin," APF, SOCP, v. 22, f. 375r–386r.

46. APF, SOCP, v. 22 (1740–1741), f. 388v.

47. APF, SOCP, v. 22 (1740–41), f. 389r.

48. Randanini, "Liber baptizatorum," f. 378v–379v.

49. Randanini to Cardinal Vincenzo Petra, September 19, 1740, SOCP, v. 43 (1740–1741), f. 585v.

50. Buocher to Orazio, October 22, 1740, BNN, MS. XI-B-70, f. 606–608, cited in De Vincentiis, *Documenti e titoli,* 463.

51. Randanini, "Loca missionis provinciarum Xantung et Peking," APF, SOCP, v. 22 (1740–1741), f. 388r.

52. Randanini, "Liber baptizatorum," f. 375–386r.

53. Buocher to Orazio, October 22, 1740, cited in De Vincentiis, *Documenti e titoli,* 463.

54. Buocher to Orazio, September 26, 1739, BNN, MS. XI-B-70, f. 600r.

55. BNN, MS XI-B-70, f. 599r.

56. Mensaert, "Les Franciscains," 274.

57. S.F. 10: 845 n.

58. Mensaert, "Les Franciscains," 181–83.

59. S.F. 9: 732–33; S.F. 10: 826 n; Mensaert, "Les Franciscains," 182.

60. Mensaert, "Les Franciscains," 183–85.

61. Mensaert, "Les Franciscains," 186 n; Joseph Dehergne, S.J., *Répertoire des Jésuites de Chine de 1552 à 1800* (Rome: Institutum Historicum Societatis Iesu, 1973), 68, 231–32.

62. Lucera was a member of the Franciscan province of Saint Agnes in Apulia. He died in a convent of Macau on March 4, 1779.

63. Mensaert, "Les Franciscains," 184.

64. Pinheiro was born in Loures, diocese of Lisbon, on March 21, 1688, and entered the Jesuit novitiate on November 9, 1704. He accompanied the Portuguese ambassador Don Alexandre Metello de Sousa to Beijing, where they arrived on August 26, 1726. He was a mathematician and served as Jesuit vice-provincial twice (1732–1735 and 1741–1745). He was named on December 20, 1739, by Father Emmanuel de Silva Tchang (Sintranus), S.J., as his successor as administrator of the diocese of Beijing. Pinheiro died June 16, 1748, at Beijing. (Dehergne, *Répertoire,* 204).

65. Mensaert, "Les Franciscains," 189.

66. Louis Fan was born in Jiangzhou, Shanxi, in 1682. He was Provana's manservant and accompanied him to Europe, departing from Beijing in October 1707 and arriving in Rome in December 1709. He returned with Provana, departing from Rome in 1719 and arriving in Beijing in 1725. He took the vows of a spiritual coadjutor on February 2, 1730, and died in Beijing on February 28, 1753. Further information about Fan is given in two articles by Paul Rule: "Louis Fan Shouyi and Macao," *Review of Culture* (Macau) 21 (2d ser.) English ed., (1994): 249–58; and "Louis Fan Shou-i: A Mission Link in the Chinese Rites Controversy," in *Actes du Septième Colloque International de Sinologie de Chantilly 8–10 septembre 1992,* ed. Edward J. Malatesta, S.J., Yves Raguin, S.J., and Adrianus C. Dudink (Taipei: Institut Ricci, 1995), 277–94.

67. Mensaert, "Les Franciscains," 190.

68. Mensaert, "Les Franciscains," 191–92.

69. Mensaert, "Les Franciscains," 274, 277.

70. Bernward E. Willeke, O.F.M., *Imperial Government and Catholic Missions in China during the Years 1784–1785* (Saint Bonaventure, N.Y.: Franciscan Institute, 1948), 108.

71. Mensaert, "Les Franciscains," 276.

72. Mensaert, "Les Franciscains," 283.

73. Mensaert, "Les Franciscains," 284.

74. Mensaert, "Les Franciscains," 284.

75. Willeke, *Imperial Government,* 141.

76. Willeke, *Imperial Government,* 78 n. 12.

77. Mensaert, "Les Franciscains," 278; and Georges Mensaert, O.F.M., "Adrien Chu, prêtre chinois et confesseur de la Foi (1717–1785)," *Neue Zeitschrift für Missionswissenschaft* 12 (1956): 6 n. 27.

78. Mensaert, "Les Franciscains," 290.

79. S.F. 9: 732; and S.F. 10: 682.

80. Antoine Gaubil, S.J., *Correspondance de Pékin 1722–1759* (Geneva: Librairie Droz, 1970), 177.

81. Otto Maas, O.F.M., "Die Franziskanermission in China während des achtzehnten Jahrhunderts," *Zeitschrift für Missionswissenschaft und Religionswissenschaft* 22 (1932): 235.

82. Antolín Abad, O.F.M., "Misioneros franciscanos en China (siglo diez y ocho)," *Missionalia Hispanica* 13 (1956): 455.

83. Maas, "Die Franziskanermission in China," 236.

84. Maas, "Die Franziskanermission in China," 236–37. See also Antolín Abad, O.F.M., "Misioneros franciscanos en China (siglo diez y ocho)," *Missionalia Hispanica* 11 (1954): 264.

85. Mensaert, "Les Franciscains," 284.

86. Abad, "Misioneros franciscanos" (1956), 457.

87. Willeke, *Imperial Government,* 106–7.

88. There is some uncertainty about Astorga's year of death. Whereas Willeke, *Imperial Government,* p. 108 n, gives the year 1801, Abad, "Misioneros franciscanos" (1956), 472, gives the year 1797. Further information on Astorga is found in Willeke's article, "Documents Relating to the History of the Franciscan Mission in Shantung, China," *Franciscan Studies* 7 (1947): 171–72.

89. Abad, "Misioneros franciscanos" (1956), 473.

90. Maas, "Die Franziskanermission in China," 329.

91. Willeke, *Imperial Government,* 33f. Also see Joseph Krahl, S.J., *China Missions in Crisis: Bishop Laimbeckhoven and His Times, 1738–1787* (Rome: Gregorian University Press, 1964), 296–99.

92. The perpetuation of Catholicism in villages in central and southern Hebei (formerly Zhili) province is treated by Richard Madsen in *China's Catholics: Tragedy and Hope in an Emerging Civil Society* (Berkeley and Los Angeles: University of California Press, 1998).

Postlude

1. *Sinica Franciscana,* vol. 8, *Relationes et epistolas Fratrum Minorum Hispanorum in Sinis qui a. 1684–92 missionem ingressi sunt,* ed. Fortunatus Margiotti, O.F.M. 2 parts (Rome: Segreteria delle Missioni, 1975), 853.

Chinese-Character Glossary

Aijin Hui 哀矜會
Aijing Shizijia Hui 哀敬十字架會
An Duoni 安多尼
anchasi 按察司
Anhai cheng 安海成
Ba Duoming 巴多明
Ba Lianren 巴璉仁
bagua 八掛
baiding 白丁
Bailian She 白蓮社
baique 敗闕
Bao Zhongyi, Zhian 鮑仲義，質菴
bao 報
baofu 包袱
Baogang 寶崗
Baotuquan 趵突泉
bazi zhengyan 八子正言
Benming zhai 本名齋
Bi Fangji, Jinliang 畢方濟，今梁
Bi Jia 畢嘉
Bian Shuji 卞述濟
bian 辯
Boxing xian 博興縣
bu pian 不偏
bu Ru pi Fo 補儒闢佛
Bu Ru wengao 補儒文告
bu Ru yi Fo 補儒易佛
bu 補
buzhengshi 布政使
ce 冊

173

chao xing 超性
chaoxing xing 超形性
charen 查人
Chen Shance, Jingzhi 陳善策，敬之
Cheng Guan 成瓘
Cheng Jili 成際理
chengzi 呈子
Chenjialou Sheng Ruose Tang 陳家樓聖若瑟堂
Chiping xian 茌平縣
Chongzhen 崇楨
chuan 傳
da zhu 大主
Dai laoye 戴老爺
Danshui 淡水
danzi 單子
Dao Chuan 道傳
Dao shuai yu xing; xing ming yu Tian. 道率於性。性命於天。
daotai 道臺
Daotong 道統
de xing 德性
Dengzhou 等州
Dezhou 德州
di wang xian sheng 帝王賢聖
diezi 碟子
ding 訂
Dingtou 頂頭
Dong [Tianzhu] Tang 東《天主》堂
Dong huizhang 董會長
Dongchang fu 東昌府
Dong'e xian 東阿縣
Dongguan 東莞
Dongping zhou 東平州
Du Tingfen, Yiling 堵廷棻，伊令
dui zi 對字
en xian 恩縣
en 恩
Ershi 二氏
Fa Anduo, Shengxue 法安多，聖學
Falisaie 法利塞俄
Fan Shouyi, Lihe 樊守義，利和
Fang Hao 方豪

Fang Jige 方濟各
Fang Quanji 方全紀
Feicheng xian 肥城縣
fengshui 風水
Fo Lao yi kongji xu wuwei jiao 佛老以空寂虛無爲教
Fuyin Tang 福音堂
gai xian yi zhe 改絃易轍
Gan Lichuan 甘粒傳
Gangjian huizuan 鋼鑑會纂
Gaodousi hang 高都司巷
gaosheng 高聲
gaoshi 高示
Gaoyuan xian 高苑縣
gong chuan 公傳
Gong Gong 共工
Gong Shangshi, Guanruo 龔尙實，觀若
gongjiang 工匠
gongshi 公師
gongshi 工師
Gu Jiafen 谷家憤
Gu Jiao 古教
Gu Ruohan 谷若翰
guanhua 官話
Guo [Lixing'a] 郭《里星阿》
Guo Nabi 郭納璧
Haidian 海淀《海甸》
Han Chengliang 韓承良
He Ruling 何如苓
He Tianzhang, Qiwen 何天章，起文
Hebei 河北
hegui 合軌
Henan 河南
hengshi 衡石
Hongjialou Shengxin Tang 洪家樓聖心堂
Hongjialou 洪家樓
Huaian fu 淮安府
Huainanzi 淮南子
Huaiyin 淮陰
Huang Yilong 黃一農
Huatajie 花塔街
huipiao 回票

huizhang 會長
hun po 魂魄
Ji Li'an, Yunfeng 紀理安，雲風
ji Tian 祭天
ji 祭
Jiading 嘉定
Jiang Chenxi 將陳錫
Jiang Kun 蔣焜
Jiangjunmiao jie 將軍廟街
Jiangle 將樂
jiaohua huang 教化皇
Jiashan xian 嘉善縣
Jiaxing fu 嘉興府
jie 節
jiezhi 接旨
Ji'nan fu 濟南府
Ji'nan fuzhi 濟南府志
Jing Mingliang 景明亮
jing Tian [zhu] 敬天《主》
Jingzhou 景州
Jiu yishi zhi pi long xumu zhong ren. Shi zhi bulü shi ting sishi fuhuo.
救一世之疲聾墟墓中人。使之步履視聽死屍復活。
jiushu deng shi xian dasheng ji 救贖等事顯大聖跡
Jiyang 濟陽
juan 卷
jue Fo bu Ru 絕佛補儒
juren 舉人
Kang Andang 康安當
Kang Hezi 康和子
Ke Ruose, Yilin 柯若瑟，亦臨
Kong 孔
Kongzijiao 空子教
Ku Hui 苦會
Laiwu xian 萊蕪縣
Laizhou fu 萊州府
Lanxi xian 蘭谿縣
Lao Hongen 勞弘恩
laoye 老爺
Li (Gu) Anding, Weizhi 利《顧》安定，惟止
Li Andang, Kedun 利安當，克敦
Li Anning, Weiji 利安寧，惟吉

Li bei 理輩
Li Bing, Zhang Yuan 李炳，長源
Li Jiao 理教
Li Shan 歷山
Li Shouqian 李受謙
Li Shude 李樹德
Li Song 李松
Li Wei 李煒
Li Xiufang, Yaming 李秀芳，雅明
Li Yeshi 李冶世
Li Yufan 黎玉範
Li Zhizao 李之藻
Li 李
li 理
Liangxi 梁谿
liang 兩
Licheng xian 歷城縣
Liezi 列子
Liji, Zhengyi 禮記，正義
Ling xian 陵縣
ling xing 靈性
lingli 伶俐
lingwei 靈位
Linqing fu 臨清府
Linqu xian 臨朐縣
Lishan 歷山
lishu 曆書
Liu Biyue 劉必約
Liu Junzi 六君子
Liu Mingde [dazhu] 劉明德《大主》
Liu Ruowang 劉若望
Liu Zizhen 劉自珍
liushi 鏐石
Lixia 歷下
Luo Wenzao 羅文藻
Luojia hang 羅家巷
luying 綠營
Ma Guoxian 馬國賢
Mai Ningxue, Zhiwen 麥寧學，止文
Mei Shusheng 梅述聖
Mei 梅

Meng Erya 孟爾雅
Meng Jialou 孟家樓
Meng Ruwang 孟儒望
Mengyin xian 蒙陰縣
Min Mingwo 閔明我
Ming-Qing jian Yesuhui shi yizhu tiyao 明清間耶穌會士譯著提要
Mingwu 鳴梧
Moxiang shenggong 默想神功
Muyang xian 穆洋縣
nainai 奶奶《嬭嬭》
Nan Huaide 南懷德
Nan Huairen 南懷仁
Nan Xuan 南軒
Nan'an xian 南安縣
nanguanli 南關裡
Nanxuntu 南巡圖
Neiwufu 內務府
Nian 年
Ningde xian 寧德縣
Niu San Jiaohuazi 牛三叫化子
Nü Gua (Wa) 女媧
Pan Gu 盤古
Pan Guoguang 潘國光
pi Fo bu Ru 闢佛補儒
pi 闢
pian 偏
pian 篇
piao 票
Pihoujiao 皮厚教
Pingyin xian 平陰縣
Poligu 坡里谷
Pulimen 普利門
Putai xian 浦台縣
Putai 蒲臺
qi 氣
Qian Chenjialou 前陳家樓
Qian Shisheng, Saian 錢士升，塞菴
Qing shi biannian 清史編年
Qingcaohe 青草河
Qingcheng 青城
Qinghe 清河

Qingzhou xian 青州縣
Quanzhou 泉州
Quzhou xian 曲周縣
ren xue 人學
Rence Hui 仁慈會
Ru li 儒理
Ru que 儒缺
ru zai 如在
Ruan Yuan 阮元
Run Wangbi 閏王弼
Sanli zhuang 三里莊
Sanshan lunxue ji 三山論學計
Shandong sheng 山東省
Shandong tongzhi 山東通志
Shang Huqing, Wei Tang, Shiji, Zhangtang 尙祜卿，韋堂，識己，章堂
shangyu 上諭
Shanhai jing 山海經
Shanyangfu 山陽府
Shen Dongxing 沈東行
Shen Nong 神農
Sheng Fangjige Hui 聖方濟各會
Sheng Fangjige Shengsu Hui 聖方濟各聖素會
sheng hao 聖號
sheng huang 聖皇
Sheng Jiao 聖教
Sheng Leisi Hui 聖類思會
Sheng Mu Hui 聖母會
Sheng Mu Tang 聖母堂
Sheng Mu 聖母
Sheng Ruose Tang 聖若瑟堂
sheng wang 聖王
Sheng Yi'najue Hui 聖依納爵會
Shengjiao guicheng 聖教規程
Shengjiao rike 聖教日課
Shengjiao xiaojing jie 聖教孝經解
Shengjiao zong du jingwen 聖教總牘經文
shengren 聖人
Shengshen Beixiu Yuan 聖神備修院
Shengsu guitiao 聖素規條
shengyuan 生員
Shenshunmen 神順門

shenwei 神位

Shi Duolu, Zhenduo 石鐸祿，振鐸

Shifozha 石佛閘

Shiji 史記

Shisan jing zhushu jiaokanji 十三經注疏校勘紀

shiwei 侍衛

Shoudu xian 壽光縣

shulue 疏略

Shunde xian 順德縣

Si Ju 四句

Sishu zhangju jizhu 四書章句集註

Su Laolengzuo 蘇老楞佐

Su Na, Deye 蘇納德業

Sui Ren 燧人

Sun Yuanhua 孫元化

Taian zhou 泰安州

Taiji 太極

Taixi shuifa 泰西水法

Taixi Yesuhui shi zhe 泰西耶穌會士著

Taiyuan 太源

Tang Menglai 唐夢賚

Tian Ming 天命

Tian Ru yin 天儒印

Tian 天

Tianjiao mingbian zixu 天教明辨自序

Tianjingzha 天井閘

Tianqu [Tianzhu] Tang 天衢《天主》堂

tianshen bao shen bailengyun 天神報娠白稜孕

Tianshen Hui 天神會

Tianxue chuhan 天學初函

Tianxue lueyi 天學略義

Tianzhu Shangdi zhi hao 天主上帝之號

Tianzhu Yesu wanmin zhi dajunfu 天主耶穌萬民之大君父

Tianzhu zi 天主子

Tianzhujiao dongchuan wenxian sanbian 天主教東傳文獻三編

Tianzhujiao dongchuan wenxian xubian 天主教東傳文獻續編

tidu 提督

Tixing Ancha Shisi 提刑按察史司

Tong Guowei 佟國維

tongding 同訂

tongxin 同心

tongzhi 同知
tuoyu 唾餘
Tushu jikan 圖書季刊
Wan Jiguo, Daojin 萬濟國，道津
wang dao 王道
Wang Ermu 王二木
Wang Hui 王翬
Wang Jingting 王景亭
Wang Ruwang 汪儒望
Wang Shizhen 王世貞
Wang Zhongmin 王重民
Wang Songfen 王誦芬
Wang Zengfang 王贈芳
Wang 王
Wanwu benmo yueyan 萬物本末約言
Wei Dazhong, Tinggeng, Kongshi, Kuoyuan 魏大中，廷鯁，孔時，廓袁
Wei xian 濰縣 (Shandong)
Wei xianggong 魏相公
Wei xianzhi 濰縣志
Wei Xuelian 魏學濂
Wei Xuequ, Qingcheng 魏學渠，青城
weili 委吏
Weixian 威縣 (Zhili)
weizhengtang 委正堂
Wen Dula, Daoji 文度辣，道濟
Wenshang xian 汶上縣
wen 文
wu Dajun Dafu 吾大君大父
Wu Jiaji 吳嘉記
Wu laoye 伍老爺
Wu Xiangxiang 吳相湘
wu 武
Wucheng xian 武城縣
Wulin 武林
Wuyuanzui tang 無原罪堂
Xi xian 西賢
xianggong 相公
xiangzhu 香燭
xiao 孝
xiaomi 小米
Xiaonanmen 小南門

xie dang 邪黨
xiejiao 邪教
xieshuo 邪說
Ximen 西門
Xin Jiao 新教
Xincheng xian 新城縣
xing wu de ren 行惡的人
xing zhi li 性之理
Xinglijiao 性理教
Xinshixue 新史學
Xintai xian 新泰縣
Xinzhen 新鎮
Xitu 西土
xiucai 秀才
Xu Guangqi, Wending 徐光啓，文定
Xu Risheng 徐日昇
Xuan Ying 玄應
xunfu 巡撫
Yang Dele 樣德樂
Yang Guangxian 楊光先
Yang Liansheng 楊聯陞
Yanggu xian 陽穀縣
Yangjiazhuang 揚家莊
Yangrenli dongyue 楊仁里東約
Yanshen zhen 顏神鎮
Yanzhou fu 兗州府
Yanzhou fu 奄州府
yaofang 腰房
Yaotou 窯頭
Ye Zongxian, Ruohan 葉宗賢，若翰
Ye Zunxiao 葉尊孝
Yesu Ku Hui 耶穌苦會
Yi da chuan 易大傳
Yi Daren 伊大任
yi zhe 義者
Yidu xian 益都縣
yiduan 異端
Yin Degong 尹得功
yin xing 因性
Yinreng 胤礽
Yinti 胤禔

yinxing xing 因形性
Yiqiejing yinyi 一切經音義
Yizhou fu 沂州府
You Chao 有巢
Yu xianggong 于相公
Yuan Xi jinshi 遠西進士
yue jing potiao 月經破調
Zaoqiangxian 棗強縣
Zeng Leisi 曾類斯
Zhan Chengjie 展成傑
Zhang Baoluo 張保羅
Zhang Changzhu 張常住
Zhang Xingyao, Zichen, Yi'najue 張星曜，紫臣，依納爵
Zhangqiu xian 章邱縣
zhanli dan 瞻禮單
Zhao Chang 趙昌
zhen 貞
Zheng Chenggong 鄭成功
Zheng Chuan 正傳
Zheng Jing 鄭經
Zheng Min 蒸民
Zheng Shifan 鄭世蕃
Zheng Zhilong 鄭芝龍
Zhengding fu 正定府
Zhengxue liu shi 正學鏐石
zhengxue 正學
Zhenkong jiaxiang wusheng fumu 眞空家鄉無生父母
zhennü shengyi 貞女聖異
zheren 哲人
zhi jin wei Tian Ru he che 至今謂天儒合轍
zhi qi zhong 執其中
zhi ren 至人
zhi 旨
Zhi 直
Zhili sheng 直隸省
zhixian 知縣
zhizhou 知州
Zhong Tianshen zhi Muhuang Ben Hui Tang 眾天神之母皇本會堂
Zhong Tianshen zhi Muhuang Tang 眾天神之母皇堂
zhong 中
Zhongguo lishi ditu ji 中國歷史地圖集

Zhongguo renmin da cidian 中國人民大辭典
Zhongguo renmin dacidian 中國古今地名大辭典
Zhongguo Tianzhujiao shi renwu chuan 中國天主教史人物傳
Zhu en 主恩
Zhu Xi 朱熹
Zhu Xingyi 朱行義
zhu 主
Zhu 朱
Zhuan Xu 顓頊
Zhujiang 珠江
zhun 准
zhuzai 主宰
zibo 自搏
Zigong 子貢
zipu 自撲
Zisi 子思
Zizhi tongjian gangmu qianbian 資治通鑑岡目前編
zong huizhang 總會長
zongbing 總兵
zu wei wu Ru bu wang 足爲吾儒補亡
zuo chaoting 做朝廷
Zuochuan 佐傳

Bibliography

Primary Literature

Aleni, Giulio. *Sanshan lunxue ji* (Record of the learned discussion of the Three Mountains). 1 juan. Hangzhou, ca. 1627. In *Tianzhujiao dongchuan wenxian xubian,*.edited by Wu Xiangxiang, 1: 419–93. Taipei: Taiwan Xuesheng Shuju, 1966.

Archivo Storico della Sacra Congregazione per l'Evangelizzazione dei Populi o 'de Propaganda Fide, Vatican. Scritture Originali nella Congregazione Particolare dell'Indie e Cina (SOCP) and Scritture riferite nei Congressi (SRC).

Archivum Romanum Societatis Iesu, Rome. Japonica–Sinica (Jap.-Sin.) 163 and Fondo Gesuitico.

Biblioteca Nazionale Vittorio Emanuele III–Napoli (BNN).

Brooks, E. Bruce, and A. Taeko Brooks, trans., *The Original Analects: Sayings of Confucius and His Successors.* New York: Columbia University Press, 1998.

Brueyre, Benjamin (Li Xiufang Yaming), S.J. Letter of September 30, 1847, in *Annales de la Propagation de la Foi.* 21: 306–11. Lyon, 1849.

Castorano [Orazio] [Fr. Caroli Horatii a. Castorano]. Regul. Observan.ae S. Francisci ad Sinas Missionarii Apostolici. "De rebus Sinensibus. Monumenta Papyracea Sinensia ex museo March.s de Sterlich." Mss. adservatum in B. St. Bon. Continet plura documenta sinica, et quaedam etiam italica et hispanica. Mss. collecta a P. Carolo Orazi de Castorano qui omnibus aliquam praefatiunculam seu summariam descriptionem praemisit lingua italica.

De Vincentiis, Gherardo. *Documenti e titoli sul privato fondatore dell'attuale R. Istituto (antico "Collegio dei Cinesi" in Napoli) Matteo Ripa sulle Missioni in China nel secolo XVIIIe sulla constituzione e consistenza patrimoniale della antica fondazione.* Naples: Melfi & Joele, 1904.

Fernández-Oliver, Michael, O.F.M. "Declaration faite a Monsieur le Cardinal de Tournon par le Reverend Père Michel Fernandez." In *Anecdotes sur l'état de la Religion dans China ou Relation de M. le Cardinal de Tournon,* 2: 309–24. Paris, 1739.

Gaubil, Antoine, S.J. *Correspondance de Pékin 1722–1759.* Geneva: Librairie Droz, 1970.

Ji'nan fangzhi (Gazetteer of Ji'nan prefecture). Edited by Jiang Kun; compiled by Tang Menglai. 54 juan. Ji'nan, 1692.

Ji'nan fangzhi (Gazetteer of Ji'nan prefecture). Edited by Wang Zengfeng; compiled by Cheng Guan. Ji'nan, 1840.

Karlgren, Bernhard. *The Book of Odes: Chinese Text, Transcription, and Translation.* Stockholm: Museum of Far Eastern Antiquities, 1950. Originally published in *Bulletin of the Museum of Far Eastern Antiquities (BMFEA)* 16 (1945) and 17 (1946). The glosses appear in *BMFEA* 14 (1942): 71–247, 16 (1944): 55–169, and 18 (1946): 1–198. Reprinted in 1 vol. as *Glosses on the Book of Odes.* Stockholm: Museum of Far Eastern Antiquities,1964.

Legge, James, trans. *The Chinese Classics.* 5 vols. Oxford: Oxford University Press, 1893.

Li Andang [Antonio Caballero, O.F.M.]. *Wanwu benmo yueyan* (A brief summary of the beginning and end of all things) is preserved in the Bibliothèque nationale de France (Paris), Chinois 6971. Canton, ca. 1680.

Li Yufan [Juan-Bautista Morales, O.P.]. *Shengjiao xiaojing jie* (Filial piety explained in terms of Christianity), a Chinese text with Spanish translation. Manuscript in the Vatican Library, Borgia Cinese 503.

Lu Xiangshan (Jiuyuan). *Lu Xiangshan quanji* (The complete works of Lu Xiangshan). 36 juan. 1521. Reprint, Hong Kong: Kwong Chi Book Co., n.d.

Mencius. Translated by D. C. Lau. Harmondsworth, England: Penguin, 1970.

Meng Ruwang (José Monteiro, S.J.). *Tianxue lueyi* (A summary of the Heavenly Teaching). In *Tianzhujiao dongchuan wenxian xubian* (A continuation of a collection of writings from the Eastern mission of the Catholic Church), edited by Wu Xiangxiang, 2: 839–904. Taipei: Taiwan Xuesheng Shuchu, 1966.

Ripa, Matthaeus. "Diario a. 1713–21." Manuscript in Archivum Archidioecesis de Hankow in Sinis, section A. Archivum Generali Ordinis Fratrum Minorum, Rome.

———. *Giornale de' viaggi fatti da me D. Matteo Ripa diviso in tre parti,* 3: oct. 1717. Archivum Generale Ordinis Fratrum Minorum, Rome.

———. *Giornale (1705–1724).* Edited by Michele Fatica. Vol. 1 (1705–1711) Introduzione, testo critico, e note. Vol. 2 (1711–1716) Testo critico, note, e appendice documentaria. Naples: Instituto Universitario Orientale, 1991–96.

Ruan Yuan. *Shisan jing zhu shu* (Notes and commentary on the Thirteen Classics). A photolithographic edition based on *Shisan jing zhu shu jiaokanji.* Originally printed in 1806, 2 vols. Beijing: Zhonghua Shuju Chuban, 1980.

Shandong tongzhi (Gazetteer of Shandong province). 1911. Reprint, Shanghai: Shangwu Press, 1934–35.

Shang Huqing and Li Andang [Antonio Caballero, O.F.M.]. *Tian Ru yin* (Imprints of the Heavenly Teaching and the Literati Teaching). Ji'nan, 1664. Slightly variant copies in the Biblioteca Apostolica Vaticana, Beitang Library (National Library of China–Beijing), Bibliothèque nationale de France, and Zikawei Library (Shanghai Library).

———. *Zhengxue liushi* (The touchstone of True Knowledge), 1698. Copies in the Biblioteca Apostolica Vaticana and Bibliothèque nationale de France. Reprinted in the collection *Tianzhujiao dongchuan wenxian sanbian* (Third collection of documents on the spread of Catholicism to the East), edited by Wu Xiangxiang, 1: 89–266. Taipei: Taiwan Xuesheng Shuju, 1972.

Shang Huqing. *Bu Ru wengao* (A warning to repair the deficiencies of the Literati), 1664. Copy in the Sinologisch Instituut (Leiden) transcribed from a manuscript in the Zikawei Library (Shanghai Library).

————. *Tian Ru yin zheng*, preface by Run Wangbi, after 1664. Copy in the Zikawei Library (Shanghai Library).

Shengjiao zongdu jingwen (General collection of prayers of the Holy Teaching). Ji'nan, 1701.

Shi Duolu (Pedro de la Piñuela, O.F.M.). *Moxian shen gong* (The pious exercise of meditation). Reprinted by the Confraternity of the Cross of the Bu Ru Tang. Jinan, 1699.

Sinica Franciscana. Vol. 2, *Relationes et epistolas Fratrum Minorum Saeculi 16 et 17*. Edited by Anastasius van den Wyngaert, O.F.M. Quaracchi: Collegium S. Bonaventurae, 1933.

————. Vol. 3, *Relationes et epistolas Fratrum Minorum Saeculi 17*. Edited by Anastasius van den Wyngaert, O.F.M. Quaracchi: Collegium S. Bonaventurae, 1936.

————. Vol. 5, *Relationes et epistolas Illmi D. Fr. Bernardini della Chiesa O.F.M.* Edited by Anastasius van den Wyngaert, O.F.M., and Georgius Mensaert, O.F.M. (Rome: Collegium S. Antonii, 1954),

————. Vol. 6, *Relationes et epistolas primorum Fratrum Minorum Italorum in Sinis (Saeculis 17 et 18)*. Edited by Georgius Mensaert, O.F.M., in collaboration with Fortunato Margiotti, O.F.M., and [Antonius] Sixto Rosso, O.F.M. 2 parts. Rome: Segreteria delle Missioni, 1961.

————. Vol. 7, *Relationes et epistolas Fratrum Minorum Hispanorum in Sinis qui a. 1672–81 missione ingressi sunt*. Edited by Georgius Mensaert, O.F.M., in collaboration with Fortunato Margiotti and [Antonius] Sixto Rosso, O.F.M. 2 parts. Rome: Segretaria delle Missioni, 1965.

————. Vol. 8, *Relationes et epistolas Fratrum Minorum Hispanorum in Sinis qui a. 1684–92 missionem ingressi sunt*. Edited by Fortunatus Margiotti, O.F.M. 2 parts. Rome: Segreteria delle Missioni, 1975.

————. Vol. 9, *Relationes et epistolas Fratrum Minorum Hispanorum in Sinis qui annis 1697–98 missionem ingressi sunt*. Compiled and annotated by Fortunatus Margiotti, O.F.M.; prepared for publication and corrected by Gaspar Han (Han Chengliang) and Antolin Abad, O.F.M. 2 parts. Madrid: Segreteria delle Missioni, 1995.

————. Vol. 10, : *Relationes et epistolas Fratrum Minorum Hispanorum in Sinis qui annis 1696–98 missionem ingressi sunt*. Compiled and edited by Antonius [Sixto] Rosso, O.F.M.; prepared for publication and corrected by Gaspar Han (Han Chengliang) and Antolin Abad, O.F.M. 2 parts. Madrid: Segreteria delle Missioni, 1997.

Waley, Arthur, trans. *The Analects of Confucius*. London: George Allen & Unwin, 1938.

————. *The Book of Songs*. London: George Allen & Unwin, 1937. Reprint, New York: Grove, 1960.

Wei xianzhi (Gazetteer of Wei district). Compiled by Wang Songfen. 2 vols. 1760. Reprint, Taipei, 1976.

Xu Wending. *Taixi shuifa* (Western hydraulics). In *Tianxue chuhan* (The first collection of writing on the Heavenly Learning), edited by Li Zhizao. Vol. 3, 1505–1710. 52 juan. 1628. Reprint, Taipei: Taiwan Xuesheng Shuju, 1965.

Zhang Xingyao. *Tianjiao mingbian* (Clearly distinguishing the Heavenly Teaching [from heterodoxy]). 1711.

Zhu Xi. *Sishu zhangju jizhu* (Division into chapters and sentences and collected commentary on the Four Books). 1177–1189.

Secondary Literature

Abad, Antolin, O.F.M. "Misioneros franciscanos en China (siglo 18)." *Missionalia Hispanica* 11 (1954): 245–328; 13 (1956): 453–95; and 15 (1957): 5–55.

Alcobendas, Severjano, O.F.M. "El P. Francisco de la Concepción, Misionero de China (1696–1733)," *Archivo Ibero-americano* 2 (1942): 307–27.

Bartoli, Daniello. *Dell'historia della Compagnia de Giesu: La Cina.* Rome, 1663.

Bays, Daniel H. "Christianity and the Chinese Sectarian Tradition." *Ch'ing-shi wen-t'i* 4, no. 7 (June 1982): 33–55.

Birrell, Anne. *Chinese Mythology: An Introduction.* Baltimore: Johns Hopkins University Press, 1993.

Black, Christopher F. *Italian Confraternities in the Sixteenth Century.* Cambridge: Cambridge University Press, 1989.

Bodde, Derk. *Essays on Chinese Civilization.* Edited by Charles Le Blanc and Dorothy Borei. Princeton, N.J.: Princeton University Press, 1981.

Bridgman, Elijah C. "Latin and Chinese Inscriptions Found on the Tomb of a Roman Catholic Missionary in the Neighorhood of Canton." *Chinese Repository* 8 (1839): 389–90.

Brunner, Paul, S.J. *L'euchologe de la Mission de Chine, editio princeps 1628 et développements jusqu'à nos jours.* Münster: Aschendorffsche, 1964.

Camps, Arnulf, O.F.M. "Carolo Orazi da Castorano O.F.M. (1673–1755) on the Prophet Muhammed and on the Master Philosopher Confucius." *Neue Zeitschrift für Missionswissenschaft* 56 (2000): 35–43.

Cao Xueqin. *The Story of the Stone.* Translated by David Hawkes. Harmondsworth, England: Penguin, 1993.

Chan Wing-tsit. *A Source Book in Chinese Philosophy.* Princeton, N.J.: Princeton University Press, 1963.

Charbonnier, Jean, M.E.P. *Guide to the Catholic Church in China/Zhongguo Tianzhujiao zhinan.* Singapore: China Catholic Communications, 1989.

———. "The Interpretation of Christian History." In *Historiography of the Chinese Catholic Church: Nineteenth and Twentieth Centuries,* edited by Jeroom Heyndrickx, C.I.C.M., 37–51. Leuven: Ferdinand Verbiest Foundation, 1994.

Chaunu, Pierre. "Manille et Macao, face et la conjoncture des seizième et dix-septième siècles." *Annales, Economies Sociétés Civilisations* (Paris) 3 (1962): 555–80.

Chaves, Jonathan. "Moral Action in the Poetry of Wu Chia-chi (1618–84)." *Harvard Journal of Asiatic Studies* 46 (1986): 420–22.

Cordier, Henri. *Bibliotheca Sinica.* 5 vols. Paris: Librairie Orientaliste Paul Geuthner, 1922–24.

Cummins, J. S. *A Question of Rites: Friar Domingo Navarrete and the Jesuits in China.* Aldershot, England: Scolar, 1993.

Daniel-Rops, Henri. *The Church in the Eighteenth Century.* Translated by John Warrington. Garden City, N.J.: Image Books, 1966.

D'Arelli, Francesco."The Catholic Mission in China in the Seventeenth and Eighteenth Centuries, Archives and Libraries in Italy." *East and West* 47, nos. 1–4 (December 1997): 293–340.

De Groot, J. J. M. *The Religious System of China.* 6 vols. Leiden, 1892–1910. Reprint, Taipei: Literature House, 1964.

Dehergne, Joseph, S.J. "Les missions du nord de la Chine vers 1700." *Archivum Historicum Societatis Iesu* 24 (1955): 251–94.

———. "La Chine du sud-ouest: Guangxi (Kwangsi) et Guangdong (Kwangtung), étude de géographie missionnaire." *Archivum Historicum Societatis Iesu* 45 (1976): 3–55.

———. "Les Jésuites de Chine et la dévotion à saint Joseph." *Cahiers de joséphologie* (Montreal) 15, no. 1 (1967):. 145–54.

———. *Répertoire des Jésuites de Chine de 1552 à 1800.* Rome: Institutum Historicum Societatis Iesu, 1973.

Dong Zuobin. *Zhongguo nianli zongpu* (Chronological table of Chinese history). 2 vols. Hong Kong: Hong Kong University Press, 1960.

Fang Hao. *Fang Hao liushi zidinggao* (The collected works of Marius Fan Hao, revised and edited by the author on his sixtieth birthday). Taipei: Taiwan Xuesheng Shuju, 1969.

———. *Zhongguo Tianzhujiao shi renwu chuan* (Biographies of historical personages in the Chinese Catholic Church). 3 vols. Hong Kong: Gongjiao Renlixue Hui, 1970–73.

Fang Yi et al. *Zhongguo renmin dacidian* (Comprehensive dictionary of Chinese biographies). Shanghai: Commercial Press, 1921. Reprint, Taipei: Commercial Press, 1979.

Goodrich, L. Carrington, and Chaoying Fang, eds. *Dictionary of Ming Biography.* New York: Columbia University Press, 1976.

Handlin Smith, Joanna F. "Benevolent Societies: The Reshaping of Christianity during the Late Ming and Early Ch'ing." *Journal of Asian Studies* 46, no. 2 (1987): 309–35.

Haeger, John Winthrop. "The Intellectual Context of Neo-Confucian Syncretism." *Journal of Asian Studies* 31 (1972): 499–513.

Hearn, Maxwell K. "Document and Portrait: The Southern Tour of Paintings of Kangxi and Qianlong." In *Chinese Painting under the Qianlong Emperor: The Symposium Papers in Two Volumes,* edited by Ju-hsi Chou and Claudia Brown. Published in *Phoebus* (Arizona State University) 6, no. 1 (1988): 91–131, 183–89.

Heeren, J. J. "Bishop Della Chiesa and the Story of His Lost Grave." *Journal of the North-China Branch of the Royal Asiatic Society* 54 (1923): 182–99.

Hibbert, Christopher. *Rome: The Biography of a City.* London: Viking, 1985.

Huang Yilong. "Zhongxiao beifang yu shizijia: Mingmo Tianzhu-jiao-tu Wei Xuelian qiren." *Xinxue* 8, no. 3 (1997): 43–94.

Huang Zhiwei. "The Xujiahui (Zi-ka-wei) Library / Xujiahui Zangshulou," translated by Norman Walling. *Tripod* (Hong Kong), July–August 1992, 23–35.

Hucker, Charles O. *A Dictionary of Official Titles in Imperial China.* Stanford, Calif.: Stanford University Press, 1985.

Hummel, Arthur, ed. *Eminent Chinese of the Ch'ing Period.* Washington, D.C.: United States Government Printing Office, 1943.

Hunter, William C. *Bits of Old China.* London: Kegan Paul, Trench, 1885.

Jensen, Lionel M. *Manufacturing Confucianism.* Durham, N.C.: Duke University Press, 1997.

King, Gail. "Christian Charity in Seventeenth-Century China." *Sino-Western Cultural Relations Journal* 22 (2000): 13–30.

Krahl, Joseph, S.J. *China Missions in Crisis: Bishop Laimbeckhoven and His Times, 1738–1787.* Analecta Gregoriana vol. 137. Rome: Gregorian University Press, 1964.

Latourette, Kenneth Scott. *A History of Christian Missions in China.* London: Society for Promoting Christian Knowledge, 1929.

Lin Fujun and Shi Song, eds. *Qing shi biannian* (Annals of Qing history). 3 vols. Beijing: Zhongguo Renmin Daxue Chubanshe, 1988.

Maas, Otto, O.F.M., "Die Franziskanermission in China während des achtzehn Jahrhunderts." *Zeitschrift für Missionswissenschaft und Religionswissenschaft* 22 (1932): 225–49.

Madsen, Richard. *China's Catholics: Tragedy and Hope in an Emerging Civil Society.* Berkeley and Los Angeles: University of California Press, 1998.

Margiotti, Fortunato, O.F.M. "Congregazioni laiche gesuitiche della antica missione cinese." *Neue Zeitschruft für Missionswissenschaft* 18 (1962): 255–74 and 19 (1963): 50–65.

Matti, Leonard von, and Franco Barelli. *Rom: Kunst und Kultur der "Ewigen Stadt" in mehr als 1000 Bildern.* Cologne: Verlag M. DuMont Schaubert, 1975.

Mensaert, Georges, O.F.M. "Adrien Chu, prêtre chinois et confesseur de la Foi (1717–1785)." *Neue Zeitschrift für Missionswissenschaft* 12 (1956): 1–19.

———. "Les Franciscains au service de la Propagande dans la province de Pékin, 1705–1785." *Archivum Franciscanum Historicum* 51 (1958): 161–200, 273–311.

———. "Le Père Pie Liu minor, missionnaire au Shensi. D'après sa correspondance (1760–1785)." In *Der einheimische Klerus in Geschichte und Gegenwart. Festschrift P. Dr. Laurenz Kilger OSB. zum 60. Geburtstag darbegoten,* edited by Johannes Beckmann, S.M.B. Schöneck-Beckenried, Switzerland: Administration der Neuen Zeitschrift für Missionswissenschaft, 1950.

Mungello, D. E. *The Forgotten Christians of Hangzhou.* Honolulu: University of Hawaii, 1994.

———. *The Great Encounter of China and the West, 1500–1800.* Lanham, Md.: Rowman & Littlefield, 1999.

Naquin, Susan. "Funerals in North China: Uniformity and Variation." In *Death Ritual in Late Imperial and Modern China,* edited by James L. Watson and Evelyn S. Rawski, 37–70. Berkeley and Los Angeles: University of California Press, 1988.

———. *Millenarian Rebellion in China: The Eight Trigrams Uprising of 1813.* New Haven: Yale University Press, 1976.

———. "The Transmission of White Lotus Sectarianism in Late Imperial China." In *Popular Culture in Late Imperial China,.* edited by David Johnson, Andrew J. Nathan, and Evelyn S. Rawski, 255–91. Berkeley and Los Angeles: University of California, Press, 1985.

New Catholic Encyclopedia. New York: McGraw-Hill, 1967.

Pelliot, Paul. "Les Franciscains en Chine au seizième et au dix-septième siècle." *T'oung Pao* 34 (1938): 191–222.

———. *Inventaire sommaire des manuscrits et imprimés chinois de la Bibliothèque Vaticaine.* Revised and edited by Takata Tokio. Kyoto: Instituto Italiano di Cultura Scuola di Studi sull'Asia Orientale, 1995.

Pérez, Lorenzo, O.F.M. "Los Franciscanos en el extremo Oriente. Noticias bio-bibliogràficas. 4. Santa Maria, Fr. Antonio Caballero de." *Archivum Franciscanum Historicum* 2 (1909) 548–60; 3 (1910): 39–46; 4 (1911): 50–61; and 5 (1911): 482–503.

———. "La venerable orden tercera y la Archicofradia del Cordón en el Extremo Oriente." *Archivo Ibero-Americano* 33 (1930): 43–68.

Pfister, Louis, S.J. *Notices biographiques et bibliographiques sur les Jésuites de l'ancienne mission de Chine, 1552 à 1773.* Variétés Sinologiques59. Shanghai: Imprimerie de la Mission Catholique, 1932–34. Reprint, Taipei: Chinese Materials Center, 1976.

Pinot, Virgile. *La Chine et la formation de l'esprit philosophique en France (1640–1740).* Paris: Librairie Orientaliste Paul Geuthner, 1932.

Rosso, Antonio Sisto, O.F.M. *Apostolic Legations to China of the Eighteenth Century.* South Pasadena: P. D. & Ione Perkins, 1948.

———. "Pedro de la Pañuela, O.F.M., Mexican Missionary to China and Author." *Franciscan Studies* (St. Bonaventura, New York) 8 (1948): 273–74.

Rule, Paul. "Louis Fan Shou-i: A Mission Link in the Chinese Rites Controversy." In *Actes du Septième Colloque International de Sinologie de Chantilly, 8–10 septembre 1992,* edited by Edward J. Malatesta, S.J., Yves Raguin, S.J., and Adrianus C. Dudink, 277–94. Taipei: Institut Ricci, 1995.

———. "Louis Fan Shouyi and Macao." *Review of Culture* (Macau) 21 (2d ser.) English ed., 1994: 249–58.

Schneider, Robert A. "Mortification in Parade: Penitential Processions in Sixteenth- and Seventeenth-Century France." *Renaissance and Reformation* 10 (1986): 123–46.

Spence, Jonathan D. *Ts'ao Yin and the K'ang-hsi Emperor, Bondservant and Master.* New Haven: Yale University Press, 1996.

Standaert, Nicolas. "Confucian–Christian Dual Citizenship: A Political Conflict?" *Ching Feng* 34, no. 2 (June 1991): 109–14.

———. "Inculturation and Chinese–Christian Contacts in the Late Ming and Early Qing." *Ching Feng* 34, no. 4 (December 1991): 1–16.

Streit, Robert, O.M.I. *Bibliotheca Missionum.* Vol. 5, *Asiatische Missionsliteratur 1600–1699.* Freiburg im Breisgau: Herder, 1929.

———. *Bibliotheca Missionum.* Vol. 7, *Chinesische Missionsliteratur 1700–1799.* Freiburg im Breisgau: Herder, 1931.

Tan Qixiang, ed. *Zhongguo lishi ditu ji / Historical Atlas of China.* Vol. 7, Yuan and Ming; and vol. 8, Qing. Sponsored by the Chinese Academy of Social Sciences. Hong Kong: Sanlian Shudian / Joint Publishing, 1992.

Ter Haar, B. J. *The White Lotus Teachings in Chinese Religious History.* Leiden: Brill, 1992.

Tiedemann, R. G. "Christianity and Chinese 'Heterodox Sects': Mass Conversion and Syncretism in Shandong Province in the Early Eighteenth Century." *Monumenta Serica* 44 (1996): 339–82.

Van Damme, Daniel, O.F.M. *Necrologium Fratrum Minorum in Sinis.* 3d ed. Hong Kong: Tang King Po School, Kowloon, 1978. 1st ed. compiled by Joannes Ricci, O.F.M. (1934); 2d ed. compiled by Kilian Menz, O.F.M. (1944).

Väth, Alfons, S.J. "P. F. Antonio Caballero de Santa Maria über die Mission der Jesuiten und anderer Orden in China." *Archivum Historicum Societatis Iesu* 1 (1932): 291–302.

Verhaeren, H., C.M. "Boite aux renseignements nova et vetera: Notes bibliographiques." *Bulletin catholique de Pékin* 30 (1943): 183–90.

———. "Ordonnances de la Sainte Eglise/ *Shengjiao guicheng.*" *Monumenta Serica* (Peiping) 4 (1939–40): 451–77.

Wakeman, Frederic, Jr. *The Great Enterprise.* Berkeley and Los Angeles: University of California Press, 1985.

Walsh, Michael. *Butler's Lives of Patron Saints.* Wellwood, England: Burns & Oates, 1987.

Wang Zhongmin. "*Shang Huqing chuan*" (Biography of Shang Huqing). *Tushu qikan.* New ser. 5, no. 1 (March 1944): 49.

Wylie, Alexander. *Notes on Chinese Literature.* Shanghai, 1867. Reprint, New York: Paragon, 1964.

Willeke, Bernward H., O.F.M. "Documents Relating to the History of the Franciscan Missions in Shantung, China." *Franciscan Studies* (St. Bonaventura, N.Y.) 7 (1947): 171–87.

———. *Imperial Government and Catholic Missions in China during the Years 1784–1785.* Saint Bonaventure, N.Y.: Franciscan Institute, 1948.

———. "Studia preliminari pro 'Sinica Franciscana.'" April 6, 1986.

Wyngaert, Anastase Van den, O.F.M. "Les dernières années de Mgr della Chiesa." *Archivum Franciscanum Historicum* 38 (1945): 82–105.

———. "Mgr. Fr. Pallu et Mgr. Bernardin della Chiesa, le serment de fidelité aux vicaires apostoliques, 1680–1688." *Archivum Franciscanum Historicum* (Florence) 31 (1938): 17–47.

———. "Le patronat portugais et Mgr. Bernardin della Chiesa." *Archivum Franciscanum Historicum* 35 (1942): 3–34.

Xu Zongze. *Ming-Qing jian Yesuhui shi yizhu tiyao* (A summary of Jesuit translations made in the late Ming and early Qing periods). Taipei: Zhonghua Shuju Gufen Youxian Gongxi, 1958.

Yang Liansheng. "Daojiao zhi zibo yu Fijiao zhi zipu" (The self-pummeling - of Daoism and the self-beating of Buddhism). In *Tsukamoto hakushi shoju kinen Shoju Kinen Bukkyo-shi gakuronshu* (Essays on the history of Buddhism presented to Professor Zenryu Tsukamoto on his Retirement*),* 962–69. Kyoto: Research Institute for Humanistic Studies of Kyoto University, 1961.

Yuan Ke. *Dragons and Dynasties: An Introduction to Chinese Mythology.* Selected and translated by Kim Echlin and Nie Zhixiong. London: Penguin; Beijing: Foreign Language Press, 1991.

Zang Lihe, ed. *Zhongguo gujin diming dacidian* (Comprehensive dictionary of ancient and modern Chinese place names). Shanghai: Commercial Press, 1931. Reprint, Hong Kong: Commercial Press, 1982.

Index

About the Author

D. E. Mungello, the grandson of Italian and German immigrants to the United States, completed his doctorate at the University of California at Berkeley. His research in Sino-Western history led to three years of study in Germany as an Alexander von Humboldt fellow and a Herzog August Bibliothek fellow. He has published several books, including *Curious Land, The Forgotten Christians of Hangzhou,* and *The Great Encounter of China and the West, 1500–1800* (Rowman & Littlefield, 1999). He is the founder and editor of the *Sino-Western Cultural Relations Journal.* His first teaching position was at Lingnan College in Hong Kong, and he currently is professor of history at Baylor University in Waco, Texas.

DATE DUE